T0395754

PLACE REINVENTION

Place Reinvention
Northern Perspectives

Edited by

TORILL NYSETH
University of Tromsø, Norway

ARVID VIKEN
Finnmark College, Norway

Routledge
Taylor & Francis Group

LONDON AND NEW YORK

First published 2009 by Ashgate Publishing

Published 2016 by Routledge
2 Park Square, Milton Park, Abingdon, Oxon, OX14 4RN
711 Third Avenue, New York, NY 10017, USA

Routledge is an imprint of the Taylor & Francis Group, an informa business

British Library Cataloguing in Publication Data
Place reinvention : northern perspectives.
    1. Urban renewal--Europe, Northern--Case studies. 2. Place
    marketing--Europe, Northern--Case studies. 3. Sociology,
    Urban--Europe, Northern.
    I. Nyseth, Torill. II. Viken, Arvid.
    307.3'4'0948-dc22

Library of Congress Cataloging-in-Publication Data
Place reinvention : northern perspectives / edited by Torill Nyseth and Arvid Viken.
    p. cm.
    Includes bibliographical references and index.
    ISBN 978-0-7546-7475-7
    1. Place marketing--Scandinavia--Case studies. 2. Tourism--Scandinavia--Case studies.
    I. Nyseth, Torill. II. Viken, Arvid.

    G155.S35P53 2009
    914.80068'8--dc22
                                     2009009822

ISBN 13: 978-0-7546-7475-7 (hbk)

Contents

List of Figures

List of Tables

List of Contributors

Karl Benediktsson is professor in human geography, University of Iceland. His main research field is in land conflicts, fresh food trade, and rural space in Papua New Guinea as well as post-productionist agriculture, coping processes, landscape, nature and place-reinvention in Iceland. Among his publications are international journal articles in *Sociologia Ruralis* and *Geografiska Annaler* and the monograph *Harvesting Development, The Construction of Fresh Food Markets in Papua New Guinea* (2005).

Elin Berglund is a PhD student at the Royal Institute of Technology, Stockholm, Sweden. Her research field is cultural economy, place identity and city marketing.

Anniken Førde is associate professor at the Department of Planning and Community Studies at the University of Tromsø. Her research field is gender studies, rural development, innovation and tourism. Among her publications are articles on rural entrepreneurship and a co-edited book on cross diciplinarity.

Brynhild Granås is a PhD student in the Department of Sociology, University of Tromsø. Among her publications are *Mobilities and Place* (edited with J.O. Bærenholdt 2007) and *Place Reinvention in the Nordic Peripheries, Dynamics and Governance Perspectives* (2007, eds with Torill Nyseth).

Yvonne Gunnarsdotter is associate professor at the Department of Urban and Rural Development, Swedish University of Agricultural Sciences, at Uppsala University, Sweden. Her research is in rural development, ecotourism, gender, and male identity building in rural Sweden. She has published in both international journals and had contributions in books, for instance in the book *Ecotourism in Scandinavia. Lessons in Theory and Practice.*

Magnfríður Júlíusdóttir is assistant professor at the Department of Geology and Geography, University of Iceland, Reykjavik. Her reasearch field is gender studies in geography, and she has done field research in Africa as well as in Iceland and published reports and journal articles on this subject. She is appointed as representative of the editorial board of NORA, Nordic Journal of Gender Research.

Turid Moldenæs is associate Professor at the Department of Political Science, University of Tromsø. Her research field is in organizational theory, narrative theory and constructions of local identity. Among her publications is the book *I Sitt Bilde? Identitet og Identitetsproduksjon i Lokalsamfunn* (2006) and in the journal *Systemic Practice and Action Research*.

Mai Camilla Munkejord is a PhD student at Finnmark college in Alta. Among her work is an article in the journal *Sociologia Ruralis* (2006) and several papers on rurality and gender.

Kristina Nilsson is assistant professor and senior lecturer in spatial planning at the Department of Urban and Rural Development, Swedish University of Agricultural Sciences, Uppsala, Sweden. Her research in field is urban and rural planning and sustainable place development. She has published on issues such as managing complexity in spatial planning, recreation and spatial planning, methods in place development etc.

Torill Nyseth is associate professor at the Department of Planning and Community Studies, University of Tromsø. Her research field is in local democracy, public policy, governance and administration and in urban development and design. She has also been a college lecturer and worked as a municipal planner. In addition to many journal articles and contributions in political science, entrepreneurship, urban planning and governance, among them in *Local Government Studies* and *Planning Theory and Practice*, she has published the book *Dugnad og Demokrati* (2000 with Toril Ringholm, Asbjørn Røiseland and Nils Aarsæther), *Nærdemokrati: Teori og Praksis* (2002, with Nils Aarsæther), *I disiplinenes grenseland* (2007, eds with Svein Jentoft, Anniken Førde and Jørgen Ole Bærenholdt), and *Place Reinvention. Dynamics and Governance Perspectives* (2007, eds with Brynhild Granaas).

Krister Olsson is senior researcher at the Royal Institute of Technology, Stockholm, Sweden. His research field is city marketing, cultural heritage management and cultural economy. Among his publications are contributions to the books *New Urbanism & Beyond: Contemporary and Future Trends in Urban Design* (Haas, 2006, ed), *Reshaping Regional Planning* (Snickars, Olerup and Persson, 2002 eds), and in journals such as *Plan* and *Town Planning Review*.

Gry Paulgaard is associate professor in pedagogics at the University of Tromsø. Her research field is youth identity with modernity and place enactment. She is a member of the steering committee of the "Arctic Youth Research Network". She is also participating in a Nordic Research project; Young people in the Barents region – work and welfare. Among her many publications are articles in *Young, Nordic Journal of Youth Research*, several books and book chapters. She is a member of steering committee for the research School "Citizenship, Encounters and Place Enactment" (CEPIN) at the University of Tromsø.

Paul Pedersen is chair researcher at Norut Science Ltd in Tromsø. In the last years he has concentrated on labour market analyses, analyses of migration, and evaluation of consequencies of specific rural and ethnic development policies. He has published books and articles on this. A recently finished project is called The Revitalization of Coastal Sami identity, and a book is forthcoming based on this research. He is also participating in a Nordic Research project; Young people in the Barents region – work and welfare.

Arvid Viken is associate professor at Finnmark College. His research field is tourism development in which he also has many publications. Among those are the books *Turisme, Postmoderne Kultur og Tradisjon* (2000) and *Turisme, Miljø og Utvikling* (2004) and many articles in international journals, for instance *Annals of Tourism Research, Sosiologi Idag, Acta Borealia* and *Polar Records.* He has also been Rector at Finnmark College.

Preface

The title of this book – *Place Reinvention: Northern Perspectives* announces a focus on place and place development – a topic that currently is hot in most social sciences all over the world, also in the marginal northern parts of Europe where most of studies in this book originate from. This collection of essays is a contribution to the discourse on reinvention that is affecting almost every place these days, the urban mega-cities as well as rural townships. The book's focus is on how places are reinventing themselves within the context of globalization and a new economy. It has become more important than ever to appear as attractive, not only towards newcomers and potential investors but also in respect of the inhabitants. This new and expanding discourse on place making is addressed through a critical and analytical social science perspective.

Empirically, the analyses in this book are unfolded along the northern European periphery, in Norway, Sweden, and Iceland. The book originates from a series of Nordic research projects and networks that have focused on restructuring, renewal and reinvention of place and space. The idea of the book is to further develop the theories of place reinvention through case studies that illustrate the diversity of the phenomena. The studies demonstrate that places in the North are still strongly involved in production industries; however, less dominant than before and complemented by a variety of new industries. Many of the transformations that have been observed happen within the spheres of the traditional industries. A cultural economy is also evolving, side by side with heavy industry and traditional modes of production.

The book is multidisciplinary in the sense that the authors come from sociology, social anthropology, cultural geography, political science and planning, but also in the sense that many of the presentations draw on theories crossing different disciplines.

The editors would like to thank all our fellow contributors for their thorough work in several rounds of drafting and editing. Apart from the work of the contributors the creation of this book has depended on numerous other forms of support. In additon to the support from NORDREGIO who financed the research on place reinvention and the funding from the Norwegian Research Council to the project 'Globalization from below', the Department of Planning and Community Studies at the University of Tromsø and Alta College have been our main sponsors. We also would like to thank Ashgate Publishing for their professional response during the editing and production process, and thank John Hobson for his excellent proof-reading.

Torill Nyseth and Arvid Viken
Tromsø, 2009

Chapter 1

Place Reinvention at the Northern Rim

Torill Nyseth

Marginal places, those towns and regions which have been 'left behind' in the modern race for progress, evoke both nostalgia and fascination.

Rob Shields: *Places on the Margin* (1991)

Into the Zones of Otherness

In the introduction to his book *Places on the Margin* Rob Shields (1991) characterizes marginal places as left behind, and that those places on the margin form a 'mythic heartland ... a zone of Otherness' (Shields 1991, 4). Shields' 'margin' is located on the rim of the British Isles and in North America. This book is about the Otherness of places on the 'margin' of Europe, nearly as far as you can get from the European metropolis and still be in Europe. According to Berg and Kearns (1998, 129) there is a tendency that '... geographies of other people and places become marked as Other – exotic, transgressive, extraordinary, and by no means representative ...'. One of the consequences of this, Kitchen (2005, 6) remarks, is that the theoretical production 'casts much of the world's geography into silence'. This book tries to break this silence. It challenges the centre–periphery conceptions, relating empirical studies to trends that have removed the material basis for such stances; basically the globalization and mobilities turn in the comprehension and constitution of the world. Through 12 case studies of places in northern Norway, Sweden and on Iceland, marginality becomes questioned, their uniqueness exotic and at the same time marked by urban winds. However, as will be argued here, these areas are not left behind in these enacted peripheries. According to Bærenholdt, 'People connect and live together over distances to such an extent that we can envision a globalization from below, which has been going on for centuries in the region' (Bærenholdt 2007, 256). Borders that physically were lines of separation becomes points of connection, producing new places and borderlands. New industries like tourism and traditional industries like fishery merge and form new niches like fish tourism, building networks to markets far away, and re-image the localities in their making. Routes become more important than roots (Friedman 2002). 'Marginal' in a global world has become an anachronism – impossible. Every place is a global space.

In this book the approach to these processes of changed marginality is performed through the concept of place reinvention – a concept that relates to ideas like place branding and place promotion and at the same time questions the rationale behind them.

Beyond Place Branding

A standard approach to place transformation in postmodern society is through place marketing perspectives. Re-imaging of place is often understood within the discourse of entrepreneurial managerialism (Harvey 1989). Terms such as place marketing, place branding, and competitive place identities (Anholt 2007) are among those that have emerged in this field. As Brenner and Theodore (2002) point out, it is a part of the true neo-liberal vision that a place should be branded and marketed. The practices of selling and promotion of place are therefore tightly linked to entrepreneurial strategies. As a part of the cultural shift, places have to represent themselves as interesting and entertaining, not only places where you can live a good life. In the global competition between places local actors are fighting to attract industrial investors and offer them the best possible terms to convince them to invest in their specific place. Place marketing is a broad entrepreneurial ethos which has permeated the common affairs of particular places.

Place reinvention goes beyond the concept of place branding and represents a critical perspective on certain aspects of branding as a practice. While branding is an active strategic and deliberate policy for changing the image of a place, place reinvention is underpinned by more contingent and discrete processes of change. Branding means narrowing down a place's identity into fancy logos and slogans – it is selective story-telling (Sandercock 2003), a form of collective impression management (Jensen 2007, 12). Place images tend to be characterized by simplification, stereotyping and labelling (Shields 1991, 47). Branding places is a way of inscribing a certain logic in space – both symbolically through logos, slogans and so on, and materially through construction of buildings, infrastructure and landmarks. Place branding activities must be based on an understanding of demand patterns and images of place consumers, and on identifying the position of the place in the view of competitors. As with place myths, the branding process is a process of creating an evocative narrative with a spatial referent through selective narration – the act of representing the place in a favourable light. Places are packaged and sold as a commodity (Ward 1998, 1). Place promotion has therefore been labelled the carnival mask of late capitalist urbanization (Harvey 1989, 35). Place promotion reduces the complexity involved in local histories and identities inherent in their formation. In order to create a more attractive place image social and cultural meanings are selectively appropriated and problems are played down. Place branding does not do justice to the richness and diversity of places and their peoples. Place reinvention is more than fine words and this quotation from Stephen Ward leads us to a broader understanding of the concept:

> Yet marketing, narrowly defined, is not enough. Behind the fine words and images there has to be at least some physical reality of buildings, public spaces and activities that give some genuine promise of a re-invented city (Ward 1998 193).

An important part of our argument is therefore that changes in the symbolic representation of place involved in branding and re-imaging strategies often are contested.

Place Reinvention Practices

The focus in this collection is what can be called the practices of place reinvention; practices that involve both economic and symbolic transformations constituting a changed sense of place. Processes of reinvention are related to changes in industrial bases and the representational changes accompanying these changes. This means that the focus is not so much on landscapes, townscapes and architecture but rather on how economic restructuring is followed by a changed symbolic and redefined meaning of place. The term 'reinvention' indicates that something has been left behind and has to be recreated, renewed or redefined. Several known processes have over the years changed the character of most places, processes that are going on all the time. Some processes change the raison d'être of the place – the genus locus of a place, for instance the industrial basis or status, whereas other processes are more related to changed landscapes and townscapes, and often these two processes are merged; townscapes change due to shifts in industrial bases. Changes in the modes of production followed by an ongoing restructuring of the local economy may lead to changes in place identities and place images.

Places are put under an innovation imperative according to Thrift (2008). This may lead them to boost their attractions in the form of place marketing – or as we emphasize in this volume to a series of other forms of innovation. Place reinvention is a concept that focuses both on inventions and interventions as vehicles for change of both urban and rural places (Robinson 2006, 251). Inventions are the more continuous changes going on all the time, while interventions are linked to those more direct, planned and intentional processes attempting to achieve change. Inventions are not only a label that fits the larger cities. We find many rural places in this collection to be experimental, innovative, open, fluid and dynamic places concerned with re-imaging the place to adapt to a new global context.

Places never reach a position of completion; they are always an ongoing affair, always in the making. Place reinvention addresses the numerous ways places are being produced and reproduced. The concept goes beyond place branding and directs attention towards the relationship between symbolic and imaginative change and planned regeneration. By place reinvention we mean transformations resulting from interplay between actors such as industries, authorities and the public, between projects of construction, promotion and consumption, and processes related to information, identity and imagery. Reinvention of places is a matter of intention, intervention and hazard; it is both planned and something that just happens as more or less unintended consequences of other ongoing processes. Thus, new place images are not only results of strategic development processes aiming at profiling and promoting place, but also products of people's everyday life, and local and national politics.

It is this complex dialectics between material space and discursive representation that we try to catch in the notion of place reinvention. Through the concept of place reinvention the aim is to give attention to the complexity involved in place transformation which the branding literature seems to ignore or simplify. We relate place reinvention to particularly two dimensions, a material and a symbolic, which will be elaborated in the following section. The political implication of such reinventional processes will be discussed thereafter.

Analytical Dimensions of Place Reinvention

Material production of place

Perceptions of place reflect activities going on in many spheres, including production, consumption, everyday life and cultural spheres. Concerning the production sector the perspective has changed significantly in recent years – about what production is, its relation to consumption, to authorities and to place. Traditional industries are no longer seen as a necessity for every community, nor is mass production seen as a key to industrial success. This has produced a view of towns and cities as sites of consumption more than of production (Lash and Urry 1994). This theory has recently been discussed by Thrift (2008) who argues that sites of consumption also are sites of production, as there are obvious links in-between, in an economy where the consumers take part in the production. This tight relationship also indicates that production is something going on in most places; it is a function of the existence of social life in places. Thus, towns are still obviously also sites of production. Due to the industrial turn called post-Fordism, technology has become more flexible and adaptable, and enables small-scale production being profitable (Piore and Sabel 1984; Lash and Urry 1994). Companies wherever located can be integrated in huge international production systems. In many places production has changed from being locally based for a local market, to production adapted to global specialization and diversification, and for international markets. Therefore, in most places the industrial base is in a process of change; traditional industries become technologically more advanced and effective, and do not employ as many people as before.

Most of the places discussed in this collection have always been oriented towards an international market as they have a history as fishery villages or mining towns. Integrated in an extremely open economy, very much depending on natural resources and international markets, the northern regions have always been part of national and international economic systems, and thus have long traditions in adapting to changing economic trends. In this book places that have depended on fish markets are, for instance, represented by Vadsø, Båtsfjord, Berlevåg, Sørøya in Norway and Fjarðabyggð in Iceland. Others that have been depending on global markets for minerals are Pajala and Kiruna in Sweden and Narvik and Kirkenes in Norway.

Several of the places have also experienced industrial restructuring, being transformed from exclusively manufacturing sites to places with diverse industrial platforms. Several of the studies will demonstrate that places in the North still are strongly involved in production industries, however less dominant than before and complemented by a variety of new industries. In Chapter 2, Karl Benediktsson emphasizes that restructuring in a small Icelandic community is all about jobs, jobs, jobs – and only jobs in the manufacturing sector counts. In 2008 this small community, Fjarðabyggð, has been transformed from a small fishing village to a site for international aluminium production. Being recognized as places in rich areas of natural resources like oil, gas and hydro-electric power, many of the places in the North undergo processes of restructuring that take the form of re-industrialization. In Kirkenes (Chapter 4), near the Russian border, the town is preparing for an oil era, and an old iron ore mine has been reopened more than ten years after it was closed down and a process of restructuring the local economy started. There is a historic continuity in local economic development that marks certain places, particularly where the economy is based on natural resources of some kind. The social relations embedded in a place supports some forms of production and resist others. Thus, as old industries are vanishing, the cultural and social capital of people tend to live on. There is therefore a tendency for local production systems to survive, sometimes only culturally or in the form of continuity of businesses, partly in new forms.

Oil, gas, minerals, fish, waterfalls and so on produce not only hard currency in a global market, but also a highly materialized and embodied sense of place. In Narvik people still frequently wash their windows to get rid of the dust from the coal storage, and in Båtsfjord fish still represents the 'smell of money'. On the other hand, materiality is also changing its meaning. In Sørøya big fish has been transformed into something almost erotic, at least for male tourists.

In many places the industrial base is a combination of production for national and/or international markets and production for locals and travellers. From a production point of view, most places are diversified, multifaceted and complex industrial systems. They are not passive containers even if some of them are competing with other localities and forced to attract capital by offering tax breaks, cheap land and free infrastructure. However, what these local economies are labelled vary according to local traditions, international trends and political opportunities.

Symbolic production of place

Place promotion is intimately linked to image communication (Gold 1994). In *The Economies of Signs and Space* Lash and Urry (1994) develop a new paradigm for understanding how economic development is connected to images. The shift towards a cultural and experience economy means that, to an increasing degree, cultural values are added to products. The idea of a 'cultured' economy lays the ground for the semiotic focus in efforts to develop place. Signs, images and symbols of place are carrying place specific cultural values, and must be understood as cultural expressions. Place marketing is, according to Philo and Kearns (1993), characterized by making use of 'imageneering' concepts or symbols to construct competitive place images. Place marketing involves quite specific interpretations of what are the symbolic attributes of a place, and implies a symbolic communication of these interpretations. Such symbolic communication is not only directed towards the target group of an external market, it also demonstrates locally how our place should be understood. In this collection, an example of the analyses of symbolic representations in marketing is found in Chapter 7 where Granås discusses the uniqueness of Narvik communicated through 'strong experiences'. However, place reinvention, even the most explicit place marketing campaigns as the one in Narvik, is never a promotional campaign only. The case also exemplifies how the ascription of meaning to the place is regulated by the positioning of the place within extensive symbolic relations of north and south as well as centre and periphery.

The symbolic production of place is not only obvious in place promotion and selling of place, also physical regeneration and the construction of flagship projects of particular architectural value can be powerful symbolic representations of place (Hubbard 1996). In Chapter 3 Kristina Nilsson analyses the relocation of the city centre in Kiruna as an example of an extreme make-over of a town. Even if the reason is industrial – to get hold of the iron ore in the soil beneath the city centre – the symbolic implications are numerous. Nilsson discusses four different place images that have turned up in the local discourse that demostrate how different actors perceive quite different futures for Kiruna as a place, from a dark mining town to an image of a completely new and modern townscape.

Re-imaging processes then involves physical reconstructions as well as semiotic work (cf. Short 1999, 46). In Kirkenes, to attract investors, workforce and tourists, the question of town make-over has been raised, and the semiotics and narratives of the town has already changed – it has become a border town with lots of signs of a cross-border region (called Barents Region) and Russian co-existence such as street names being spelled in Cyrillic and the Russian language is heard all over. However, more important than semiotic changes, are shifts related to narratives and discourses. Through the construction of symbolic boundaries global flows allow people to construct their 'locality' in a range of ways (Appadurai 1990).

Through symbolic expressions places also communicate their identity (Philo and Kearns 1993), an important aspect in their struggle to be attractive. This is particularly demonstrated in Chapter 11 (by Pedersen and Viken) where place reinvention is linked to a particular event, an ethnic festival (Riddu Riđđu in Gáivuotna). The festival has brought about a revitalization of the coastal Sami culture and in marketing the place as a site for international indigenousness. In this case reinvention of place involves renegotiation of local identities. Symbolic production of place is also analysed in Chapter 9 (by Paulgaard), which focuses on a film called *Cool and Crazy* – a film about a male choir in the small fishing town Berlevåg. The film produced a changed image of the place. The uniqueness of place is here demonstrated by the authenticity and universality of the 'Other' through close-up pictures of quite ordinary men singing in a snow storm with icicles hanging from their beard. The symbolic construction of place is here demonstrated through difference – the film reinvented the place into a more exotic site in sharp contrast to depressing images of a place where the fishing industry is bankrupt and were young people have moved out.

Where cultural industries are replacing manufacturing industries, for instance tourism, signs and images of place are decisive. In the case demonstrated by Førde (in Chapter 6) the traditional fishing village Sørøya is transformed into a tourist resort based on fish tourism. In marketing this destination the slogan 'The Land of the Big Fish' was developed, playing with erotic signs and male obsession with catching the big fish using a female figure holding a big cod. The cultural power to create an image has become more important as traditional institutions have become less relevant mechanisms of expressing identity (Zukin 1995).

Political production of place

Politics is territorial but these territories are simultaneously real, imaginary and symbolic (Keith and Pile 1993, 224). To enhance the attractiveness of a place pro-growth economic development is defined as the basic strategy. Places are products of social and industrial activities, but today place development is also a question of choice, and matters for political negotiations, policy making and planning. Thus, place development tends to be on the political agenda. Places are scenes where structural development patterns intersect and trigger off new regimes. And more than before places as such are areas for political interests, negotiations and governance. This also reflects changes in the social composition of the local population with regard to class, gender, race and age. Social stratification is expressed in new ways, for instance through gentrification of working-class areas. With economic restructuring follows a recomposition of class distinctions and social cleavages; political behaviour changes and new groups may enter positions of power where they are able to impose their preferences, values and perspectives upon a place. New place images may therefore mobilize and legitimate particular sets of actions or policies (Jessop 1997), and there is a potential of new conflicts produced by place brands (Mommaas 2002). Images are social constructions, and as such never neutral. To produce images, is to enact power.

A renewed focus on place development has emerged in a period with major shifts in the political culture, defining new rules of the game for local governments (Clark 2003). Transformations in the classic left–right dimension to political pragmatism (Beck 2002), new public management, and new modes of governance all affect the way 'place images' are perceived and produced. Place transformation is a field that is not governable through 'government' alone. New governance regimes appear as consequences of a break with established ways of understanding politics. A number of different processes are intertwined, many beyond formal systems of 'conductors'. Chapter 5 (by Júlíusdóttir and Gunnarsdotter) shows how new forms of governance, for instance in the form of public–private partnerships, evolve even in quite small and remote Swedish villages as Pajala, as a part of a reinventing strategy aiming at transforming the town into a 'Cultural Municipality'. This reorganization of local development issues changed the profile of the policy involved from culture as a matter of art and identity towards culture as business.

A particular form of political production of place is illustrated in Chapter 4 (by Viken and Nyseth) about the border town Kirkenes. One of the narratives told here is the image of a political place, a place for international politics. Its localization close to the Russian border has in a sense always marked the town as of national political importance. The fall of the Soviet Union and the opening of the border to Russia have, however, made Kirkenes into a political destination. Diplomacy, cross-border cooperation and political meetings are going on all the time and ministers and high-profile politicians are visiting Kirkenes almost on a daily basis these days.

Places can be planned, and even moved or relocated as in one of the cases in this book (the Kiruna case). This is a highly political issue and a matter of negotiations and governance. One aspect of this is how local citizens can be involved in promotion strategies directed towards targeted consumer groups in external markets. This question is analysed in Chapter 8 (by Olsson and Berglund) based on a study of urban planning in the Swedish town Arboga. The authors argue that knowledge on how local citizens actually experience and value the practice of city selling is limited. Traditional methods of citizen participation, like public meetings often do not involve large groups of citizens even if they become affected by place reinvention. The authors argue that systematic mapping of common interests through survey data analyses in urban planning could complement traditional methods of public participation.

Politics is also about the driving forces, which in regard to place reinvention are numerous. Some of them are related to economic crises in the local economy. One example is the enforced restructuring of three mining towns: Kiruna in Sweden (Chapter 3 by Nilsson) and Narvik in Norway (Chapter 7 by Granås), and in Kirkenes where this situation led to a close-down (Chapter 4 by Viken and Nyseth). Another example of this is demonstrated in Chapter 11 (by Pedersen and Viken), where crises in fisheries and agriculture in this coastal Sami area gave rise to an ethnic reinvention process. In several of the towns in Iceland, Pajala in Sweden, and in several of the Norwegian cases, the reasons for problems in the 1990s were blamed on others, the market, the authorities and on globalization of markets. For instance, the major decline in fish resources in the many fish-dependent communities on the coast of Iceland and North Norway is elaborated in several of the case studies in this book. At a more profound level, overall changes in the economy, for instance the cultural shift, such as a shift from Fordist mass production and industrial manufacturing towards a cultural economy, are also important drivers affecting the places in the North. Among the deeper changes are also those related to globalization and increased competition expressed, for instance, through different processes such as global tourism at one end of the spectrum, discussed in Chapter 6, and at the other end the revitalization of local identity could also be linked to another consequence of globalization. The global discourse on indigenous rights was one of the driving forces behind the international indigenous festival Riddu Riđđu discussed in Chapter 11. Drivers can also be political; an intentional and strategic change. Place promotion policies have become a mandatory part of economic development policies in even the most remote communities in the North partly as a consequence of tourism but also to attract new inhabitants from more urban regions of Europe.

A Narrative Approach

There has been a change of direction towards narrative in social sciences that also has inspired the approach of this book which contains a number of case studies, or 'case stories' from the northern rim of Europe. Most knowledge can be seen as narratives, and narration is a way of mediating information – facts as well as fiction; 'narratives is natural mode of human consciousness – in contrast to ... logic and reason' (Bowman 2006, 8). Narratives are both modes of constructing reality, and a means for conveyance and politics. Narratives are central in human communication and in the way we present and interpret each other. Narratives represent a way 'in which people make sense of the world and construct identity by ascribing meaning and ordering events in a logical manner' (Gilpin 2008; cf. Czarniawska-Joerges 1995; Czarniawska 2002). Even though narratives demand narrators, there is also a tendency for stories to live their own life reducing its authors to co-authors; they are something that circulates among people giving meaning to events, space and human actions.

There are at least three ways in which this book can be said to have applied a narrative approach, using a scheme presented by Czarniawska-Joerges (1995). The first is that each chapter represents narratives from the field, narratives about places on the northern rim. These stories go into the body of knowledge about these places, and into the discourse concerning restructuring, place marketing, identities and so on. The second way the narrative approach is revealed is through referring to particular narratives in the field, narratives that people tell and that are important in their lives. The last way narratives can be studied, also demonstrated in this book, is to reveal how stories constitute and influence interpretations of social life which adds to the construction of the place.

In Chapter 11, Moldenæs make use of an autobiographical approach in constructing the origin myth of the small town Båtsfjord on the coast of Finnmark in Norway. Through this approach the story of how the identity of the place was created is expressed through the actors' self-presentations towards an external audience. There are also other narratives and other forms of narrative analyses appearing in the chapters. People's perceptions of place give rise to what Somers (1994) calls ontological narratives – people's personal experiences. Narratives from women's lives are for instance presented in Chapter 12 (by Munkejord), in Chapter 5 (by Júlíusdóttir and Gunnarsdotter) and in Chapter 6 (by Førde). People also tell about their places as such: local history, events, legends and material realities are important in the stories people tell in interviews concerning the place where they live, stories they more or less share as members of a community. Somers (1994) calls this type public narratives. A third form of narratives – what Somers defines as conceptual narratives – are stories that are inscribing in academic or public discourses. Such stories are demonstrated in Chapter 5 when public officials claim that Egilsstaðir and Pajala are on their way into the cultural economy, or when an informant in Kirkenes says 'Kirkenes is a hybrid community'. The choice of one type of these narratives is determined by the educational background or the profession people have. Such professional narratives are demonstrated in Chapter 8 (by Olsson and Berglund) where the small Swedish town of Arboga is described according to its historical and cultural profile with a street pattern from the Middle Ages. We also find this form of narrative demonstrated in Chapter 7 (by Granås) in the professional marketing of Narvik. A particular form of narratives is the meta-narratives – grounded in grand theories or ideologies (Somers 1994). Meta-narratives are often inscribed in discourses, for instance academic discussions concerning place, region or cultural economy. In this way narratives about local changes are narratives about adaptations to international or global trends, and how global trends are embedded in local performance and culture. Such narratives are for instance represented in Chapter 4 (by Viken and Nyseth) in the narrative about the multiculturality of Kirkenes.

Narratives in the form of self-presentations about the urban character of the towns located in this peripheral part of Europe seem to flourish (cf. Throgmorton 2003). One is about the town as a site of opportunity and excitement. This is illustrated in the optimistic plans that tell about a prosperous future of the small village Fjardabygd in Iceland as a site for a new aluminium smelter (Chapter 2, by Benediktsson), about Båtsfjord as a world site for fisheries (Chapter 10), and Kirkenes as a hub in a future oil industry (Chapter 4). Another narrative has almost an opposite tone – the nightmares narratives addressing challenges related to unemployment, out-migration, economic crises or diminishing fish resources. In several of the chapters in the book such stories are told: about crises in the fisheries in the 1990s, about falling prices of iron. In several of the cases one can see the contours of a narrative of victimization (cf. Gilpin 2008) – others are blamed for the crises: public authorities, globalization or the 'market'. A fifth type of narrative is about 'town ghosts', for instance in Berlevåg the cinematic narrative where people refer to the community of good old days. Also this is a type of narrative in Kirkenes – the 'good old days of mining', when everything was arranged by the company – a narrative that is said to have blocked the way for innovation and development; in such a dependent climate people sat passive, waiting for someone to get things in order, create jobs and services, and so on. We also find examples of narratives that represent matters for local pride and boasting, for instance about 'big fish' (in Chapter 6) about the never-ending business success stories in Båtsfjord (Chapter 10), and about the community and fellowship through the harsh living conditions in Berlevåg, and narratives that try to sell the places, for instance by promising 'strong experiences' (Narvik), or conveying dreams about an 'international hub' (Kirkenes).

The focus in this book will be what masterframes and discourses that are taken into use to create new images of the places; how new contested identities are produced and negotiated; whose images they represent and interests they gain; and how the images relate to the places as they traditionally are known. For instance this book contains stories of revitalization of cultural heritage in the construction of particular indigenous (coastal Sami) identity, another about the awakening of the border-culture between Sweden and Finland. Uniqueness is often found in history.

Aims and Structure of the Book

Empirically, the analyses in this book are unfolded along parts of the northern European periphery, in Norway, Sweden and Iceland. The book originates from a series of research projects and networks that have focused on restructuring, renewal and reinvention of place and space. The idea of the book is to further develop the theories of place reinvention through case studies that illustrate the diversity of the phenomenon but also to develop and question analytical categories that can enhance our understanding of place reinvention. The book is multidisciplinary in the sense that the authors originate from sociology, social anthropology, human geography, political science and planning, but also in the sense that many of the presentations draw on theories crossing different disciplines.

The empirical examples highlight how transformations of place are interwoven in global structures and networks even in remote areas in the northern periphery. This book invites the reader into processes of reinvention that cope with the impacts of, but also add to, global trends through meta-narratives and discourses.

A part of our concern is to understand more of the dynamics behind processes of place reinvention that goes deeper than place promotion – focusing on a narrow and commodified understanding of place transformation, removed from its social and cultural structures. Place reinvention is a much broader concept linking place making to both material and symbolic processes of change, and to the discourses and narratives that are linked to place images. One of our main arguments is that material and symbolic production of place are intimately linked, and not two different processes. Changes in the mode of production followed by an ongoing restructuring of the local economy may lead to changes in place identities and place images; the symbolic representation of a place. But place reinvention is also guided by traditions, norms and values. And in most places there are different narratives operating at the same time. Different actors tell different stories about the same place.

For places to appear attractive to investors, as well as inhabitants, newcomers and tourists depends on traditional economic systems and market trends, but it is also influenced by discourses and meta-narratives, for instance discourses concerning alternative economies, symbolic aspects of place, and the place branding discourse. Fishing villages are not only places where people make a living out of fishing – increasingly such places have become integrated in an experience economy, and as a consequence, such places reorient themselves through forms of branding as unique localities for visitors.

The following chapters are not divided into distinct sections as they all relate to the two dimensions of place reinvention, although to a varying degree. Chapters 2, 3 and 4 have in common reinvention of industrial towns: in the Icelandic community Fjarðabyggð, from fish to aluminium production; in Kiruna, sustained mining; and in Kirkenes, a more differentiated industrial pattern emerges at the same time as the iron mine is being reopened. The two following chapters (5 and 6) both discuss gendered practices involved in place reinvention. In Chapter 5 Júlíusdóttir and Gunnarsdotter discuss gendered processes of place reinvention in Pajala in Sweden and Egilsstaðir in Iceland. The local discourse on cultural economy is becoming part of the regional development policy and economic aims are increasingly used in arguments in support of cultural activities. The analysis focuses on the gendered outcomes of that process. In Chapter 6 Førde tells the story of how Sørøya, an island on the harsh coast of Finnmark in Norway, creates itself as 'The Land of the Big Fish'. The study shows how new place images produce new tourism projects – addressing male tourists. The result has been a considerable upswing for existing and new tourism enterprises. In Chapters 7 and 8 place marketing approaches are the issue. In Chapter 7 the construction of a new place image of Narvik in Norway is considered. Brochures aiming at appealing to new inhabitants, investors, students and tourists are analysed emphasizing how both the ordinary and unique aspects of the place are communicated. In Chapter 8 Krister Olsson and Elin Berglund look more closely into the growing practice of city marketing from a citizen perspective. Through illustrations from Arboga the authors show how findings from local citizens survey data can be used to evaluate city marketing practices. In Chapter 9 Gry Paulgaard analyses film as a medium for place image construction. Her point of departure is the film *Cool and Crazy*, about the choir in the small coastal town of Berlevåg in Norway that plays upon otherness and familiarity. Through an analysis of the film, the author discusses the power of place myths, and how they can be modified. In Chapter 10 Turid Moldenæs use a narrative approach in analysing the construction of place images in the small town of Båtsfjord in Finnmark, applying an autobiographical approach. This story is about construction of a proud and strong place attachment. In Chapter 11, Paul Pedersen and Arvid Viken analyse how the ethnic festival Riddu Riđđu in Gáivuotna in Norway has been a catalyst for ethnic reinvention. From being a place where the Sami culture had almost vanished, Gáivuotna has turned into a strong internationally-oriented indigenous community. In Chapter 12, May Camilla Munkejord focuses on in-migrants' place perceptions in light of the urban–rural discourse. Through this analysis the value of the dichotomy is questioned; people live urban lives in this remote town. The book closes with Chapter 13 where the authors reflect upon some of the main findings that can be drawn from the case studies. To what extent are places in the European North being reinvented, and what forms does place reinvention assume in this region? What has been reinvented, and how was it done? What dynamics were behind these changes? The multiple forms and dimensions of place reinvention are discussed, concluding with emphasizing the essence of the book: how narratives reinvent place creating new materialities, social conditions and images.

References

Anholt, S. (2007), *Competitive Identity: The New Brand Management for Nations, Cities and Regions* (Basingstoke: Palgrave Macmillan).

Appadurai, Arjun (1990), 'Disjuncture and difference in the global economy', *Theory, Culture & Society*, 7, 295–310.

Bærenholdt, J.O. (2007), *Coping with Distances. Producing Nordic Atlantic Societies* (New York: Berghahn Books).

Beck, U. (2002), *Globalisering og Individualisering* (Oslo: Abstrakt forlag).

Berg, L. and Kearns, R. (1998), 'Amerca unlimited', *Environment and Planning D: Society and Space*, 16, 128–32.

Bowman, W.D. (2006), 'Why narrative? Why now?', *Research Studies in Music Educations*, 27, 5–20.

Brenner, N. and Theodore, N. (2002) 'Cities and the geographies of actually existing neoliberalism', *Antipode*, 34(3), 349–79.

Clark, T.N. (2003), 'Globalisation and transformation in political cultures' in: Hambleton, R., Savitch, H.V. and Stewart, M. (eds), *Globalism and Local Democracy. Challenges and Change in Europe and North America* (New York: Palgrave Macmillan).

Czarniawska-Joerges, B. (2004), *Narratives in Social Research* (London: Sage).

Friedman, J. (2002), 'From roots to routes. Tropes for trippers', *Anthropological Theory*, 2(1), 21–36.

Gilpin, D.R. (2008), 'Narrating the organization self: Reframing the role of the new release', *Public Relation Review*, 34, 9–18.

Gold, J.R. (1994), 'Locating the message: place promotion as image communication', in: Ward, S. and Gold, J.R. (eds), *Place Promotion. The Use of Publicity and Marketing to Sell Towns and Regions* (Chichester: Wiley & Sons Ltd).

Harvey, D. (1989), 'From managerialism to entrepreneurialism: the transformation in urban governance in late capitalism', *Geografiska Annaler* 71B(1), 3–17.

Hubbard, P. (1996), 'Urban design and city regeneration: social representations of entrepreneurial landscapes', *Urban Studies*, 33(8), 1441–6.

Jensen, O.B. (2007), 'Culture stories: understanding cultural urban branding', *Planning Theory*, 6(3), 211–36.

Jessop, B. (1997), 'The entrepreneurial city: re-imaging localities, redesigning economic governance, or restructuring capital?', in: Jewson, N. and Macgregor, S. (eds), *Transforming Cities. Contested Governance and New Spatial Divisions* (London: Routledge).

Kitchen, R. (2005), 'Disrupting and destabilizing Anglo-American and English-language hegemony in geography', *Social and Cultural Geography*, 6, 1–15.

Keith, M. and Pile, S. (1993), *Place and the Politics of Identity* (London: Routledge).

Lash, S. and Urry, J. (1994), *The Economies of Signs and Space* (London: Sage).

Mommaas, H. (2002), 'City branding', in: Heuben, T., Vermeulen, M. and Patteeuw, V. (eds), *City Branding: Image Building and Building Images* (Rotterdam: Nai Publishers).

Philo, C. and Kearns, G. (1993), *Selling Places. The City as Cultural Capital, Past and Present* (Oxford: Pergamon Press).

Piore, M.J. and Sabel, C.F. (1984), *The Second Industrial Divide: Possibilities for Prosperity* (New York: Basic Books).

Robinson, J. (2006), 'Inventions and interventions: transforming cities – an introduction', *Urban Studies*, 43(2), 251–8.

Sandercock, L. (2003), *Cosmopolis II: Mongrel Cities in the 21st Century* (London: Continuum).

Shields, R. (1991), *Places on the Margin: Alternative Geographies of Modernity* (London: Routledge).

Short, J.R. (1999), 'Urban Imagineers: Boosterism and the Representation of Cities', in: Jones, A.E.G. and Wilson, D. (eds), *The Urban Growth Machine. Critical Perspectives, Two Decades Later* (New York: State University Press), pp. 37–54.

Somers, M. (1994), 'The narrative constitution of identity: A relational and network approach', *Theory and Society*, 23, 605–49.

Thrift, N. (2008), *Non-representational Theory. Space, Politics, Affect* (Oxon: Routledge).

Throgmorton, J.A. (2003), 'Planning as persuasive storytelling in a global-scale web of relationships', *Planning Theory*, 2, 125–51.

Ward, S. (1998), *Selling Places: The Marketing and Promotion of Towns and Cities* (New York: Routledge).

Zukin, S. (1995), *The Culture of Cities* (Cambridge: MA: Blackwell).

Chapter 2

The Industrial Imperative and Second (hand) Modernity

Karl Benediktsson

Introduction

Are towns in the Nordic periphery heading out of an industrial era and into a future of a different kind? How do their own inhabitants answer that question? Some 35 years have now passed since American sociologist Daniel Bell (1973) confidently asserted that the structures of industrial society were giving way to a different kind of societal organization: the 'post-industrial society', based on service occupations and information handling. Numerous others have since presented broadly similar arguments, and ever more intricate labels continue to roll off the academic production lines.

Many people living in the towns of the North are not entirely convinced by the (admittedly somewhat grand) narratives of postindustrial society, with the corresponding emphasis on immaterial economic activities. Theirs are localities whose existence has always been based largely on the utilization of the material bounties of nature – fish, timber, minerals, etc. For the best part of the 20th century, the industrial processing of these resources seemed to be the 'natural order' of economic life. No wonder perhaps that many people in these towns harbour deep suspicions towards suggestions about the disappearance of the industrial era. But yet, times are obviously changing. New technologies have not only reduced the need for industrial labour, but also worked towards a deterritorialization of knowledge processes that are so important in the new economy. A global marketplace has brought in new actors in faraway countries, instigating new relational networks between places, firms and individuals. At a micro level, social and cultural changes have deeply affected gender roles and prevailing ideas about the good life.

This chapter looks at a particular instance of adjustment to a new environment. This is Fjarðabyggð, a coastal municipality of East Iceland which has been enthusiastically reinventing itself through heavy industry, precisely of the kind which is presumed to be on the wane. The empirical material upon which the chapter is based consists of recorded focus group sessions, where 'ordinary' people discussed the state of and prospect for their localities, and some interviews with leading persons in the communities. The fieldwork took place in early 2006. The importance of everyday discursive production of local space as an arena of meaningful economic engagement – of place as social context – will be highlighted in the analysis below, through direct quotations from the fieldwork material. Preempting the conclusion, a common concern in this local setting is uncertainty and how to avoid it – themes that are central to recent ideas about 'second modernity'; yet the solutions seem to have more in common with the 'first'.

Modernity reinvented?

Among the theories about current socioeconomic changes that were mentioned briefly at the beginning of the chapter, the theory of second modernity is somewhat distinctive. Based on Ulrich Beck's (1986) ideas about the pervasive impact of increasingly mobile risks and the central role of reflexivity in modern society, this is less a theory about epochal change towards post-modernity than of a changed complexion of modernity. First modernity, according to this line of thinking, is a social order "based on nation-state societies, where social relations, networks and communities are essentially understood in a territorial sense" (Beck and Lau, 2005, p. 526). The transition to second modernity has meant that

> [t]he collective patterns of life, progress and controllability, full employment and exploitation of nature ... have now been undermined by certain interlinked processes: globalization, individualization, the gender revolution, underemployment and global risks (Beck and Lau, 2005, p. 526).

Society is thus characterized rather by fluid networking, mobility and cosmopolitanism than by territorially bounded and cohesive entities (cf. also Urry, 2000). This is not an argument about 'place' having lost its significance for inhabitants, but that its meaning has to be renegotiated within a framework of fluidity and ongoing changes: a shift in logic from structures to flows (Lash, 2003). Marx's famous aphorism, about all which is solid melting into air with the advent of capitalism, is thus even more true in the second modernity than in the first, which did after all provide a modicum of stability for a good part of the 20th century (Beck, Bonβ and Lau, 2003). In this account, the transition to second modernity is seen as the direct result of the success of, and contradictions inherent in, the first.

A defining characteristic of the move towards second modernity is reflexivity: this is reflexive modernization (or perhaps simply re-modernization – see Latour, 2003). The concept of reflexivity has often been used in a broadly positive sense, to signify increased contemplation by individuals and collectivities of their life's conditions and how to cope with them (see e.g. Aarsæther and Bærenholdt, 2001; Lash and Urry, 1994; Ray, 1999). In the formulation of Beck and his colleagues, the term "does not mean that people today lead a more conscious life" (Beck, Bonβ and Lau, 2003, p. 3) and are thus better able to master their fortunes. Quite the opposite – it signifies disenchantment and loss of certainties: "Simple modernization becomes reflexive modernization to the extent that it disenchants and then dissolves its own taken-for-granted premises" (Beck, Bonβ and Lau, 2003, p. 3). Old, purified and powerful modern binaries such as nature/society, state/ market, and work/leisure, are called into question. Previously taken-for-granted categories of nation-state, family, gender, company and so on, are destabilized.

What then about the meaning of locality or local community? In fact, local practices and discourses are something of a blind spot in the otherwise comprehensive theorization of Beck et al. In a manner of much classical social science, it is directed towards an explanation of the 'whole', but "without showing the least interest in the practical and local conditions making this 'whole' visible" (Latour, 2003, p. 40). That lacuna seems indeed problematic. In the empirical discussion which follows I attempt to bring to life these practical and local conditions and concerns. My discussion is centred on questions about how local actors define their situations in local development discourse and how they act on them; how place is animated as a social context through everyday discursive practices. Can we really say that places in the north fit the blueprint of second modernity?

As most other theories about a new kind of modernity (or post-modernity), the second-modernity thesis has been developed with reference to the world's old industrial heartlands – in this case Germany and Western Europe – regions of intensive restructuring of industries, labour markets and welfare state functions during the late 20th century. The experience of deindustrialization is central in the thesis. That process has also impacted upon localities in the northern periphery, many of which were in fact latecomers to industry. This certainly applies to the case study locale presented here. The fish processing industries of Iceland have been 'rationalised' through technology and changes in management. But how well are the localities in the north, such as the fishing villages on the Icelandic coast, placed to enjoy the benefits of a new economic situation – of moving into service occupations and cultural activities? And, even if these activities are found to hold some promise, to what extent do the people of the north accept the premises of the new social order – with stress on flexibility and change rather than standardization and stability? As we will see from the discussion of Fjarðabyggð, the development discourse in this part of Iceland reveals a somewhat uneasy relationship between these two models.

Fjarðabyggð: A simple yet complex locality

The name Fjarðabyggð is in fact a recent invention. This is the official term that represents a rather young municipal entity, created in 1998 through the amalgamation of three previously separate townships together with some farms – Reyðarfjörður, Eskifjörður and Neskaupstaður/Norðfjörður (Figure 2.1). Each is located in its very own fjord (as the names imply) and each has its own distinct character. In 2006, the municipality was further enlarged to include two fjords to the south and one to the north, adding two smaller towns and some farms.

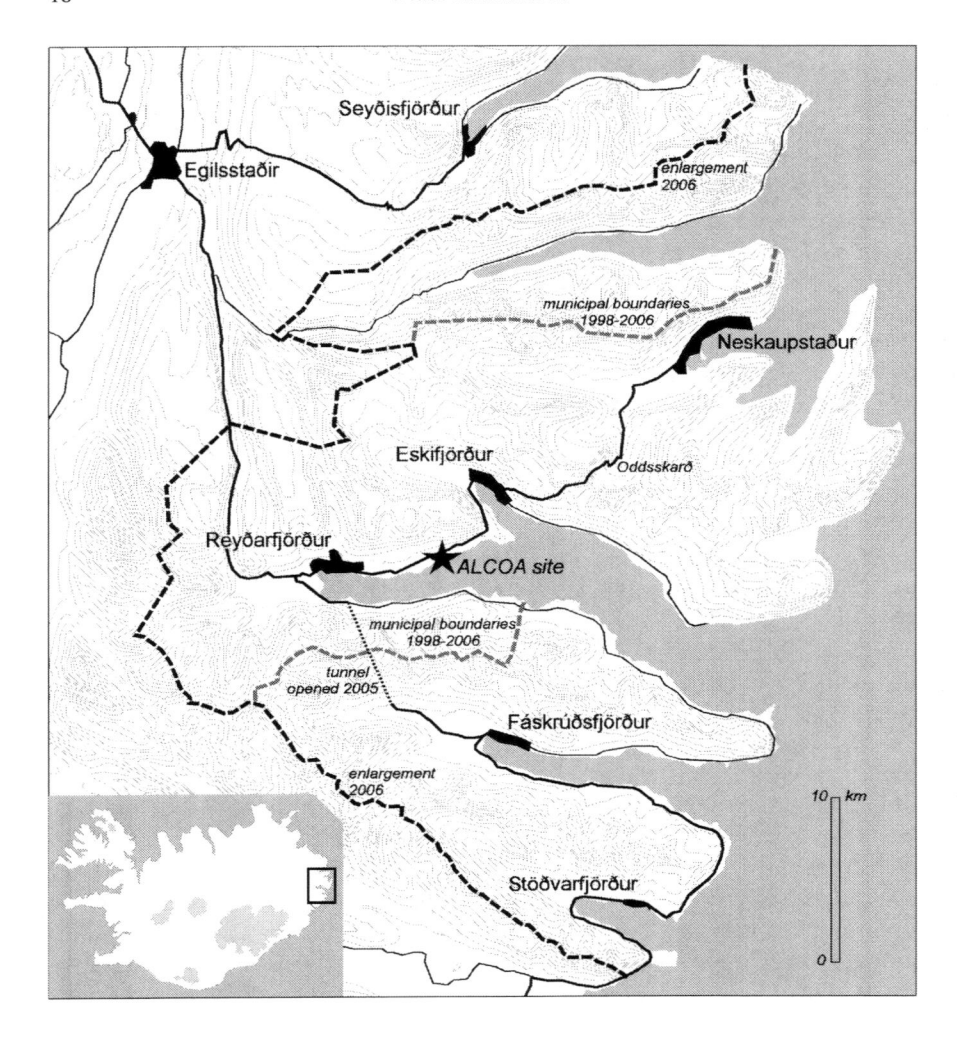

**Figure 2.1 The area included in the amalgamated municipality of
         Fjarðabyggð in 1998**
Source: © Fjarðabyggð.

The towns of Fjarðabyggð have many things in common. Yet each has its very
own history, which is reflected in both social life and in the material fabric.
Reyðarfjörður (or Búðareyri as the village was originally called) has until recently
been the smallest of those towns. Up until a few years ago, one would have been
inclined to describe it as a stagnant place at best, or even as a declining place.
Population fluctuated, but was usually between six and seven hundred. Apart from
a few early 20th century buildings, most of the housing was from the mid-20th

century, and from the 1970s. Most of the residential housing stock consisted of detached houses, with one rather heavy-looking block of flats built according to standardized plans in the 1970s as communal housing for working class families, but during the 1970s a concerted effort was made in Iceland to bring industrial modernity to the fishing villages through state-supported investments in the name of regional policy (Benediktsson and Skaptadóttir, 2002; Hall, Jónsson and Agnarsson, 2002).

In 2006, at the time of my fieldwork, 'stagnation' was not a term that would come to the visitor's mind. The whole village looked rather like one large construction site. New residential houses were being built, some obviously rather cheaply and without much consideration to either design or site. A large 11-storey block of flats had already sprung up. A new building combining shops and offices, that had been given the name Molinn, had been opened in 2004, with an enlargement already underway two years later. A new school was under construction and also a large sports hall, which was going to contain a fully-fledged indoor football field when completed. Large cement silos on the quay and a newly completed bypass for truck traffic were further signs of the construction frenzy which was taking place here. And population? Over 1400 at the beginning of 2006, according to Statistics Iceland (2008), up from less than 700 just a year before. Most of this remarkable increase, however, consisted of a multinational army of construction workers residing at a large camp just outside town. Most numerous were the Polish workers.

The neighbouring town of Eskifjörður, home to some 1000 people, was a much more settled place in 2006 than Reyðarfjörður, even if numerous new residential building sites told the observer that this was indeed also a town in the midst of great changes. An old trading place, Eskifjörður has a core of 19th century seaside warehouses and other buildings which have escaped the urge to erase anything vaguely 'pre-modern' which is so evident in many Icelandic seaside towns and villages. Other buildings are of varying age, telling a story of a gradual development. The ubiquitous petrol station/kiosk is here, as well as a few other shops and small service establishments, a reduction factory and freezing plant. Eskifjörður is also a container port for East Iceland. The older part of town is spread along the steep side of the fjord, but most of the new housing under construction in 2006 was being built on the flats in the valley behind.

Located at the very eastern edge of Iceland, the elongated fjordside town Neskaupstaður (population 1400) was the largest of the towns of Fjarðabyggð at the time of fieldwork. As numerous other fishing localities in the country, it came into being in the late 19th century, following the relaxation of a rather draconian piece of legislation that to all extents and purposes prevented people from being permanently occupied with anything but farming (Hálfdanarson, 1993; Hall, Jónsson and Agnarsson, 2002). Neskaupstaður enjoyed a favourable location for coastal fishing and grew rapidly in the early 20th century (Geirsson, 1983). It was for a long time the leading community not only for this part of the eastern fjords, but for the whole of East Iceland. It is, however, somewhat removed from the two towns described previously, both geographically and mentally. The mountain pass Oddsskarð (632 m a.s.l.) is a considerable barrier to interaction, even if a road was constructed through the pass in the middle of the 20th century and improved with a short tunnel in 1978. Still however, this easternmost town in Iceland is at the 'end of the road'. The visitor approaches from the west, passing a few farms and then some large fish factories. Then there is a large gap in the town's fabric, owing to a large snow avalanche that occurred in 1974, which demolished the old fish reduction plant and took the lives of twelve workers. Continuing into the town proper, the houses are strung along two main streets for some 2 kms, protected from further avalanches by a formidable wall in the steep mountainside above.

Neskaupstaður is a rather tidy if somewhat bland town, that has embraced 'modern' times in a physical sense. The hospital and the junior college are located in the eastern part. Seashore warehouses and boatsheds are mostly absent, giving a quite different feel to the town to that of Eskifjörður. One does not sense that the past is highly valued. A scatter of shops is found along the seaside street.

A few farms are found in the fjords, but these have (up until recently) been overwhelmingly fishing communities. The main exception has been Reyðarfjörður, where services were a somewhat larger part of the economic structure than in the other towns. Eskifjörður and Neskaupstaður are very much 'company towns', although they have also stood for very different political leanings.

In Eskifjörður, the company Eskja has long dominated. Established as a family concern by one Aðalsteinn Jónsson (popularly known as Alli ríki – Alli the rich), it is now one of the country's larger fisheries firms, but unlike many of those it is still very much bound to the locality of origin. Eskifjörður is thus a town built on private capital and has a reputation for rather conservative politics.

Neskaupstaður, on the other hand, used to be known in Iceland as 'Little Moscow', due to the strong power base of socialists. In the middle of the 20th century the town was associated with a troika of powerful political personalities, who together shaped its destiny. One was a national parliamentarian (and at times the Minister of Fisheries), another was the town's mayor, and the third was at the helm of the town's largest firm, Síldarvinnslan. This company was itself the outgrowth of a fisheries cooperative, SÚN, which still exists and also wields considerable economic power. Like Eskja in Eskifjörður, it is now a highly commercialized fisheries firm and one of the country's largest. Besides this, public service employment is important, through the regional hospital (now rather inconveniently located here, but not necessarily during earlier times when sea travel was most common) and local junior college. The college is based on an older vocational school, and the town has a certain blue-collar tradition and a rich industrial history, not least in servicing the fishing fleet.

The economic makeup of Reyðarfjörður has always been more mixed than that of the other two towns. Reyðarfjörður originated as a coastal gateway to the large inland farming region of Fljótsdalshérað. In the first half of the 20th century it was home base to a large cooperative, Kaupfélag Héraðsbúa (KHB) and commerce, transportation and public services have been comparatively large. Although always a part of the economy, fisheries have been less important than in the other towns. Some small-scale food processing and other industries have existed besides it.

It would not be accurate at all to present these towns as if they had not undergone any changes since their early days. They have certainly not stood still, any more than other Icelandic local communities. Many of the older generation told of the change from a close-knit community where people knew each other well – even rather too well – to a much more fluid society today, where children for instance were no longer active participants in the economy as they used to be.

Locational and socio-political differences notwithstanding, these three towns have now united in a single municipal entity, and have plunged headlong into a 'reinvention' phase based on heavy industry. Like the road hugging the coast of the East Fjords, the metaphorical road to industrial development has been a long and winding one. Already in the 1970s and early 1980s, a government working group had reasoned that Reyðarfjörður would be a suitable place for locating heavy industry (Staðarvalsnefnd um iðnrekstur, 1983). The fjord offered good conditions for a port that could handle very large freight vessels and ample electrical power could be generated within the district. At that time, however, the smallness of the town's workforce was seen as a hindrance to the development of a major industrial project, such as an aluminium smelter. A smaller industrial plant was planned, but this did not materialize. When large-scale aluminium smelting again became a strategy of choice by political power brokers, which happened around 1990 (Skúlason and Hayter, 1998), Reyðarfjörður was seriously considered. Again nothing happened. Local frustration grew. Finally in 1997 the then Foreign Minister (and Member of Parliament for East Iceland) announced that the multinational giant Norsk Hydro was eager to build a very large smelter in Reyðarfjörður, powered by a hydropower plant that had been on the drawing board for some years. This would however have destroyed a wetland area of great ecological importance in the highlands. A very divisive battle ensued between environmentalists and those speaking for development of large-scale industry. The proposed hydropower scheme was shelved – but an even bigger one drawn up: the Kárahnjúkar dam. And then, in 2002, Norsk Hydro backed out. Morale in Reyðarfjörður sank to new lows. But in 2003 another multinational corporation appeared on this contested ground, namely the US-based Alcoa. An agreement was signed. Local despondency turned to euphoria and jubilation, that to many other Icelanders reached almost bizarre proportions. Youth paraded through town wearing sporting hats made of aluminium foil, and a local car owner ordered a personalized number plate with the letters ALCOA.

A story jokingly told in the focus group session held by the author in Neskaupstaður can be taken as a gentle critique of the mentality engendered by the history of 'industrial dreaming', which is presumed to have prevailed in Reyðarfjörður especially:

An old man in Reyðarfjörður asks his grandson: 'Little fellow, what to you want to do when you grow up?' The boy answers: 'I am going to do just like you have done, grandpa. I am going to sit and wait. For an aluminium smelter.'

The people of Reyðarfjörður, mind you, are at pains to tell you that this is a very wrong impression and based on ingrained prejudices towards their community – in fact, there were, and to some extent are, considerable rivalries between the three main towns of Fjarðabyggð. But, as a focus group participant in Reyðarfjörður – a man in his late thirties – reminisced:

> ... already when I was just a small boy, there was always something just about to come, some heavy industry ... Then that faded away, and perhaps two-three years passed, and then the discussion began again about something big. I experienced this right from my childhood.

From Fish Industry to 'Real' Industry?

And now industry has finally arrived – big time. A rather huge aluminium smelter has been erected on the shores of Reyðarfjörður, some 5 kms east of the town. It started operating in 2007. The people interviewed in Fjarðabyggð in 2006, when construction activities were reaching their peak, were understandably enough very much preoccupied with the immense economic and social changes that were taking place in the municipality. The demand for labour was great and just about every firm and individual entrepreneur had been drawn into the project's orbit. Most people saw this as a very welcome break from the stagnation allegedly prevailing in the past. They also perceived a changed attitude of other Icelanders towards their own community. Reyðarfjörður and the other towns of Fjarðabyggð were no longer seen as merely some moribund fishing towns:

> I feel that [Reyðarfjörður] is no longer an irrelevant *extremity* [in the eyes of other Icelanders]. It has become a place.

When asked whether they had been in favour of the project, and if so why, most replied that they had indeed been positive from the outset, for very simple reasons:

> I looked at it this way: If this would not have come, the town would have continued to shrink. The community and the services ... it would all have gradually collapsed. But with this you get expansion. There are more jobs. You have more jobs to choose from. You do not have to accept whatever job you may be lucky enough to get.

But it was all happening very suddenly. A woman in Reyðarfjörður contemplated the changes to the identity of her home town:

> The fish is gone, the smell of fish is gone ... We have suddenly moved from being a fishing place to industrial labour.

One of the major concerns of those who questioned the emphasis on heavy industry is that it would transform the localities into single-industry towns that would inevitably become quite vulnerable to market forces which they can in no way control. The aluminium industry is of course in many ways almost an epitome of globalization. A handful of large, multinational corporations controls the mining of bauxite, its processing into alumina and smelting to make aluminium (Skúlason and Hayter, 1998). These corporations keep a close watch on the cost of energy around the world, which is the decisive locational factor for smelters. As for the market for the finished product, price fluctuations have also been significant, and related to the general ups and downs of the large industrial economies. Few interviewees were overly worried about changing fortunes. Some brushed aside rather lightly the question of potential uncertainties:

> You simply think that it [the smelter] will never close down!

But one must perhaps be careful not to exaggerate the level to which this actually represents a radical change in these resource-based communities. Some focus group participants referred an economic past which certainly was always rather risky and changeable anyway, like this middle-aged man:

> Of course we are born and raised in an economy dependent upon a single sector – fisheries. We know that situation well. We know that when the catches fail, there is less money and less activity – we know all of that. The cod has sometimes failed, or the capelin, or the whole lot, and this has alternated with booms, and we have lived with that. Therefore ... whether this kind of dependence will be different?

Of course, if this factory closes down, then that is not like the cod, which comes back during the next season. The factory would be gone for good. So that would perhaps be a risk, but this factory would maybe have built up such an environment around itself that we would be better able to cope with losing it.

Similar reasoning often came up in the group sessions, where the participants exchanged their views:

> A: We have never had anything but a single something to build on. We have never had other things.
>
> B: Well, many small things ...
>
> A: But all these small things have always lived on the fisheries. We have never known anything else. And always when the fish is gone, in all villages, when the fish is gone, nothing is left. It does not matter if the place was doing well before. Look at Stöðvarfjörður [a small village, now part of the municipality of Fjarðabyggð]. It was for a while one of the richest places in Iceland. If you

wanted to look at the most recent car models, you would go to Stöðvarfjörður. You did not go to Reykjavík for that. This is a fact. And then the fish was gone, and nothing was left.

The new industry was thus compared favourably with the fisheries and related industries, where fluctuations of nature – and, to a lesser extent, international markets – were an inevitable source of uncertainty.

But even if the sentiments were thus positive for the most part, it was of course not the case that all inhabitants of these three towns turned out to be in favour of the industrialization project. In Norðfjörður, a man in his forties, with very strong ideological convictions, alleged that a pernicious

> ... brainwashing ... has been taking place here: we are being told 'it is aluminium or nothing'!

This propaganda had in his view led local people to neglect other and perhaps more innovative strategies for making a living, waiting instead for the one-off solution. The same person also hinted that his own life had not been entirely pleasant since the debates started:

> I am of course nearly expelled from this community here for holding these opinions, which ... I have been trying as best I can to make heard.

Another man had very serious reservations about the nature of jobs associated with the project:

> I cannot say that it was my most cherished dream that the sons and daughters of Norðfjörður would be working in a giant factory ... This was never my dream, far from it. And this means that if I were a young man here, then I would be looking for another place to live, certainly. I am here because I am a village person by nature, not a factory slave.

Some of the most serious doubts aired about this industrial 'reinvention' project have been related to its gender implications. Critics of the project have often pointed out that, as such industrial jobs have traditionally been culturally coded as male, it is likely that the project will exacerbate already-existing gender imbalances. For some time, the male-to-female ratio has been quite skewed in many rural areas and smaller coastal villages of Iceland, but even more so in East Iceland than elsewhere. A woman observed that gender imbalance in local economic life was not exactly a new phenomenon, but had been a persistent feature of local culture for a long time:

> I argue that these coastal villages, they are really very male-centred communities, everything is somehow based on the male viewpoint.

When recruitment for the smelter started, Alcoa put great emphasis on the company's commitment to gender equality, by explicitly seeking to recruit women (Alcoa, 2006). One of their advertisements showed a young, smiling woman, with a toddler on her arm. She was the manager of Alcoa's Reyðarfjörður office. A special 'Women's Day' was also held at the plant in October 2006, where local women were encouraged to visit the site and be informed about the job opportunities that are opening up. According to the company's public relations office, a surprising number of women turned up.

Another prominent question was where the workforce for the plant was going to come from. The local labour market is quite small and the interest of Icelanders in 'Fordist' industrial work has been dwindling, it seems, as witnessed by the numerous international labourers found not only in the fishing industry, but in most larger workplaces. A local politician scoffed at the suggestion that the new jobs would be filled by international labourers:

> ... there are those who talk much but think little, and who do not know the local context, they of course say that there will be some four hundred new jobs in the aluminium plant, and that nobody wants to work in an aluminium plant, and there will be only Turks, and such things. But, see, this simply is not like that.

Others recognized the staffing of the new plant by foreign labour as a distinct possibility and even likelihood, but saw it not as a problem but simply a healthy development towards a more diverse community.

A Place for 'Knowledge'?

Although the large-scale industrial project had been the overwhelming preoccupation of people in the three towns when they were interviewed in 2006, there seemed to be a growing realization in the communities that general socioeconomic change would require considerable intellectual 'retooling'. Alongside the industrial processing of material resources, new attitudes, skills and practices geared for the processing of somewhat ethereal symbols and meaning would have to be developed. Increased education and the raising of the region's relatively low level of (formal) knowledge was mentioned by most people as vital for the future well-being of the community.

During the past few years, despite an overwhelming penchant for energy-hungry industrial developments, the Icelandic central government has, in its regional policy statements, in fact at least frequently referred to ideas of the knowledge economy. Some regional and local authorities have taken up the challenge of designing an institutional architecture appropriate to their knowledge needs. One such initiative was the establishment, in June 2006, of the East Iceland Knowledge Network. Headquartered in the inland town of Egilsstaðir, the Network was based on an earlier and quite successful distance learning network, that had revealed a latent need for education in the towns and rural areas of the region. This previous organization had offered courses in fields as diverse as digital photography and Danish smørrebrød, in addition to providing general assistance to distance learners studying at colleges and universities in Reykjavík or elsewhere. The new Knowledge Network was supposed to build on this, not least to broaden the possibilities for local people to undertake tertiary studies at the universities. It was also meant to serve as a vehicle to promote local research and development, in collaboration with two existing small research centres elsewhere in the region, one of which is located in Fjarðabyggð (in Neskaupstaður).

This initiative had generally been well received. Yet there was some scepticism aired by those who were interviewed in 2006. While nobody really suggested that increased tertiary education was a negative thing in itself, there was a pervasive sentiment that the move towards knowledge-based occupations and emphasis on university education had led to a serious devaluation of the forms of knowledge and kinds of jobs that were more commonly found in the coastal towns. The local politician referred to above forcefully expressed a feeling, which is common in regional towns and rural areas, that urban Iceland has lost its bearings:

> It is simply a fact that ... those doing non-vocational studies ... those types generally do not at all know what they want. They have no idea! ... The mollycoddling attitude towards university studies is becoming a societal disease, in my opinion. ... We live today in a society where we educate five plumbers against five hundred lawyers! This is pure nonsense! Meanwhile, our country needs thousands of skilled industrial workers.

The term '101 Reykjavík' – which refers to the postal code of central Reykjavík, immortalized in a novel and film by the same title – is indeed often invoked in regional Iceland to portray the alleged alienation of the latte-sipping urban cultural and economic elite from the 'real' folks in the fishing towns whose industriousness keeps the whole economy going, according to this sentiment.

To wrap this up: a rather simple vision of the 'industrial community' and the need for a single, strong economic base seems to prevail in Fjarðabyggð. Again, the local politician stated this clearly:

> This is very simple, really. I have always thought that it is the economic life which is the basis for everything, and if you really want to analyse and understand a development process, you start by looking at what is happening there.

And the economy was indeed limping. Thus:

> People realised that they needed something else – more vigororus, safer, bigger – in order to reverse the trend.

Local development, in other words, is in this vision first and foremost about jobs; preferably industrial jobs that result in a material, tangible output. Knowledge, in this view of the world, is a kind of Überbau on top of a solid Grundlage – which in this case is to be made of aluminium. Apart from the sheer size of the aluminium project, which would provide hundreds of jobs in an instant, there was the expectation of multifarious spin-offs. Industrial jobs of the old type were generally seen as more convincing – offering more security and stability – than an admittedly somewhat vaguely defined 'knowledge society' or 'cultural economy' could provide.

Into the Post-construction Period

> I must say – and I have thought quite a lot about this – that I can not at all predict what this community will look like in three to five years.

There has been considerable flux in Fjarðabyggð during these heady last years, as attested by the quote above, which comes from one of the focus group sessions in early 2006. When this is written, in late 2008, the dust from the construction phase is now gradually settling. Most of the international construction workers have left. The aluminium smelter is fully operational, with the last smelting pot taken into use in April 2008 (Morgunblaðið, 9 April 2008). At the start of the megaprojects in East Iceland, the Icelandic parliament decided that a social impact monitoring programme should be carried out for six years, from 2004 to 2009. The researchers published an interim report in 2008, where the situation as of the end of 2007 and beginning of 2008 is described in some detail (Jóhannesson et al., 2008).

The completion of the smelter coincided with a drastic cut in fishing quotas and layoffs in some of the larger fisheries firms in the area. The new, large industrial establishment undoubtedly softened the blow for the communities. Hiring of production workers to the smelter started for real in late 2006. Contrary to some predictions, nearly all who applied for these jobs were Icelanders. Of the 410 persons employed at the smelter at the end of 2007, more than half had been recruited from East Iceland (Morgunblaðið, 9 April 2008). The remainder had come mostly from Reykjavík and vicinity, some of those being young people from the east, who used this opportunity to return to a place with which they had emotional affinities (Jóhannesson et al., 2008).

The impacts on education levels and on the gendering of the local labour markets are among the issues discussed in the monitoring report. As for education, the lack of fisheries some 42% of the staff that had been hired to the smelter in March 2008 had only finished compulsory schooling. At the other end, 17% had a tertiary degree (Jóhannesson, 2008). While the education level of the company's workforce as a whole is thus somewhat lower than that in the Icelandic labour market as a whole, the report concludes that the project has led to a definite increase in education levels in the towns of Fjarðabyggð. It is also pointed out, however, that this has coincided with a general trend towards higher education in the country as a whole.

As described previously, the aluminium company explicitly tried from the start to recruit women. There has been some success in this regard: in early 2008 the share of female workers was 28% (Jóhannesson et al., 2008), which is considered to be quite high in this male-dominated sector. The new industrial employer has so some extent compensated for contracting employment in the fish processing sector, where women have held many jobs. On the whole, however, the monitoring report found that women had not been involved nearly as much as men during the construction phase, nor indeed do they expect as much as men from the project in terms of local development impacts. There are also much more critical than men of its environmental impacts.

The contours of the post-project communities are thus only beginning to emerge. As hoped, the project has led to some migration of permanent settlers to Fjarðabyggð – quite apart from the influx of foreign construction workers. This in itself was indeed a sudden and very welcome reversal of a persistent trend for these small towns. Population increase has also provided a boost for retailing and services in the towns, and contributed to a much more optimistic climate in the communities than had been the case before (Jóhannesson et al., 2008). The temporal duration of those impacts is open to question, however. Longer time is needed for judging whether these places, even if their economies are now more robust than before, have reinvented their images and identities in such a way as to be able to continue to attract new settlers after all available jobs at the ALCOA factory have been filled – and hold on to those who live there currently. The capital area still exerts a strong influence on all other regions of Iceland. Also it must be noted that, while the project had been 'sold' to people in East Iceland as one that would eventually benefit the whole region, the benefits have not trickled down to other places in the east. Rather the contrary: Some 'backwash effects' were noticeable in the settlements lying beyond the immediate impact zone.

Conclusion: Second-hand Modernity?

In this chapter, I have presented empirical material from three small Icelandic towns that are in the midst of a far-reaching 'reinvention' phase. While each has certain historical specificities, the three towns in Fjarðabyggð described above have many things in common. These are, or were until quite recently, closely circumscribed local communities with strong identities. Their response to uncertainty and stagnation was to unite in the drive for getting a large – very large – industrial establishment to settle in their midst. Following success in this regard, they have been rather slow in formulating a convincing image for projecting outwards to people who might want to visit or settle. Perhaps there has not been that much real reflexivity.

Yet the local people do not see themselves as entering 'second modernity'. It would be more accurate to say that their reinvention strategy is aimed at finally entering the first one. Although large-scale introduction of stern trawlers and the standardization of fish processing in the 1970s has sometimes been characterized as the belated entrance of Icelandic coastal communities into the Fordist economy of first modernity, the reliance on fisheries has continued to mean a large degree of uncertainty and risk. The goal of fully-fledged industrialization, which allegedly brings much more stability than that which can be achieved even through 'industrialised' fisheries, has beckoned for a long time.

But while the people of Fjarðabyggð have been busily, and for the most part enthusiastically, changing their place both in material terms and as a locale for socioeconomic activity, the inevitably concomitant radical changes to the 'sense of place' are only now becoming apparent. Among some at least, these changes are viewed with a slight trepidation. But then again, there is not exactly anything new in such radical changes in this context. These are not communities that have existed in some unchanged form since time immemorial: one must be careful not to lapse into a "romantic essentialism of place" (Massey, 2004, p. 11). On the contrary, before this last bout of reinvention, the towns had changed their complexions considerably since they were first formed in the late 19th and early 20th century.

A certain construction of a 'proper' place, and of possible ways in which their own marginal position can be dealt with, prevails in the discourses of local people. Thinking back to Latour's (2003) critique of the interest by Beck et al. in the universalities of 'society', I have sought to highlight how "practical and local conditions" (Latour, 2003, p. 40) inevitably enter into the everyday discursive construction of contextual modernities, in places which are striving to reinvent themselves. Sweeping generalizations about social change must be tempered by an acknowledgement of 'practical and local conditions'. Even so, it is appropriate to ask whether the process of social change underway in these communities could in fact be characterized as a kind of 'reflexive modernization' that is the defining feature of second modernity?

As Scott Lash (2003) has usefully pointed out, first modernity involves individuals that are reflective, while true reflexivity is the product of second modernity. The people who live in the towns of Fjarðabyggð do indeed reflect constantly upon the conditions of their lives and communities. They are far from secure about themselves or their communities, but on the contrary are very much preoccupied with uncertainty. They are aware of their somewhat marginal position in a risky global environment, while quite correctly pointing out that risk has always been present here. They do realize that gaps in education levels and knowledge-based activities increasingly set them apart from the metropolitan Reykjavík, and the globalized world at large. There are those who do see certain opportunities in tourism and in linking up with other parts of the cultural economy.

But the industrial imperative of first modernity is still an irresistible prospect for most local people. To use the formulation of Lash (2003, p. 49), they are working with a "logic of structures" that is characteristic of the first modernity, rather than the "logic of flows" which is associated with the second. In these towns, there seems to be a somewhat more continuity in thinking than Ulrich Beck and other theorists of a radically different 'second modernity' would presume. The communities discussed in this chapter seem to be intent on leaving behind the structures of an uncertain fisheries-based first modernity, but one wonders whether they are about to enter an industrial 'second-hand modernity'.

References

Aarsæther, N., and Bærenholdt, J. O. (eds) (2001). *The Reflexive North.* Copenhagen: Nordic Council of Ministers.

Alcoa. (2006). Viewed 6 November 2006 at http://www.alcoa.com/iceland/ic/ home.asp.

Beck, U. (1986). Risikogesellschaft: Auf dem Weg in eine andere Moderne. Frankfurt am Main: Suhrkamp.

Beck, U. (1998). *Democracy Without Enemies.* Cambridge: Polity Press.

Beck, U., Bonβ, W., and Lau, C. (2003). 'The theory of reflexive modernization – Problematic, hypotheses and research programme'. *Theory, Culture & Society,* 20(2), 1–33.

Beck, U., and Lau, C. (2005). 'Second modernity as a research agenda: Theoretical and empirical explorations in the "meta-change" of modern society'. *British Journal of Sociology,* 56(4), 525–557.

Bell, D. (1973). *The Coming of Post-industrial Society: A Venture in Social Forecasting.* New York: Basic Books.

Benediktsson, K., and Skaptadóttir, U. D. (2002). 'Coping Strategies and Regional Policies – Social Capital in the Nordic Peripheries – Country Report Iceland' (Working Paper No. 2002:5). Stockholm: Nordregio.

Fjarðabyggð (2008). Yfirlitskort af gömlu Fjarðabyggð. http://www.fjardabyggd. is/media/files/fjardabyggd_yfirlitskort.pdf (Web document) Accessed 15 June 2008).

Geirsson, S. (1983). Norðfjörður: Saga útgerðar og fiskvinnslu. Neskaupstaður: Samvinnufélag útgerðarmanna & Síldarvinnslan.

Hall, A., Jónsson, Á., and Agnarsson, S. (2002). Byggðir og búseta – Þéttbýlismyndun á Íslandi. Reykjavík: Hagfræðistofnun Háskóla Íslands.

Hálfdanarson, G. (1993). Íslensk þjóðfélagsþróun á 19. öld. In Hálfdanarson, G. and Kristjánsson, S. (eds), Íslensk þjóðfélagsþróun 1880–1990 – Ritgerðir (pp. 9–58). Reykjavík: Háskóli Íslands.

Jóhannesson, H. (ed.), Leiknisdóttir, A. M., Jóhannsson, E., Heiðarsson, J. Þ. Ólafsson, K., Hallgrímsson, T., and Sigurbjarnarson, V. (2008). Rannsókn á samfélagsáhrifum álvers- og virkjunarframkvæmda á Austurlandi. Rannsóknarrit nr. 5: Áfangaskýrsla II – Stöðulýsing í árslok 2007. Akureyri: RHA.

Lash, S. (2003). 'Reflexivity as non-linearity'. *Theory Culture & Society*, 20(2), 49–57.

Lash, S., and Urry, J. (1994). *Economies of Signs and Space*. London: Sage Publications.

Latour, B. (2003). 'Is re-modernization occurring – And if so, how to prove it? A commentary on Ulrich Beck'. *Theory, Culture & Society*, 20(2), 35–48.

Massey, D. (2004). 'Geographies of responsibility'. *Geografiska Annaler*, 86 B, 5–18

Morgunblaðið, 9 April 2008: Síðasta kerið gangsett í álveri Alcoa. Retrieved 29 Sept. 2008 from http://mbl.is/mm/frettir/innlent/2008/04/09/sidasta_kerid_gangsett_i_alveri_alcoa/.

Ray, C. (1999). 'Endogenous development in the era of reflexive modernity'. *Journal of Rural Studies*, 15(3), 257–267.

Skúlason, J. B., and Hayter, R. (1998). 'Industrial location as a bargain: Iceland and the aluminium multinationals 1962–1994'. *Geografiska Annaler*, 80 B(1), 29–48.

Staðarvalsnefnd um iðnrekstur (1983). Staðarval fyrir orkufrekan iðnað: forval. Reykjavík: Iðnaðarráðuneytið.

Statistics Iceland (2008). 'Population in urban nuclei by sex and age 1 January 1998-2008'. http://www.statice.is/Statistics/Population/Urban-nuclei-and-zip-codes (website), accessed 15 June 2008.

Urry, J. (2000). *Sociology beyond Societies: Mobilities for the Twenty-first Century*. London: Routledge.

Chapter 3

Place Reinvention by Real Changed Image: The Case of Kiruna's Spectacular Make-over

Kristina L. Nilsson

Introduction

The physical relocation of the iron ore mining town of Kiruna in the very north of Sweden is the starting point in this chapter. In the 1970s the town was depressed from declining mining activities and a decrease in the number of inhabitants. Today, the high global price of iron has driven the mining company to extend the mine underneath the existing town. This in turn will cause ground deformation and necessitate a relocation of a third part of the town, including the city centre, during the next 30 years. Since the idea was launched in 2004, Kiruna has had widespread media attention and authorities, professionals and tourists visit Kiruna to hear what is going to happen and also to be part of this experience. One question is: has all this impending development already made a reinvention of Kiruna?

When Kiruna was established 100 years ago it was designed and achieved the standing as a model town. The current planning process is based on a political vision of a *future* model town, as a conception of a sustainable city. The various functions in the town are expected to be integrated to obtain good living conditions in an ecological, social and economical manner for all its inhabitants (Kiruna 2006). The main question in this chapter is to explore the town image of Kiruna. The relocation and the reinvention are seen in the theoretical perspective of institutionalism and urban regimes. Are the various stakeholders able to pool resources, build institutions and eventually a regime that has the capacity to produce a common vision of the future town – a reinvented Kiruna?

Empirical evidence for the chapter is based on activities concerned with the relocation of the town of Kiruna together with earlier documents presenting Kiruna and its development. The analysis forms a part of a larger research project which concerns managing of planning problems with sustainability visions and different stakeholders cooperating in the process. The investigation is carried out as a single-case study (Yin 1994) and in an *intensive* methodological way (Danermark et al. 1997, 237). This *intensive* method combines interviews, together with an analysis of documents, records, plans and available statistics. Kiruna provides an extreme case. However, the type of great changes, filled with uncertainties for both planners and the local community, exist in most urban planning situations. The Kiruna example provides a particularly obvious case that makes it interesting to illustrate the reinvention of a town caused by great physical changes – a spectacular make-over. The next section provides the framework for the analysis based on regime and institutional theories. The third part presents the case study focusing on the issues in this chapter – images of Kiruna town. Fourthly, the reinvention of Kiruna is analysed and lastly the governance of the process is discussed.

Theoretical Perspectives: Regime and Institutional Theories

To study the reinvention of Kiruna in a theoretical perspective of regimes and institutions I have focused on the actors' and stakeholders' aims of producing discourses, both deliberately and unconsciously. A theoretical perspective on regimes also concentrates on informal groups creating coalitions for carrying out decisions and plans. The concept of urban regime is frequently defined as consisting of three elements (Stone 1989): firstly, a capacity to make a difference; secondly, a group of actors who work together in the same purpose and thirdly a relationship between these actors that makes cooperation possible (Stone 1989, 4). Stone has also developed a typology for the concept of urban regimes; he identifies, for instance, the 'middle class progressive regime'. In this type of regime you have a purpose for example, a better environment, conserving building heritage, urban aesthetics and new resources.

Another perspective on the activity of planning is through describing the institutions governing the planning processes or other societal changes. North (1990) gives a basic definition of *institutions* as the setting of boundaries of forms of human cooperation. Institutions reduce uncertainty by structuring everyday life, and they provide and limit the number of choices for the individual. The institutions can be formal such as rules for people, or informal boundaries such as conventions and norms for behaviour. Both institutions and organizations provide a structure for human cooperation. North (ibid.) defines organizations as groups of individuals unified by striving together to achieve certain objectives. The institutions consist of the basic rules for the game, which are human shaped; North argues that the most important task for societal institutions is to reduce uncertainties by creating a structure for joint efforts between human beings.

An institutional approach has been developed within the work of 'communicative' planning theory (Healey 1997). Planning institutions have the capability for providing a foundation for institutional capacity; the 'capacity of organizations to create new relationships for engaging in purposeful, collective action' (Healey 1998). These institutional capacities are evolving in 'continual interaction between the social worlds of city actors – citizens, businesses, pressure groups, activity groups, political parties, government departments and agencies, etc' (Cars et al. 2002, 4). These authors outline the key qualities of the capacity that can be seen in the institutional relations and qualities of new governance. Broadening the stakeholder involvement is seen as a means to facilitate the flow of knowledge and helps building up intellectual capital and relationships of trust which can lead to the establishment of consensus. It can also enhance the capacity to act through opening up access to resources and sources of power (Healey 1998).

To be able to identify, analyse and compare the different images of the new Kiruna I have used discourse analysis of written documents and papers as well as some oral descriptions from interviews. Foucault (1982) is one of the founding fathers of discourse analysis. According to him, discourse is a collection of statements governed by rules for the construction and evaluation of statements. Both discursive thinking and discursive practices create a discourse. Hajer (1995), states that a discourse refers to a set of meanings, metaphors, representations, pictures, narratives, statements and so on, that in some way together produce a special version of expectations. 'A discourse is also a specific ensemble of ideas, concepts and categorizations that are produced, reproduced and transformed in a particular set of practices and through which meaning is given to physical and social realities' (Hajer 1995, 44). The language is one important part of discourse building and analysis. However, the language does not represent reality, but contributes to shaping it (Bergström and Boréus 2000, 221). The discourses in the study are interpreted as various images. The concept of 'image' is then defined as a mental perception that exists in an individual's or group's mind: something one remembers or imagines. The subject of an image need not be real; it may be an abstract concept, such as an illustration, graph, function, or 'imaginary' entity.

Kiruna Relocation

Kiruna is a small town, with approximately 20,000 inhabitants, located in the very north of Sweden at the timberline of the mountain area (Kiruna 2008a). The town was established in 1905 for the purpose of hosting the workers involved in mining iron ore. Since then the mining and the number of inhabitants have increased and also fluctuated in response to the demand for iron. The iron mine has for a long time been run by a state-owned company, LKAB (Loussvaara-Kiirunavaara Aktiebolag), which is the main industrial platform of Kiruna. Approximately a quarter of the inhabitants in the entire municipality are directly employed by LKAB. This gives the company a powerful position as the municipality is dependent on the prosperous development of LKAB. In some way the location is living in a symbiotic relationship with the iron company.

In March 2004 the mining company (LKAB 2004), informed Kiruna municipality and the community about increased mine subsidence, caused by earlier mining activities. They also reported their future plans for extensive mining activities which will mine the ore-body that extends underneath the existing town. This underground mining causes ground deformation making it highly unstable for buildings above the mine. These occurrences threaten the existing urban structure and will most likely result in the relocation of as much as one-third of the town's built up structure.

Figure 3.1 Kiruna is located in a harsh northern climate area
Source: © Anders Wallmark.

A relocation of such a large part of the urban structure is something extraordinary that will demolish the heritage of the town in its urban grid and architecture. On the other hand the new situation provides an opportunity to rebuild a large part of the town and a completely new city centre in a sustainable way. Both these proposed developments were probably the reason why the municipality information office sent out a press release saying that the centre of Kiruna had to be relocated. This news provoked an enormous reaction and Kiruna was invaded, not only by national mass media, but also by the European press. We can also imagine that parts of the population were proud – suddenly this small unknown town in the north was the focus of attention by many journals, TV and radio programmes. However, others were frightened about what was going to happen to their local environment.

The expansion of the town has been and still is directly dependent on the ore mine and its fluctuating value on the worldwide market. Today's strong global interest in minerals has resulted in a high price for iron which, in turn, has initiated the desire of the mining company to expand the mine. The local planning administration has a process of comprehensive planning in progress, based on the assumption that it will be necessary to move or rebuild a large part of the built environment (Kiruna 2006). The existing railway and the main European road, from the Baltic Sea on the east coast to the Norwegian coast in the west, will also have to be realigned as they both cross the unstable zones. Because of this, planning processes are in progress for a new railway line (Banverket 2006) as well as a new highway (Vägverket 2007).

When Kiruna was founded 100 years ago it was designed to be, and was in reality built as a model town. It has a recognized status as a national cultural heritage site because of its unique grid plan and its collection of buildings of high architectural value. In addition, the urban area is surrounded by values of high national interest such as environmental significance, an abundance of unexplored mineral resources, national road, railway and airport infrastructure, as well as important pasture areas for reindeer herding of which is undertaken by the Sami, the indigenous people of northern Sweden, Norway, Finland and Russia. All these various interests of the territory are often over-lapping and interrelated and sometimes also compete with each other. With the national interest concentrated on Kiruna the possibilities to find new locations for the new urban area have been a challenge.

The major changes in Kiruna are planned in cooperation with several important actors. There are obviously also some stakeholders who are not taking part in the process, but some of their interests are taken care of by others. The stakeholders are competing for the territory in, around and even below the existing town. The largest stakeholder groups in the development of future employment and the living environment are of course the local community of Kiruna as well as non-governmental organizations.

There is a broad time span between the different activities. On the one hand there is a political long-term vision. The town has existed for more than 100 years. The municipality looks both backwards at the original model town and envisages forwards for a similar period of time. This is the reason why the planning administration and the leading politicians have worked out the vision for as long a period as the next 100 years. Moreover, representatives of the mining company estimate where the extraction of iron ore will be in 100 years' time. On the other hand, there is a short-term reality in the location of the new railway line, which had to be decided in 2006 and the railway must be physically rebuilt before 2012.

All this, together with major global, regional and local uncertainties, expectations of a long-term sustainable development, and tight deadlines, create a very complex situation. The complexity is based on the large amount and variation of factors interwoven as a multi-dimensional web. A web consisting of all the unpredictable components, with the variety of technical, environmental and social conditions that must be integrated taking into account various actors' values and perspectives and the stakeholders' wishes. However, since the real world is infinitely complex, it is also inevitably analytically inexhaustible.

Images of Kiruna

According to whom you speak to or for what purpose Kiruna is described, the town is given several types of images. These various images are interesting to analyse and compare for the understanding of what is taking place in Kiruna today. The images are interpreted by analysing interviews, written documents and media news from the perspective of discourse theory (Hajer 1995). The examinations of both oral talks and written texts provide stronger discourses than others you can find among the population, among the authority officers and in contemporary documents and media. The four main images found are; *the dark mining Kiruna, the space age Kiruna, the deformed Kiruna* and *new Kiruna.*

The dark mining Kiruna

This image is here called the dark *mining* town since it is based on the mine as the dominating industry and employer. The town is located approximately 200 km north of the Arctic Circle and is in fact dark during most of the winter time. During the hundred years of operation the mine's production has heavily fluctuated in relation to market conditions that have influenced the town both physically and socially. The decades of 1960s and 1970s illustrate how the mining activities within the space of a few years have gone up and down and, concomitantly, so have the number of inhabitants. The down periods with unemployment and empty houses also support, metaphorically, the *dark* designation.

For the duration of the 1960s and early 1970s the town extended greatly. In 1979 the mine was at its height and the town had almost 25,000 inhabitants. This decade made it possible for a large part of the population to move from the central parts of the town, which had poor sanitation standards, to modern standards in the then newly-built Lombolo area. This new large residential area was built up with 100 apartments in multi-family houses and 500 in single-family houses (Kiruna 2000).

However, a few years later iron ore production decreased to only a third of the best years. With a reduction of the iron market, the Kiruna ore could not compete with the price of ore from the open cast mines in Brazil. The town was shrinking and some of the newly-built residential areas in Lombolo became empty. Many houses had windows covered with boards, and 14 multi-family houses were even pulled down – parts of the area looked like a ghost town. These depressive times are still part of the memory of a majority of the local community. The self-confidence of the inhabitants reached its lowest point. However, the area acquired a new role; at that time Sweden had accepted many refugees and immigrants and some of them were placed in Kiruna and Lombolo (Kiruna 2000).

During these years Kiruna had an image of a deprived town. Both the mining company and the municipality had to be supported by the state to survive. Many people left the town for jobs in the southern part of Sweden, at least the younger ones. The town looked even physically depressed with the empty buildings and residential blocks. The deprivation was a part of the image of the 'dark mining town'. This image was widespread and, today, it still is attributed to the town.

The space age Kiruna

A complete contrast to the 'dark' image is Kiruna's connection with space technology and satellite data, and it is frequently spoken of as 'Sweden's space capital'. *Esrange*, Kiruna Space Centre is located approximately 40 kilometres out of town. The centre is the base for launching and the control of satellites and tests of space vehicles. The

Figure 3.2 The *dark mining Kiruna* is well illustrated with the 'ghost town'
Source: © Anders Wallmark.

Institute for Space Physics (Institutet för rymdfysisk, IRF) has also been located here since 1956. IRF is a national authority exploring the space and atmosphere, and constructs instruments to measure the northern lights and sun wind. Also located here is the Department of Space Sciences, a joint institution of Umeå University and Luleå Technical University. Future space engineers and scientists are educated here in cooperation with IRF (ESA 2004). The municipality of Kiruna has also started a space education programme for upper secondary school level at Esrange.

All the space activities have been strategically located in Kiruna because of the high regularity of clear skies, the northern lights, proximity to the North Pole and large unsettled areas. All this facilitates communication with satellites in polar circuits. Additionally, Esrange is also enticing other space activities. The Swedish military force will use the Space Centre to test unmanned aircraft. ESA (European Space Agency) has built up a satellite control station in Salmijärvi, close to Esrange and Kiruna town. From this place communication and data exchange takes place with the European satellite Envisat. There are also future visions for strengthening the image of high technology and space activities, for example the development of space tourism. The facilities are open to the public and part of the local tourism programme. In 2012, the British company, Virgin Galactic, plans to start flights from Kiruna, bringing tourists out into space. The reason the company chose Kiruna seems mainly related to the skills that are to be found in space operations and tourism at Esrange (Swedish National Space Board 2008).

Figure 3.3 Can the *space age Kiruna* provide tourist trips out into space in the future?

Source: © Kirstina L. Nillson (chapter author).

The space discourse was supported by a press release with images of this space age place. The 'Innovative Space Town of Kiruna – Spaceport' is described as 'activities that among other things will contribute to establish Space Campus Kiruna as an international innovative environment for research, education and development of enterprises'. The global space town of Kiruna has 'activities that develop the national and international cooperation and attendance in the space town of Kiruna – within trade and industry, research and education' (Ministry of Enterprise 2008). The space age image is also highlighted when Kiruna is presented as having something more than its mining industry. Surprisingly, also officers at LKAB show off the image of space age Kiruna, which I perceive as a way of challenging the image of the town as centered around the strong relationship and responsibility between the mining company and the municipality.

The deformed Kiruna

The global demand for iron has given a new belief in the future for the mining company to extend the mine and be able to increase the production of iron ore. In 2005 LKAB decided to invest in a new pellets plant in Kiruna which was finished in 2008, one of the greatest investments ever for the company. As a consequence of the mine extension, there are on-going investigations to clarify the spread of the ore bodies for future mining and how these can influence the existing and future urban structure. The plans for extension of the mine will, as presented in the introduction, threaten the built-up parts of the town. The ground has already been deformed which is one reason for naming this image 'the deformed Kiruna'. It is a widely held perception that with a relocation of the centre the existing townscape will be 'deformed', and so will cultural values and social solidity.

As presented above, there are manifold and often over-lapping and competing interests in terms of land-use of local, regional and national importance. The national infrastructure of main roads are managed and financed by the National Road Admininstration that has conducted a Road Plan (Vägverket 2007). The railway lines are managed and financed by the National Rail Adminstration that has conducted a Railway Plan (Banverket 2006). The National Board of Housing, Building and Planning (Boverket) have a ministry assignment to support the regional board and the municipal planning administration and have reported their examination (Boverket 2007). The mining is controlled and receives exploration permissions from The Mining Inspectorate of Sweden (Bergstaten). The County Board and the National Heritage Board also have made an assignment (Riksantikvarieämbetet 2008) taking responsibility for managing heritage values in an appropriate way, and the Swedish Board of Agriculture (Jordbruksverket) through the County Board is responsible for the Sami people and the commercial reindeer interests.

Figure 3.4 The cracking ground is a reminder of the *deformed Kiruna*
Source: © Thomas Nylund.

The municipality of Kiruna is, by the general municipal planning monopoly, the planning authority and is responsible for managing all of these various interests and conflicts in a comprehensive plan, although, as we have seen much of the infrastructure planning is advocated by regional and national authorities in consultation with the municipality. The national planning authorities also visited Kiruna to be informed. This has resulted in a lot of meetings, seminars, consultations and workshops to manage the complex conditions in the plan for the relocation. The national authorities have to handle all the various consequences of the deformation. The authorities have produced several documents that point out the national interest in the resources and heritage that are threatened by the ground deformation.

In 2006, as part of the comprehensive municipal planning process, a local questionnaire survey was conducted. The aim was to collect views and responses from the local inhabitants regarding Kiruna's urban environment. The inquiry was very general and was called 'What is your view of Kiruna?' The survey was presented to give the inhabitants an opportunity to influence the shape and character of the townscape now and in the future. People were asked to highlight the qualities of the buildings that are to be developed or buildings that should be protected in the present Kiruna and moved if necessary. A large part of the respondents (94 per cent) responded by saying that the most important place with an obvious Kiruna atmosphere was the church, the town hall and the outlook over the surroundings. A viable interpretation of this result is that a large part of the local community probably does not approve of the deconstruction of the existing town. The answers are seen by the municipality as an important foundation for the spatial planning.

The new Kiruna

The massive event that the relocation of a large part of this small town will be, has provoked amazing reactions. First of all the media, both national as well as international, went to Kiruna to report on this extraordinary project of relocating almost a whole town. In the next phase a number of professional experts went on a pilgrimage to this town in the far north of Sweden searching for commissions and to be invited to be a part of developing the 'new Kiruna', to implement the overall vision of a sustainable model town that had already been laid down by the municipal planning officers together with the local politicians.

As an input to the comprehensive planning process LKAB, the mining company hired architecture and infrastructure consultants to carry out a spatial planning proposal called 'New Kiruna'. The aim of the project was to envision a new post-modern town in an area where the urban structure would not hinder further extension of the mine. The proposal illustrated a townscape with winding streets along the mountain slopes, a tropical garden and an in-door skiing hill under a glass roof. The visionary and well illustrated proposal was attractive to the local community. The proposal has also been presented and intensively discussed and criticized in national architectural journals and in a design programme on television.

Figure 3.5 The proposal of *new Kiruna* with its winding streets
Source: © LKAB.

In this discourse LKAB 'proclaimed that the town will successively be moved to the northwest in order not to prevent future extraction of the ore and so that the buildings, infrastructure and facilities did not have to be removed again' (LKAB 2008a, 2008b). The consultants phrase it this way: 'An urban development to the northwest will unify the desire of a functional and attractive shape of the town with well functioning communications to the centre ... and the continuing mining and smooth commodity transports' (LKAB 2006).

Some parts of the local community are excited about the new Kiruna. From the questionnaire survey mentioned earlier (Kiruna kommun 2007) one can deduce that several inhabitants are looking forward to the new Kiruna. For the future shape of the town some respondents mentioned that the planners should look at international examples: 'don't be so conservative and cowardly!' and 'the old urban built environment is an example', 'people are in greater numbers moving to good environments and living qualities'. Others see that there can be a future Kiruna without the mining company LKAB as the driving force, which is exemplified with the quotation directed to the local planners: 'think that people will live in Kiruna also after LKAB, don't build the town to favour LKAB, but think about people's well-being in the future. Times can change quickly!' Some respondents asked for an urban environment that appeals to youngsters and women.

All national authorities are apprehensive of, and keep up-to-date with, what happens in Kiruna. Besides the officials involved in the planning there have been study tours from the authorities as well as consultant companies. It seems as if all people in Sweden concerned with planning and architectural issues have visited Kiruna since the ideas of town relocation was launched. These study visit groups, are by and large, expecting to hear about and discuss a new Kiruna city shape.

Images Discourse Groups

The four different images of Kiruna exist side by side and are not divided by definite borders. The images are initiated and promoted by different groups in the town and among authorities at different levels. The power of the images varies in accordance with the hierarchical or political positions of the stakeholders (cf. Flyvbjerg 2001).

As illustrated above the Kiruna population and economy have fluctuated, with the most recent down period in the 1980s. One can still identify the image of the small, deprived and dark town in Norrbotten County – a part of the country identified with harsh climate and high unemployment. This perception is particularly in circulation in southern Sweden, has existed for decades and is probably not easy to get rid of. However, it is not an accurate representation of Kiruna. The current high conjuncture in the mineral market has made Kiruna an economically wealthy town.

Surprisingly, the idea of relocating the town has not severely antagonized the local community. One could expect adverse reactions, but in Kiruna the people know how important the mining and LKAB are. A great deal of the local community remembers the situation during the critical economical periods when a large part of the miners risked losing their jobs. They had earlier experienced disruption when the housing district, Ön, close to the mine, was pulled down because of ground deformation. The discourse of 'dark mining Kiruna' is taking a passive position in regard to the future prospects, as it does not have enough energy to gather support and in that way lacks power (cf. Lukes 1986).

A hundred years ago, when the town was established, the mining company LKAB took responsibility for the entire locality. It was necessary to have a functional society. The first director of the mining company LKAB, Hjalmar Lundbom, became a legend and both the longest street as well as a school is named after him and his charming residence is a tourist attraction. Hjalmar Lundbom was a great friend of art and gathered the well-known Swedish and international artists from that time in his own home. He was convinced that a strong social and cultural society would create a well-functioning town. He was also interested in educational issues and started a school to improve the education of the sons of the miners. Lundbom was highly appreciated by most people in the Kiruna area, not least by the Sámi people (Kiruna 2000).

Even if later managing directors have not felt the same personal responsibility for the local society, LKAB has always shown an interest in a well-functioning local community. This is probably the reason why people have always trusted the mining company and still seem to be trustful, despite the dramatic scenario envisaged. Also the authorities have always had a strong economical interest in maintaining civilian society and stimulating industry and trade in Kiruna. So the inhabitants have not had to take the same responsibility for the industrial development as other urban communities in the region.

The image of the 'deformed town' is mainly supported by parts of the local community and authorities on local, regional and national level. The local community is worried about the 'deformation' of the existing town and its cultural and social values. The big changes will break the settled structure both physically and socially. The questionnaire survey conducted in 2006 (Kiruna 2007), demonstrated that people highly appreciated the Kiruna urban grid and the monumental buildings such as the church and the town hall. For the authorities and town developers the challenge will be to build a new town and at the same time preserve the character and most of the environments and buildings that are considered as architecturally valuable.

As this discourse is supported by the municipality and authorities on various levels and geographical location, it could be interpreted as an institution (Healey 1997; Cars et. al 2002). However, even if the people in and outside Kiruna share a view of what could be destroyed in the town, they have not agreed on solutions for the future. For the population it is much about feelings for the home town with its social networks and buildings that 'always have been there'. This contrasts with the more intellectual and technical cooperation between the authorities. Their 'deformation' image is continued by several official documents (Kiruna 2006; Vägverket 2006; Riksantikvarieämbetet 2007). This group has formal power (Lukes 1986) by legislation, national policies and societal positions.

Those holding on to the discourse of 'deformed Kiruna', have a joint view of protecting the existing social and cultural values that are threatened by 'new Kiruna'. There is a mutual struggle to either save as much as possible, to move buildings of interesting cultural heritage and entire building sites and/or recreate similar environments in the new parts of the town. In this sense, together, different groups build up power to influence the future shape of the town. The common discourse is here interpreted to strengthen the forms for human cooperation in correspondence with what North (1990) calls an institution. However, institutions are connected to the ability and power to make a difference. That is what Healey calls 'capacity of organisations to create new relationships for engaging in purposeful, collective action' (Healey 1997).

The image of the space age town is based on an expansion of the Space Centre at Esrange which will exert even more influence on the Kiruna town and its future development. There exists a small discourse that space activities in Kiruna territory could be even more prominent. This discourse is rooted in a sincere and factual cooperation of many institutes, departments and schools at Esrange – a cooperation that, from a practical viewpoint, forms a new organization. They have already organized the actors in a collaborative effort to strengthen the Centre.

One can easily see that the discourse group of 'New Kiruna' has a powerful position with the mining company as a driving force together with construction actors. After 'New Kiruna' had been presented and discussed, LKAB and their consultants built a cooperation making them capable of producing joint proposals. LKAB had the economic capacity to engage a well known and notable architect. This cooperation can be seen as a coalition, a term used for groups searching other like-minded partners in order to realize a common goal. The ways of cooperation in coalitions are often conceptualized as partnerships (Peters 1998). A coalition, as I see it, is a shorter form of cooperation than an institution, with the objective of realizing something in the near future. The LKAB-based coalition has also been supported by media – always interested in exciting news, in this case the proposals for the 'New Kiruna'. So, the new Kiruna image has had and still has a strong position among the Swedish public.

Today the economic situation for the mining company is at the top due to the high global price for iron. LKAB, is still the main industry and the main employer. It has always been said 'when the company is wealthy the inhabitants are well-to-do'. That is probably the reason why the local community isn't more worried about the relocation of the town and city centre. The inhabitants are used to ups and downs and know that the mining company only does what promotes the mining interests. And not much has happened. In 2008, the only visible result is a newly-constructed electricity transformer station. You can hear people say 'nothing is happening, nothing is apparent. The local community seems to mistrust the local planning administration, the leading politicians and the mining company. The citizens think that they just talk about great changes and nothing has happened! You could hear reactions from people that LKAB had exaggerated, that the situation is not that serious. This was also felt when, two years later, the company was not willing to talk about the sketches. Nevertheless, when it was presented, the attractive illustrated proposal confused the municipality, who in fact is responsible for urban planning. And there has been some opposition. The local planning administration had suggested that the new parts of the town should be located to the east of the existing town, whereas LKAB's proposal located these to the north-west.

Among some of the people a new discussion is evolving relating to the mining company's increasing focus on efficiency. As a consequence, there are speculations that even if the urban structure is successively depleted as a result of ground deformation, the rest of the town will accommodate the displaced population. The outcome would be a smaller town without any new parts built. From this we can identify an on-going competition between the image discourses that will always change.

Kiruna Reinvented?

From the above presentation and analysis we can perceive several images of Kiruna carried by diverse groups. Some of the images are connected to each other and others are contradictory. The 'dark mining Kiruna' has connections to the 'deformed Kiruna' in the way they describe some realities and problems. The image of 'space age Kiruna' and 'new Kiruna', are connected to each other in the way they want to illustrate something new, outstanding and exciting happening with this northern town. At the same time these two groups of images are contradictory to each other. The first two represent pessimistic or realistic views while the second pair reveals a more visionary development view. The discourse group of 'new Kiruna' is based on a great enthusiasm for a new and exciting future. This image is influential and connects different groups that have the courage and power to introduce new ideas.

As claimed above the institutions can be formal as rules for people, for example the Planning and Building Act that has to be adhered to when the urban structure of Kiruna is re-planned. They can also be informal restrictions as, for instance, conventions and norms for behaviour. Societal discourses can be so strong that other aspects are hard to bring in. Both these types of institutions and organizations give a structure for human cooperation in society. The relocation of Kiruna town is extremely complex concerning all overlapping, competing and interrelated interests as a base for the spatial planning. The variety and large amount of basic data creates uncertainty rather than a more definite foundation. In such an uncertain context it is probably a natural response for the citizens to accede to image discourses that a majority of the local community supports. An institution can reduce uncertainties by creating a structure for joint efforts between human beings (North 1990). These image institutions can reduce the uncertainty enforced by structural factors influencing everyday life, and they provide and limit the number of choices for individuals.

The various images of the existing and prospective Kiruna can only be grasped as discourses and no one knows today what the future town will look like. Today only an imagined reinvention of Kiruna is present. Since there is no complete enduring movement supporting a particular collective image, no regime can be identified, in the way it is defined by Stone (1989). However, as one can understand from the future plans for Kiruna, a spectacular make-over will take place in this small mining town. There is no doubt a reinvention is going on.

The main actors involved in the planning processes, consisting of the planning administration of the municipality, the Regional Road Administration, the Regional Rail Administration, LKAB and Vattenfall (the electricity company), have conducted a joint information brochure in both Swedish and English which concludes as follows:

> The Future is Uncertain – but Exciting!
> The transformation of the city has begun and a great many important decisions will be made over the months and years to come. But no one knows exactly how great the transformation will be. Their extent will be guided partly by the development of the mine and future technical conditions.
>
> Just imagine if a technique emerges in the future enabling ground stabilization, thus stopping the ground from cracking? Another decisive factor is the world's demand for iron ore. No one in Kiruna can affect the customers' needs for LKAB's iron ore, and no one can know for sure if the demand will increase – and thereby hasten the pace of mining and cracking – or decrease – and even slow down the transformation of the city. But one thing is certain; it will be exciting to follow the development of Kiruna over the coming years. For, within ten years, the city will not be as it is today, no matter what happens!
>
> (Kiruna kommun 2008b)

Accordingly, the municipality, the local community and the local trade and industry together with the regional and national authorities have not, so far, succeeded in creating a regime for the realization of a joint image of the future Kiruna. They have only achieved one of the three elements that Stone (1989; Fahlén 1998) define as a regime. There is probably a capacity to make changes. However, the ability or will to work together and to agree on the aims have so far been limited. In this sense the local actors have insufficient capacity to bring about any real differences. I interpret the situation in Kiruna as that of various groups of actors and population supporting a variety of images that are competing with each other for the one which is authentic.

References

Banverket (2006), *Järnvägsplan, utställelsehandling.* Banverket, Norra banregionen, (BRNT 2004, 4).

Bergström and Boréus (2000), *Mening och Makt – Handbok i samhällsvetenskaplig textanalys* (Lund, Studentlitteratur).

Boverket (2007), *Boverkets uppdrag att följa utvecklingen avseende fysisk planering och byggande i Malmfälten.* Slutrapport (Karlskrona: Boverket).

Cars, G., Healey, P., Madanipour, A. and de Magalhaes, C. (eds) (2002), *Urban Governance, Institutional Capacity and Social Milieux* (Aldershot: Ashgate Publishing Ltd).

Danermark, Ekström, Jakobsen, Karlsson (1997), *Att förklara samhället* (Lund: Studentlitteratur).

ESA (European Space Agency) (2004) (http://www.esa.int/esaCP/SEM6XUW4QWD_Sweden_0.html).

Fahlén, A. (1998), *Urban regimteori*. Centrum för stadsmiljöforskning (Örebro: Högskolan i Örebro).

Flyvbjerg, B. (2001), *Making Social Science Matter – Why Social Inquiry Fails and How It can Succeed Again* (Cambridge: Cambridge University Press).

Foucault, M. (1982), *The Archaeology of Knowledge and the Discourse on Language* (New York: Pantheon Books).

Hajer, M.A. (1995), *The Politics of Environmental Discourse. Ecological Modernization and the Policy Process* (Oxford: Clarendon Press).

Healey, P. (1997), *Collaborative Planning – Shaping Places in Fragmented Societies* (Basingstoke: Palgrave Macmillan).

Healey, P. (1998), 'Building institutional capacity through collaborative approaches to urban planning', *Environment and Planning A*, 30, 1531–46.

Kiruna (2000), *Kiruna 100-årsboken, del I-II* (Kiruna: Kiruna kommun).

Kiruna (2006), *Fördjupad översiktsplan för Kiruna centralort – Samrådshandling. [Deepening of the comprehensive plan for Kiruna town]* (Kiruna: Kiruna kommun).

Kiruna (2007), Sammanställning av enkätsvar: 'Vilken är din bild av Kiruna?' (Kiruna: Kiruna kommun).

Kiruna (2008a), General information of Kiruna (http://www.kiruna.se).

Kiruna (2008b), Utvecklingsprogram för Rymdstaden Kiruna till år 2020 (http://www.kommun.kiruna.se/upload/136/UPR%202020%20Pressmeddelande%202008%2003%2026.doc).

LKAB (2004), *Brev till Kiruna kommunstyrelse* (Kiruna: LKAB).

LKAB (2006), *Nya Kiruna* (http://www.lkab.com/?openform&id=74C2) and (http://www.lkab.com/__C12570A1002EAAAE.nsf/($all)/0395C011B79D31FEC1257125004C3CF0/$file/NyaKiruna.pdf).

LKAB (2008a), *Future plans* (http://www.lkab.com/?openform&id=7492).

LKAB (2008b), *Kiruna Gruvan och samhället* (http://www.lkab.com/__C12570A1002EAAAE.nsf/($all)/44149E8E29259C70C12574D60051FBB6/$file/Kiruna_GruvanOcSamh%E4llet.pdf).

Lukes, S. (1986), *Power. A Radical View* (London: Macmillan).

Ministry of Enterprise (2008), Press release (http://www.regeringen.se/sb/d/10359/a/102039).

North, D.C. (1990), *Institutions, Institutional Change and Economic Performance* (Cambridge: Cambridge University Press).

Peters, G. (1998), 'Public–Private Partnerships as Institutions and Instruments' in: Pierre, G. (ed.), *Partnerships in Urban Governance*, pp.11–33 (Basingstoke and London: Macmillan).

Riksantikvarieämbetet (2008), *Delrapport för Riksantikvarieämbetets regeringsuppdrag att följa och stödja utvecklingen i Malmfälten* (Stockholm: Riksantikvarieämbetet).

Stone, C. (1989), *Regime Politics – Governing Atlanta* (Lawrence: Kansas University Press).

Swedish National Space Board (2008), (http://www.snsb.se/dyn_aktuellt. asp?languageId=2).

Yin, R.K. (1994), *Case Study Research – Design and Methods*, 2nd edition, (London, New Dehli: Sage Publications).

Vägverket, (2007), *Vägutredning/Förslagshandling, Kirunaprojektet*. Vägverket, Region norr. (BD-11453-10).

Chapter 4

Kirkenes – A Town for Miners and Ministers

Arvid Viken and Torill Nyseth

Introduction

Close to the Norwegian–Russian border, the small town Kirkenes recently has become a scene for the revitalization of cross-border collaboration and international politics. After the break-up of the Soviet Union, Russian relations have had significance for the industrial development, the political agenda and daily life in this town. The town is locally regarded as a centre of the Barents Region, stretching over the northern areas of Russia, Finland, Sweden and Norway. Even if Kirkenes is a small town with about 5,000 inhabitants, in some ways it fits the description that Robinson (2006, 251) gives of much larger cities: 'their internal complexity and external connections contribute to the on-going transformation of social life and economic activity ... Both inventions, dispersed and often spontaneous, and interventions, focussed and usually directed, are constantly changing the nature of urban places.' In this chapter both inventions and interventions will be discussed, or more correctly, narratives of inventions and interventions taking place in Kirkenes.

The reinvention of this mining town has been enabled and supported by global trends and local stubbornness – some locals have never abandoned the idea of a continuation of the mining activities. However, this is not the only narrative that is central to an understanding of the continued and prosperous existence of the town. To better comprehend this dynamic, theory about place narratives is taken as a point of departure. A whole variety of narratives about the past, the present and the future partly competing, partly supporting each other exists at the same time. Those focused on here are related to the town as a mining town, as a border town, as a place for international politics and as a multicultural community. The chapter starts with a description of data and methodology, followed by a brief introduction to Kirkenes' past with a focus on the period after 1990, emphasizing the major narratives that can be elaborated from this. This is followed by a theoretical discussion of narratives as direction for development. Then some major contemporary narratives are presented and analysed – their origin, how they are kept alive and how they are materialized. Before concluding the chapter, in the penultimate section, narratives as those analysed here, are discussed as a matter of path-dependency.

Analysing Narratives: Methodological Approaches

This chapter is based on a case-study focusing on different narratives that circulate in Kirkenes and how they are sustained and presented. To obtain evidence for these processes a variety of data sources are used, representing what Yin (1994) calls a robust case study. A large number of plans, letters and decisions are used as vital signs of the narratives that are studied, as well as material manifestations and statistics. However, focus group and in-depth interviews are the basic data sources conducted in 2006, supplemented with some more in-depth interviews in 2008. It was through these interviews that the contours of the narratives emerged. Collective focus and communication is one of the advantages of the focus group method (Webb and Kavern 2001, 800), and it is claimed that focus groups create a situation for data collection which is less artificial than many other kinds of data collection settings (Wilkinson 1999, 225). 'Focus groups employ "natural" communication processes such as argumentation, joking, boasting, teasing, persuasion, challenges and disagreement', says Jarrett (1993,194). These interviews revealed that the local identities were strongly related to some narratives that seemed to have been there for years, and that was more or less collectively committed to memory.

Narrative analysis comes in basically two types. One is the type of research where the researcher refers and analyses the narratives that he identifies in the fields he is studying. The other is the narratives that are constructed by the researcher on the basis of the information that is collected, from interviews or other data sources. This study combines both types; the narratives identified exist, but they are not necessarily thought of as narratives among the informants, but are constructed by the authors.

Narratives as Future Leads

Narratives represent an approach that has been applied in a series of disciplines, ranging from literary theory and folklore, to psychology, organizational theory and planning (cf. Bowman 2006). It is widely acknowledged that it is '... through narrativity that we come to know, understand and make sense of the social world, and through which we constitute our social identities' (Somers 1997, 83; Gilpin 2008; cf. Czarniawska-Joerges 1995; Czarniawska 2002). Narratives are something with which people identify, 'telling stories is how people everywhere make sense of and share meaning' (Bowman 2006, 7). In the literature of sense making, it is held that 'groups of people tend generally to see and to understand actions and events in similar ways' (Brown et al. 2008, 1038). What Somers defines as public narratives (Somers 1994), are such narratives that people share. They are shared frameworks that enable groups to 'collectively make sense of ... our social world ... through jointly negotiated narratives' (Currie and Brown 2003, 564). In fact, narratives add to the construction of past, present and future (Gilpin 2008, 11). Even though narratives demand narrators, there is also a tendency for stories to live their own life reducing its authors to co-authors; they are something that circulate among people that gives meaning to events, space and human actions.

There certainly are different types of narratives, from formal written history and literature to oral stories, myths and legends. Some narratives circulate among people or they may be made by intention, they can be public or private, formal or informal. Narrative analysis has a suspended position in the social sciences. In place analyses narratives are vital (Johnstone 1992). One example is heritage narratives. According to Bridger, heritage narratives are inevitable in such analyses because they 'give temporal persistence of a community by providing an account of its origins, the character of its people (both past and present), and its trials and triumphs over time' (1997, 69). However, such narratives are selective representations of the past that feed into and are partially driven by the demands, sentiments and interests of those in the present (Bridger 1997, 70). Thus, in most societies there are always a variety of stories about the past and multiple versions of historical events; a plurality of narratives stemming from a number of heterogeneous voices (Jensen 2007; Finnegan 1998).

Stories are a central component in narratives, and often the two terms are even reckoned as synonyms. However, narrative is a broader term, covering a variety of types of narratives, whereas stories are of a specific type related to a plot, having a start, something in between – a core – and an ending. Seen in this way, a story is an event for the listener. Bowman (2006) makes a parallel to Dewey's (1934) distinction between experience, that is something that emerges and changes over time, and 'an experience' which is the immediate excitement of an event (or story). The type of narratives that are explored in this chapter is of the first type. Such narratives are often more vague and less structured than a story. They also tend to reflect ongoing discourses (Bowman 2006, 8). Narratives are not imperatives or mantra, but a more flexible 'frame of reference' (Brown et al. 2008, 1038).

In planning theory, narratives about the future represent a particular form of analysis. Planning is by definition future-oriented, and may be seen as a form of persuasive storytelling (Throgmorton 1992). Planning can be seen as a narrative ordering of society (Law 1992; cf. Doolin 2003, 783–54). Such narratives exist in social settings and give direction to human performance. Ordering narratives tend to be strategic, but often more in the minds of the planners than in reality. There are lots of plans searching for a strategic position in Kirkenes. Most of them have, however, been of minor significance for future development. Second, ordering narratives tend to be discursive, which means that they refer to ongoing discourses and put the narrator and the reader in a meaningful political, ideological or scientific context. Discourses about the regions of Europe, border regions and globalization are relevant to Kirkenes.

Narratives are therefore related to discourses. The type of narratives that will be discussed here can all be identified as within a particular discourse. Hardy et al. (2000, 1234) gives a description of how this functions. First discourses provide people with a particular analytical approach, concepts, categories and theories. For example, people in Kirkenes have started talking about their town as hybrid, leaning towards a discourse about multiculturalism. Second, such approaches or concepts in certain ways produce the reality; the term 'border town' is a designation that is important in the creation of such a town. And third, such discourses provide people with positions: as a discourse is immersed into local narratives, the bearers of this perspective tend to take up positions within the realm of the narrative. Thus, narratives are structured and inscribed in discourses (cf. Somers 1994). And therefore, narratives are related to power and hegemonic positions. In Kirkenes there is particularly a hegemonic struggle going on between political narratives and identities and more neutral bordered positions (Viken et al. 2008). In this chapter the prime focus however is on how narratives are kept alive, and the power of the narratives in the formation of a community.

Narratives are also enacted, circulating in relations between people. In Kirkenes there are lots of stories told; the old mining era is well represented in them, and several are about the border and the border town, among others (Viken et al. 2008). Narratives are also materially heterogeneous – they enact as texts, technologies and organizational arrangements – this is often what makes narratives important in stabilizing arrangements. In Kirkenes this is a strong tangible element – there is a heritage from the mining period that is visible, and so are the new institutions coping with border issues. Lastly such ordering narratives are incomplete, according to Law (1992). This is obvious in Kirkenes; people are anticipating the future and wonder what will happen next. As was said in one interview: 'In Kirkenes people are about to jump, but nobody really knows where.' One should then add that narratives are ordering in the way that they direct people's action towards particular areas of activity.

A Reinvented Kirkenes Town – Changed Social Practices

Knowledge of the past is important to understand the narratives circulating in Kirkenes today (cf. Eriksen and Niemi 1981; Niemi 1992), at least from the more recent decades. The Norwegian–Russian boundary represents the northernmost border between national states in Europe. The Russian–Norwegian border was settled through a treaty that was signed in 1826 (Niemi 1992). Although the area adjacent to the Norwegian border was, due to international agreements, in the hands of the Finns in the period between World Wars I and II, this border has not been negotiated or contested. There has always been a significant contact between Norway and Russia, except for the Cold War era (1947–89) when the border was more or less closed, because of the international political situation. In the post-Soviet period the patterns and frequencies of contacts have been regained, and today Kirkenes stands out as a vibrant border town. However, the formality related to the border crossing and the iconography of the border have not changed significantly; the systems and symbols of the Cold War still exist (Viken 2007).

In its first 90 years Kirkenes was dominated by the mining industry that, at the most, employed around 1,500 people. Several incidents during the 1980s were crucial for the final close-down of the mining company, Sydvaranger Ltd in 1996: investments that failed, an international break-down in the iron ore market occurred, and political changes followed by growing scepticism towards subsidizing industries (as was the case in the 1980s) within the Norwegian political system. Locally the decision to close-down was never fully accepted, and the idea of reopening the mine has been kept alive and manufacturing industries have had a prioritized position locally. In 2009 the mine is to be reopened due to high market prices and new owners.

From the late 1980s to the beginning of the 21st century Sør-Varanger municipality and Sydvaranger Ltd received considerable funding to restructure the local economy. Today, more than 50 per cent of the workforce is employed in the public sector. In the private sector tourism has been growing, with approximately 250 employees in 2006, but even more important is the growth in trade and commerce, partly as a result of a Russian presence. As a sign of this, two shopping centres were constructed after the year 2000, one of them obviously having Russians as its target market. Kirkenes has rapidly become part of a border economy.

This brief overview shows that there are some predominant elements in the more recent history of Kirkenes: one an industrial and mining town and its restructuring, one about a border town, one about a political place and one about a multicultural and welcoming place. All these backgrounds are deeply rooted and reflected in contemporary Kirkenes. In many ways they circulate as narratives about the past, present and future. This chapter will focus on how the narratives not only play roles concerning place-identity and optimism, but in fact also create a series of activities, jobs, businesses and institutions.

Narratives about Kirkenes

An industrial town

> Kirkenes started as an industrial town, that is what it has been and should be. Iron is in the ore of the mountains behind, mining is in the ores of local people. There is a strong history of labour unions, managing directors, and legends about miners and unionists that creates a nostalgic aura of the past.

Kirkenes has been in a phase of renewal and transition since the mid-1980s and onwards. The central authorities saw it as their responsibility to support Kirkenes in these processes. A state grant and an investment company were set up to implement this process. Much of the grants were spent on the establishment and development of 'Kimek', the engeneering factory. Also some smaller firms were supported, but most of them did not survive more than a few years (Abelsen 2004). However, the management of the restructuring process kept alive the idea of a prolonged manufacturing community and culture. This was reinforced by many business efforts, development plans, feasibility studies and industrial initiatives (see Table 4.1). Some related to the reopening of the mine. This hope was also supported by Australian and Russian investors who tried to raise money for a restart. However, it was when a Norwegian transport company took over in 2006 that the idea was realized, this time partly based on Australian capital.

The mining narrative has been particularly strong among old people, people working within traditional industries, and people occupied by developing new industries. However, there has been a whole variety of institutions and actors contributing to the sustenance of the narrative. At one stage the municipality bought the mine and its estates and maintained an administrative staff for the old mining company. The labour union organized displays of the mining history in the first years after the abandonment, and later jubilees, for instance the 100th anniversary in 2006. In 2008 the local museum opened a playground for children modelled as a mine. There is a weighty '10 tons thinking' one informant said, referring to the manufacturing culture. The content of these narratives varies; for some it is related to reopening of the mine, for some to the mechanical industries, engineering and other manufacturing activities, and for others to the narratives about transportation and Kirkenes as a hub and a central site in a future oil era of the Barents Sea.

There are many documents concerning Kirkenes as a harbour and transport hub (see Table 4.1). For instance, there is the idea of a 45-kilometre long railway from Kirkenes to Nikel, the Russian neighbouring town closest to Kirkenes – connecting to one of the world's biggest railway systems – supported by no less than 13 major documents between 1990 and 2008, a bit less than one per year on average, the last one being produced in 2008. In addition are all the presentations given by local and national businesses, political and administrative actors at the number of conferences and seminars that are held and that circulate in various networks. However, it is unlikely that the railway will be built in the near future.

It is obvious that the production and sustenance of this narrative creates a whole economy; there are several consultancy companies that are engaged in this production, and public offices such as the Barents Secretariat, the municipality, the harbour authorities and the mining company. NOK 40 million is said to have been spent on keeping the mining company alive from 1997 to 2006, and the production of the 13 documents for a railway connection to the nearest Russian town, Nikel, is estimated to have cost NOK six million. All these future orientations create a whole business sector, providing jobs and economic benefit. And some ideas also materialize in new firms and activities such as the engineering branch of Kimek, some oil-related activities and, from 2009, 250 employees in the reopened mine.

A representative of the tourism industry illustrates the significance of the industrial culture: 'Now, I have made an alliance with an industrial actor, this is the only way to be heard in this community', he said. However, this also illustrates a problem; many admit that they supported this focus, but that it might have been wrong. The narrative of Kirkenes always being a manufacturing town has encouraged a passive attitude and hindered the development of an entrepreneurial culture. People sat waiting for somebody from outside to come and solve their problems (cf. Dale 2002). One of the stories about the restructuring of Kirkenes, is that this did not really start before the idea of mining was dead and the restructuring funds dried up. Some of the narratives represent a romantization of the past. The 'Girls on the Bridge', the cultural curator organization, admits to having contributed to this role creating expositions and performances supporting the idea of Kirkenes as a mining town after the mine was abandoned. There are also numerous stories told about the mining era, and legends and myths represented in public narratives contribute to the strength of this narrative. It is obvious that the industry culture is still powerful. However, several of the informants in 2006 used the term 'ghost' to characterize the role of the mining company and culture. This attitude may have changed with the plans to reopen the mine in 2009.

Table 4.1   Events, processes and actors in the narration of Kirkenes as a manufacturing and transport town

Mining company kept alive, 40 million NOK spent on considering reopening, sold in 2006
Plans to restart the mine: in 2001 (Australians), 2005–2006 (Russians, Australians), 1997, reality in 2009 (Norwegians, Australians)
Town jubilee in 2006, jubilee for Sydvaranger Ltd and for Nordens Klippe the labour union. Conference in February 2006 marked ten years since closure of the mine
13 planning documents discussing or exploring the ideas of a railway to Russia: in 1990, 1992, 1993 (2), 1996 (2), 1999, 2000, 2002, 2003, 2005(2), 2008
Harbour plans: for instance in 2003 and 2008
Sea route to Asia with Kirkenes as a hub
Presentations of Kirkenes: oil, mine and transport hub – to ministers and others; the municipality, the Barents Secretariat, the Industry Association, representatives of different companies

The narrative about a border town

> The fall of the Soviet Regime, has been a *glasnost* for Kirkenes. With the opening of the border Russians came to experience the West. This contact across the border has grown into a variety of projects and relationships and an encompassing economic sector. And it is probably only in its infancy.

Since the early 1990s Kirkenes has experienced a growing recognition of the significance of the border, the neighbouring country and the border region in Russia. There is no doubt that Kirkenes has turned into a border town. The narrative of the border town is furnished by smaller and bigger events reported on in the local media. There are political events, cultural events and institutions that constantly add to the narrative: seminars, expositions, festivals, theatre shows and, for example, a library with the biggest collection of Russian literature in Norway. There is also an iconography with a Russian flavour in the town – Russian signposts, Russian ships in the harbour, and the Russian language is heard all over the town. Thus there is a Russian backcloth for the everyday life of Kirkenes. The narrative about Kirkenes as a border town is well rooted and widely recognized: 'The border and the proximity to Russia mark us all' and 'almost everybody has a Russian neighbour or friend', it was said. Another claimed that ... the Russian seamen – they make an impact on the whole [town] ... They are at the public footpath; they are everywhere ... very positive, actually.' A female informant expressed the significance of the town's location on the border in this way:

> This is a borderland ... This is what makes it exciting to live here. ... Before, we used to go to Tromsø for shopping, now we go to Murmansk. Many of us have multi-visa. ... Also Archangels is so close that the town is part of everyday life ...

Table 4.2 Events, processes and actors in the narration of Kirkenes as a border town

Gorbatchov's Murmansk speech in 1987
Companies that from the 1980s had a platform in Russia: East Trade Centre, Barents Company, Kvaerner Kimek
A new regime in Russia, more open contact and interest from 1989 onwards
An emergent cross-border activity in the 1990s; an increase from about 1,000 to more than 100,000 border crossings
The Barents Declaration in 1993
Lots of Barents-based economic development projects such as the Working Group of Economic Cooperation (WGEC) and Barents 2010, and projects within forestry, customs and so on
A growing Russian-based trade and commerce in Kirkenes
Russians settled and working in most sectors in Kirkenes
Educational and cultural exchange programmes
Russian iconography; Russian sounds and signposts
Municipal strategy to be a bridgehead towards Northwest Russia
Cross-border cooperation
Russian speaking shop-assistants in most of the shops in Kirkenes

All the activities in Table 4.2 imply huge amounts of money spent on cross-border activities. In general *glasnost* led to a boom of border crossings in the early 1990s – the statistics show an increase from about one thousand before 1990 to more than a hundred thousand 15 years later. Due to a whole variety of reasons, Kirkenes has today a significant Russian population. About 90 per cent of Kimek's activities, most of the harbour activities, trading companies, several consultancy firms and 10 per cent of the retail sector are based on trade with Russians, together constituting more than one billion turnover (NOK) per year, according to representatives of Kirkenes' Industry Association. The employment factor of the border narrative is difficult to estimate, but it is huge, both in the private and the public sector. The public sector cover such policy fields as border police, border guards, secret service, customs, military and so on, and the sector is probably growing as the border-crossings and border-crossing activities increase.

It has also been an ongoing policy of the Barents authorities to encourage cross-border contacts in several spheres. The Barents Secretariat in Kirkenes has received funds for the support of such efforts in the Norwegian–Russian border regions. Over the years NOK 350 million has been spent on about 3,000 cross-border projects.[1] The municipality has for many years been involved in different cooperation projects related to Russia. One example is friendship agreements as early as 1972, and a women's cultural exchange network that started as cooperation with Nikel in the 1980s, and now includes 16 municipalities in Russia, Finland and Sweden. Also Norwegian national authorities have been involved in cross-border co-operation. In 1993, the Norwegian Foreign Minister initiated the Barents Region and Kirkenes was chosen as the headquarters for the Barents Secretariat, an agency that was constituted under the headship of the three northernmost Norwegian counties, but funded and instructed by the Norwegian Ministry of Foreign Affairs. Today, the Barents Secretariat is an information centre and a fund for cross-border cooperation, and a connection in many Barents networks.

This narrative is however contested; not everybody is happy about the border status. Some elders found it difficult to embrace the Russians that they for decades had been indoctrinated to detest. Some young people expressed alienation towards the border focus: 'It is the commercial actors who put up signs in the Russian language', one informant said, indicating that they felt it was too much. 'This still is and should be a Norwegian community', some claimed.

The narrative of a political place

> Kirkenes is a place where important political decisions are taken, and where prominent national and international politicians meet. And the town is the capital of the Barents Region. It is a politicized place.

---

1   http://www.barents.no/granted-by-us.292852-41747.html (accessed 20 September 2008).

Somehow, Kirkenes has always been a place where international politics has been important. In the early 1900s the national authorities introduced political structures that tried to prevent the Finns from becoming too strong in the area (Eriksen and Niemi 1981). Kirkenes also had a central political position during World War II and the Cold War period. However, Kirkenes has never had such a political focus as it has in the beginning of the 21st century. With *glasnost* and *perestroika*, the authorities, both at regional and national levels, looked for ways to handle the new political situation and the new opportunities that have opened up with the removal of ideological and military politics of the Cold War period (Landsem 2007). The most important event was the Kirkenes Declaration and the establishment of the Barents Region in 1993. This policy was a result of local, regional and national political processes – inspired by the European Union policy prioritizing cross-border regions. Kirkenes soon acquired a vital role in this regional politics and in the new cross-border region. There have been ups and downs concerning the national focus of this politics and the area, but with the change of national Government in 2005 the 'northern' or 'high north' areas received much greater prominence than in the previous period. This is certainly related to new prospects for the oil industry in the North, but it also reflects recognition of the area as important for trade and contact with Russia. Kirkenes is often chosen as a place to meet for politicians, bureaucrats and researchers dealing with cross-border issues and northern and international politics. It is also a popular place to visit for national politicians. For instance, within one week in April 2009, the town was visited by four Norwegian ministers and one Finnish.

> ... it is exciting because Kirkenes is constantly on the agenda, on television, in media. At the same time we see, with all the meetings that are here, that they [national politicians] actually come here, in one election campaign after another. So it is obvious that this is something for the big boys too.

This quotation expresses a pride in belonging to Kirkenes as a 'political place'. When prominent politicians or government representatives arrive, they normally are accompanied by a team and a trail of journalists, and most often gather representatives from the surrounding districts. Besides all the political meetings, Kirkenes also has become a popular site for international conferences and a destination for people who are interested in cross-border relations, Russia and international politics on a regional level. It is said that Kirkenes has turned into a political destination, and also 'this is a politicized place'. Locally, people are proud of having this status. 'After three weeks in town, I had shaken hands with one minister and spoken to a former', a newcomer claimed. It seems to be a policy for prominent people to be seen in Kirkenes.

All the political activities are viable contributions to the local tourism industry, and indirectly to the local economy of the town. The statistics shows that business and meeting/conference guest-night stays in Kirkenes increased from 17,333 in 1991, to 22,288 in 1997 to 23,915 in 2007. Even with only a 7 per cent increase between 1997 and 2007, this has been a rather stable activity over the years. However, there has been an even more significant increase in leisure travel, from 17,337 guest-nights in 1991, 20,755 in 1997, to 31,889 in 2007, an increase of 53.6 per cent in ten years. Political activities give Kirkenes unique media exposure and high value place marketing. It certainly also contributes to the image of Kirkenes in a positive way.

Table 4.3 Events, processes and actors in the narration of Kirkenes as a political town

The Kirkenes Declaration 1993 and the Barents Secretariat established
The Kirkenes Jubilee Declaration in 2003, and the 15th anniversary event in 2008
A statue of Torvalt Stoltenberg, the previous Minister of Foreign Affairs, erected in the town in 2003
The Barents Institute established in 2006
An international Barents Secretariat established in 2007
Barents International School, a university study programme established in 2007
Yearly events: The Barents 'Spektakel' – a border-oriented cultural festival since 2004; Stoltenberg Seminar since 2006; Barents Days – a political seminar since 2008
Eight Norwegian, two foreign ministers, and 15–20 high-ranking diplomats visited Kirkenes from January to September 2008
Barents Secretariat: almost a presentation per day on average, more than 20 presentations abroad per year
The Barents Secretariat set up a unit in Murmansk

There certainly is an employment factor derived from this. In 2008 the Barents Secretariat had ten staff members and the Barents Institute had four. Sør-Varanger is also one of the few municipalities having a 'Foreign Minister' on its staff – a person dedicated to cross-border work. Also in other public offices and in some NGOs there are people dedicated to work on cross-border politics, and many of those employed in the sector deal with tourism related to the border and Russia. However the employment factor of this narrative is much more indirect than for the others.

The narrative about the politicized place is the most contested. There obviously is an emerging political elite (Viken et al 2008), but most people do not identify with their presence, and are reluctant to exert any effort into making Kirkenes into a political centre of the Barents Region and so on. 'I feel that there is very much talk of Barents, Barents, Barents ... But do we really have that much to do with Barents?', a young girl said. The elite character of political activities is also exemplified in some of the seminars, where few locals attend, and the Barents Spektakel is mostly a festival for those involved in organizing the event – the performers and the political elite – it is a marvellous event for a few, but of little interest for most inhabitants. In fact, many people are concerned about the consequences of all the Russification that politicization provokes.

The narrative about an inclusive multicultural community

> Kirkenes is a multicultural site, and has been so for centuries. The Sami, Finns, Norwegians and Russians have met and lived together in peace. It is a welcoming community, also for new immigrants from countries far away.

The narrative of Kirkenes as a multicultural and inclusive community has a long history, dating back to the situation where old Sami settlements, Finnish immigrants and Russian neighbours inhabited the place. Also the mining community had its foreign element, both Swedes and Germans were, for instance, involved in the establishment of the mine and, in some periods, many miners were Finns. The shipping of the iron ore also produced many international contacts. Moreover, Kirkenes had not emerged as a local or regional place, but rather was settled by people coming from other areas of Norway. Added to that there has always been people of Russian origin in town, some that even had escaped from Russia in the wake of the Soviet revolution. Even through the Soviet period there were contacts across the border, and an interchange of people. However, with the change of politics and regime in Russia around 1990 an entirely new situation occurred. Although, the streams of people crossing the border from the early 1990s can be seen as a continuation or reestablishment of an old relationship, it had more of the character of a border area revolution. Nevertheless, the border regimes did not change much, and the border crossing is still strictly controlled, partly due to the fact that this is both a Schengen and Nato border, and partly due to a Russian border regime introduced in 2007 – a 15-kilometre border zone. Despite this, Russians work, conduct business and settle in the Kirkenes area, and many Russians have married or found a partner in Kirkenes. In 2008, there were in Kirkenes, 382 inhabitants (4.0 per cent of the population) with roots in Russia or other former Soviet Union countries, including second-generation people (data from Statistics Norway). The Russians constituted 50.6 per cent of the foreigners within the municipality. This is much higher than in the rest of the region (Finnmark) where 32 per cent of the foreigners were Russians. Among those who have immigrated to Sør-Varanger from Russia themselves, 72 per cent are women, about the same as for the whole region. This reflects a pattern with Russian women marrying Norwegian men – also a sign of inclusion. However, the number of Russians staying in Kirkenes for shorter periods of time is much higher: people working on a short time basis, seamen and different types of visitors and tourists (Flemmen and Lothrington 2007).

In the beginning, Russians came over trying to make some money through street market activities. As they often also sold alcohol (which is strongly regulated in Norway), and there was some prostitution, the authorities did not welcome these activities, neither did the commercial sector, who saw the Russian street traders as competitors. There were debates in the media, labelling these activities as problems and provoked prejudices towards Russians. 'Don't steal' written in Russian, was a common signpost in the stores in this period. The street market activities were forbidden but, in recent years have returned in a more regulated form, as a Russian market-day.

Within the municipality people realized the need for an integrative policy and put it on the agenda – and some did a tremendous job to change attitudes. But also other organizations and actors contributed to this policy. One of the most important ways of integrating Russians was to employ them – both in the public and the private sector. Thus, everybody has or has had a Russian colleague, and through jobs or neighbourhoods, people have come to know Russians, or made Russian friends. Russians soon became part of the everyday life in town. Some company managements made efforts to integrate and to create positive attitudes towards Russians. Particularly the first managing director at the engeneering factory Kimek, made an important contribution (Landsem 2007). He started an internal newsletter where he informed his employees about market efforts in Russia and he asked his employees to welcome and treat Russians as friends (Landsem 2007, 66).

Another group that worked on integration were the employees at Sør-Varanger Competence Centre that gave refugees and Russians training in the Norwegian language. Some of these also had a background in anti-racism work, and became involved in a Norwegian–Russian Cultural Centre, established in 1993 by a couple of individuals. In 1994 a Multicultural Polar Night Festival was held, a festival that was an annual event for the next five years. The Norwegian–Russian Cultural Centre closed down in 1997 because of a lack of money. In the late 1990s the curator company, the 'Girls on the Bridge', had been established with the aim of creating arts and cultural activities. In a jubilee in 2003 celebrating the creation of the Barents Region, the 'Girls on the Bridge' were asked to take part and produced a programme with a cross-border content. It was a success, particularly the border dialogues and afterwards the municipality suggested it as a yearly festival and the 'Girls on the Bridge' took the responsibility. Since then it has been an important festival related to cross-border issues, mostly with a rather avant-garde arts programme. In 2008 the festival had a Cross-Border Café where social, cultural and political issues were discussed, a youth music programme and a spectacular theatre show on a lake where one can see over to Russia. The festival is in fact called the Barents Spektakel (with a hybrid spelling playing on the different ways spectacle is spelled in the Barents Region countries). The festival has been a success, has a significant budget, and has received financial support from local, regional and national authorities. Its aim is, through art, to create cross-border understanding, contacts and activities.

Table 4.4 Events, processes and actors in the narration of Kirkenes as an inclusive town

Norwegian–Russian Cultural Centre 1993
Multicultural Polar Night Festival from 1994–98
Barents Spektakel since 2004
Since mid-1990s Russians employed in all types of industries, also in schools and kindergartens
Central actors: Sør-Varanger Municipality, private sector, Kimek, the 'Girls on the Bridge'

Not everybody welcomes the Russian 'invasion'. Young people appreciated the 'multicultural' Kirkenes, but at the same time they expressed that it sometimes went too far. One informant referred to a widow who buried her late husband according to Russian traditions; something that the relatives of the man found strange and partly distasteful. The adolescents interviewed in 2006 expressed scepticism in different ways: 'Russian seamen occupy the town', 'the Russian seamen offend young girls', and so on. However, on the other hand, they made exceptions for their Russian buddies, and most of them claimed to have Russian friends.

Another pertinent question is this: Is Kirkenes the inclusive town that it strives to be? At least the Russians are not integrated entirely. For example, there is a tendency for Russian immigrants to keep together. There is, according to Rogova (2007), who has made a study of Russians in the town, several boundaries between the Russians and the Norwegians. This however, does not mean that integrative efforts have failed; it is more a sign of the fact that Kirkenes is multicultural; not only Russians, but people from more than 50 nations are said to live in the town. The town is however not a place where cultural differences disappear and cultures totally merge. It is a town where immigrants partake, but at the same time also constitute separate minority groups.

Discussion: Narratives and Path Dependency

One of the starting points of this study was that narratives are representations driven by the needs and feelings of those producing them, and that they are developed and changed according to changing circumstances (Bridger 1997, 70). This study certainly provides evidence for such observations. The industry narrative has changed, and is more multiple and flexible than it was. When the oil industry opportunities emerged, oil industry support became the most important part of the narrative, whereas in 2006 the mining activities again were a major focus. But another side of the industry narrative is that it is resistant to being replaced and rather stable and has survived despite the fact that it has been challenged by several border-related narratives. Most remarkable is the transportation part of this narrative that has been sustained despite a lack of interest from the Russian side. This narrative is more like a dream – a fantasy situating Kirkenes as a hub in a world-based transport system. However, regardless of the degree of realism, symbolically this narrative is important, putting Kirkenes in the centre of the world. In a way, these industrial narratives constitute some kind of continuity.

The narratives in Kirkenes not only cause and transform, but also restrain the defining of legitimate scenarios for the town. This presentation also has shown how the narratives are embedded in social practices developed over time. This reflects an evolutionary approach where the economic and social development is 'path-dependent', meaning that what is happening now is based on earlier priorities and decisions (Amin 1999; cf. Cumbers et al. 2003).The narratives in circulation are such paths. Narratives regulate behaviour. Narratives – in media, in literature, in public – are part of the environment that support laws, rules, plans and policies governing peoples' lives. Elements of this can also be found in Kirkenes. And political statements of Kirkenes as a border town, an inclusive society or a bridgehead towards Russia are all examples of such narrative regulation. The regulative element of narratives is strengthened through the normative aspect providing people with norms, values, goals, means, expectations and roles. Through repetitions and figuring in a multitude of connections narratives are internalized – people are unconsciously brainwashed. The narratives become what people believe in and strive for; people in Kirkenes believe that Kirkenes is an industrial town, despite the fact that more than half of the workforce is found within the public sector; they believe in Kirkenes as a border town, although the border-related activities account for only a minor part of the local economy. The narrative of the political place also receives a lot more attention than what it economically deserves, and so also the inclusive multicultural community narrative, with only 5 per cent of the inhabitants being of foreign origin. Yet, people think that Kirkenes should be a welcoming community.

Symbols support narratives. The symbols of the industrial narrative are huge buildings from the mining period, a tall shipyard building (Kimek), Russian trawlers in the harbour, but also plans, assessments and other documents that show the significance and future opportunities of such activities. Some also have labels related to these industries, as *Lokhallen* and *Knuseverket*. The street names written in Cyrillic are one of many symbols supporting the border town image, and the 'Barents' prefix used almost everywhere symbolizes the political place narrative. Some of these symbols also support the narrative of an inclusive community. Thus, narratives colour the way people look upon their place, culture and themselves.

As often noticed, narratives are not neutral, but containers of power. The idea of Kirkenes as an industrial town is embedded in a variety of ways, and has a position tending towards hegemony. However, since the positions of narratives are constantly renegotiated, there has been a process going on emancipating the town from this narrative, seen by some as a 'ghost' (cf. Throgmorton 2003). Thus, the industry narrative is contested, particularly by the border and the political place narratives. The position of each is not only a matter of what is happening in Kirkenes, but these narratives are parts of national and international webs of discourses, actors and institutions. Kirkenes is what Healy (1999, 115) calls a 'multiplex place', it is continually being reinvented in narrative processes as a result of pressure from below and being enforced from above (cf. Rossi 2004), in connected processes of invention and intervention (Robinson 2006).

Conclusion

The discussion in this chapter implies that several narratives are governing the development of Kirkenes. There are aspects both of invention and intervention (Throgmorton 2003) in these narratives. The way the narratives reflect and are creating new activities refer to the inventive sides of the narratives. Kirkenes has in fact developed into a border town and there are, as discussed in this chapter, at least three narratives supporting these changes: a border narrative, a narrative of a politicized place, and a narrative of an inclusive community. However, these narratives are not constant and are reinvented all the time – their content is flexible and changing. This fits into the characteristic of narratives: they are multiple, flexible and represent different voices (Jensen 2007). Thus, the big overarching narratives represent continuity, their various manifestations represent change. Concerning intervention, this presentation shows that the narratives are interwoven into cross-border, international and global webs. The industry narrative is strongly influenced by what is happening in the global market, and in the transport sector, the border narrative and the politicized place narratives are dependent on the development in Russia. The narrative of the politicized place is also heavily reliant on national politics and priorities. Many informants in this study, viewed the political institution in Kirkenes and governmental actors merely as puppets.

The narratives observed in this study obviously have had different force at different stages. Before the change of the Norwegian government in 2005, the narrative of a politicized place was feeble, four years later it is much stronger. This is also the experience in other border areas. Vila (2003, 617) maintains, for example, that a socially constructed border has different significance in different situations. And as Vila goes on: 'the different constructions people make of the international divide (as a barrier, a set of opportunities, a metaphor for other – more important – personal border, etc.), enter the common sense of the region in the variety of narrative plots ...' (Vila 2003, 616).

Concerning the realization of Kirkenes' potential, people's interpretations of their place are critical for what actions they take. In this respect it is probably the industrial and border narratives that should be given priority, as they create work and employment. However, the study also indicates that these narratives are supported by the others: cross-border politics is a premise for success in the mining and transport sectors, and so is a community that welcomes foreign capital, culture and people. And none of the narratives exclude any other; they are complementary and provide an exciting platform for a flourishing borderland development.

References

Abelsen, L. (2004), *Barenstregionen – en næringsregion? En studie av regionale politiske strukturer i forhold til et integrert og funksjonelt næringssamarbeid.* Hovedfagsoppgave (Tromsø: Universitetet i Tromsø).

Amin, A. (1998), An institutionalist perspective on regional economic development. Paper. Economic Geography Research Group Seminar, July 3, Department of Geography UCL, London.

Andersen, O.J. (1996), 'Omstilling mellom kontinuitet og oppbrudd', in: Mariussen, Å., Karlsen, A. and Andersen, O.J. (eds) *Omstilling – fra løsrivning til ny forankring* (Oslo: Universitetsforlaget).

Barthes, R. (1977), *Image, Music, Text* (New York: Hill & Wang).

Bowman, W.D. (2006), 'Why narrative? Why now?', *Research Studies in Music Educations*, 27, 5–20.

Bridger, J.C. (1997), 'Community stories and their relevance to planning', *Applied Behavioral Science Review*, 5, 67–80.

Brown, A.D., Stacey, P. and Nandhakumar, J. (2008), 'Making sense of sensemaking narratives', *Human Relations*, 61(8), 1035–62.

Cumbers, A. MacKinnon, D. and McMaster, A. (2003), 'Institutions, power and space: Assessing the limits to institutionalism in economic geography'. *European Urban and Regional Studies*, 10: pp. 325–342.

Currie, G. and Brown, A.D. (2003), 'A narratological approach to understanding processes of organizing in a UK hospital', *Human Relations*, 5(5), 563–86.

Czarniawska, B. (2002), 'Narration or science? Collapsing the division in organisation studies', *Organization*, 2(1), 11–33.

Czarniawska-Joerges, B. (1995), *Narratives in Social Research* (London: Sage).

Dale, B. (2002), 'An institutionalist approach to local restructuring. The case of four Norwegian mining towns', *European Urban and Regional Studies*, 9(1), 5–20.

Dewy, J. (1934), *Art as Experience* (New York: Minton, Balch).

Doolin, B. (2003), 'Narratives of change: Discourse, technology and organisation', *Organization*, 10(4), 751–70.

Eriksen, K.E. and Niemi, E. (1981), *Den finske fare. sikkerhetsproblemer og minoritetspolitikk i nord 1860–1940* (Oslo, Universitetsforlaget).

Finnegan, R. (1998), *Tales of the City* (Cambridge: Cambridge University Press).

Flemmen, A.B. and Lothrington, A.T. (2007), 'Transnational marriages: Politics and desire', in: Jørgen Ole Bærenholdt and Brynhild Granås (eds), *Mobility and Place. Enacting Northern European Peripheries*, pp. 127–138 (London: Ashgate).

Gilpin, D.R. (2008), 'Narrating the organization of self: Reframing the role of the new release', *Public Relations Review*, 34, 9–18.

Hardy, C., Palmer, I. and Phillips, N. (2000), 'Discourse as strategic resource', *Human Relations*, 53(9), 1227–48.

Harvey, D. (1989), 'From managerialism to entrepreneurialism: The transformation in urban governance in late capitalism', *Geografiska Annaler*, 71B(1), 3–17.

Healy, P. (1999), 'Institutional analysis, communicative planning and shaping places', *Journal of Planning, Education and Research*, 19, 111–21.

Jarrett, R.L. (1993), 'Focus group interviewing with low-income minority populations: A research experience', in: Morgan, D.L. (ed.), *Successful Focus Groups. Advancing the State of Art*, pp.184–201 (Newbury Park: Sage).

Jensen, O.B. (*2007*), 'Culture stories: Understanding cultural urban branding', *Planning Theory, 6, 211–36.* (Johnstone 1992).

Landsem, L.E.I. (2007), *Barentsregionens tilblivelse. En studie av regionale initiativ til opprettelse av Barentsregionen.* Hovedoppgave (Tromsø: Universtitetet i Tromsø). Law 1992.

Mariussen, Å. (1996), 'Innledning', in: Mariussen, Å., Karlsen, A. and Andersen, O.J. (eds), *Omstilling – fra løsrivning til ny forankring* (Oslo: Universitetsforlaget).

Murphy, J.T. (2006), 'Building trust in economic space', *Progress in Human Geography*, 30(4), 427–50.

Niemi, E. (1992), *Pomor. Nord-Norge og Nord-Russland gjennom 1000 år* (Oslo: Gyldendal Norsk forlag).

Nyseth, T. and Granås, B. (2007), *Place Reinvention: Dynamics and Governance Perspectives* (Stockholm: NORDREGIO: Report nr 1/2007).

Robinson, J. (2006), 'Inventions and interventions: Transforming cities – an introduction', *Urban Studies*, 45, 251–8.

Rogova, A. (2007), *From Rejection to Re-embracement: Language and Identity of Russian Speaking Minority in Kirkenes, Norway* (Kirkenes: The Barents Institute).

Rossi, U. (2004), 'The multiplex city. The process of urban change in the historic centre of Naples', *European Urban and Regional Studies*, 11(2), 136–69.

Somers, M. (1994), 'The narrative constitution of identity: A relational and network approach', *Theory and Society*, 23, 605–49.

Somers, M. (1997), 'Deconstruction and reconstruction class formation theory: Narrativity, relational analysis, and social theory', in: Hall, J.R. (ed.), *Reworking Class*, pp. 73–106 (Ithaca, NY: Cornell University Press).

Throgmorton, J.A. (1992), 'Planning as persuasive storytelling about the future: negotiation and electric power rate settlement in Illinois', *Journal of Planning Education and Research*, 12, 17–31.

Throgmorton, J.A. (2003), 'Planning as persuasive storytelling in a global-scale web of relationships', *Planning Theory*, 2, 125–51.

Viken, A. (2007), *Celebrating the Cold War. Tourism Related to the Norwegian–Russian Boundary*, 16th NordicTourism Research Symposium, 27–29 September, Helsingborg, Sweden.

Viken, A., Nyseth, T. and Granås, B. (2008), 'Kirkenes: An industrial site reinvented as a border town', *Acta Borealia*, 25(1), 22–44.

Vila, P. (2003) 'Processes of identification on the US–Mexico border', *The Social Science Journal*, 40, 607–25.

Webb, C. and Kavern, J. (2001), 'Focus groups as research method: a critique of some aspects of their use in nursing research', *Journal of Advanced Nursing* 33(6), 798–805.

Williamson, O.E. (1955), *Markets and Hierarchies: Analysis of Antitrust Implications* (New York: Free Press).

Wilkinson, S. (1999), 'Focus groups. A feminist method', *Psychology of Women Quarterly* 23, 221–44.

Yin, R.K. (1994), *Case Study Research: Design and Methods* (Thousand Oaks, California: Sage).

Chapter 5

Gendered Places: Cultural Economy and Gender in Processes of Place Reinvention

Magnfríður Júlíusdóttir and Yvonne Gunnarsdotter

In academic and political discourse, culture and creativity are increasingly viewed as the promoters of economic reinvention of place. This is apparent in analysis of cutural policies in the Nordic countries, where an economic approach to cultural policy, which regard arts and culture as increasingly important to employment, has gained ground in regional and local development programmes. New EU and national sources for funding cultural projects, along with the decentralization of cultural policies, have promoted the role of the regions (Mitchell 2003). The cultural economy emphasis in regional development, has replaced an earlier trend in urban transformation. According to Gibson and Kong (2005), generalizations about the capacity of a cultural economy have developed into a 'normative cultural economy' approach in policy circles. It encourages cultural economy clusters, as a vital part of an emerging knowledge economy, where innovation, creativity and entrepreneurship generate economic growth and attract young talented people, the 'creative class' (Florida 2002), as residents in places with vibrant cultural activites. For a critic on Florida's thesis see Houston et al. (2008).

In this chapter our aim is to contextualize the cultural economy debate by analysing developments in two small Nordic towns in remote regions. How is culture, as an instrument for economic growth, intergrated into reinvention processes in our case studies? What contestations and power relations, especially regarding gender, are prominent in the cultural economy developments in these places?

The towns studied are Egilsstaðir in Eastern Iceland and Pajala in the Swedish Torne Valley where local views emerged from discussions in focus groups, interviews with individuals and analysis of policy documents. Despite similarities in a loosely defined peripheral geographic and socioeconomic location at the national scale, the cultural context of these places varies, especially considering Pajala's location at ethnic, cultural as well as national borders. Pajala was declared a cultural municipality at the beginning of the 1990s. The local politicians then picked up on the cultural revival that had been going on spontaneously for some years. The focus here is on analysing changes in priorities in cultural developments and its gendered outcome. The cases presented from Egilsstaðir/Fljótsdalshérað focus on a recent cultural contract with the government and the gendered use of a local resource, wild reindeer, for place marketing and income generation.

The Rise of Cultural Economy

According to Amin and Thrift (2004), the dominant position today in the use of the concept of cultural economy is how the commodification of culture offers new life to the economy through tourism, media, art, and so on. This 'cultural turn' in economic analysis has its source in discourses on postmodernity, manifested in post-industrial production and consumption, where the analysis of change by Lash and Urry (1994) has been influential. They argue that both production and consumption are characterized by increased reflexivity, with 'aesthetic reflexivity' giving more weight to culture as a symbolic process in life-style consumption. Hence design, images/signs, experience and knowledge are important components of goods and services. This is manifested in the two Nordic towns in this study with increased weight given to tourism and higher education, cultural heritage festivals and artistic events at the dawn of the 21st century. Together with service, these post-industrial activities, have replaced the former dependence on fisheries, forest- and agricultural-processing industries in people's livelihoods.

In the context of regional development, a second source of cultural economy ideas is named 'new regionalism' by both Simonsen (2001) and Ray (1998). Ray's emphasis is on influences from the European Union development policy, where different funds have been redirected from a sectoral to a territorial approach. This policy encourages people to identify and value local resources, including cultural identity. Related to these changes is regionalism, expressed in place-promotion to develope socio-economic vibrancy (Ray 1998). According to Simonsen (2001) in many studies in economic geography, culture is conceptualized as an attribute possessed by firms and places and is seen as a resource or constraint in economic development. Simonsen claims this approach is imbued with a problematic understanding of culture–place relations, as culture appears relatively stable, bounded and internally undifferentiated. This is in opposition to formulations of a progressive sense of place (Massey 1994) where places become specific articulations of multiple layers of meaning in a variety of practices, networks and spatial scales.

Simonsen (2001) suggests that studies of practice and meaning open up new understandings of cultural economy, where economy is conceptualized as 'a meaningful activity inseparable from culture' (ibid. 2001, 47). She argues that this was also the case in German 'Wirtschaftssoziologie' at the end of the 19th century. In line with this we are interested in different actors' practices and meanings regarding activities within the cultural economy framework, for instance in creating a new place identity and making a living from creativity and culture-associated work. We also take our point of departure in Ray's suggestion that the cultural economy[1] should be understood as an '... attempt by rural areas to localize economic control – to (re)valorise place through its cultural identity' (Ray

---

1   Ray uses 'culture economy', which we have changed to the current dominant term 'cultural economy'.

1998, 3). At the same time, the contested nature of place identity should not be ignored. The contestation can arise by new ideas and social relations brought about by in-migration (Kneafsey 2001), or large-scale investments in experimental art (Zukin 1995) or commerce (Lysgård and Tveiten 2005), in small towns formerly dominated by industry. Not only representations of values and identities of people and places, but also the trend of public–private governance leading cultural economy developments are contested (Harvey 1989).

Gender and Reinvention Policy

In 'new regionalism' the field of cultural economy is depoliticized, drawing attention away from how cultures are 'internally complex and continually reshaped through practice, negotiation and struggle' (Simonsen 2001, 48). Cultural economy is not merely generating new kinds of economic activities, but is taking place in localities where social relations like class and gender are imbued with power (Kneafsey 2001), which can be reproduced or changed with a policy emphasizing the transformative power of cultural economy.

In a European context, the main focus of studies on the gendered outcome of new trends in regional policy has been on rural areas, farming and entrepreneurial activities as income generation in market-led economies (Little and Jones 2000; Little 2002; Shorthall 2002; Bock 2004). Emphasis on direct competition in fund bidding, partnerships with the local private business sector and a preference for large-scale 'flagship' projects are processes that have reinforced male power within policy-making, as women are poorly represented in leading positons and networks within the private sector. The result of the above emphasis is that the praxis of rural economic policy is increasingly masculine in style and direction (Little and Jones 2000).

In the Nordic countries, special action programmes have aimed to increase female entrepreneurship and, despite gender mainstreaming being the official policy in the EU and in individual Nordic countries, gender equality has recently been treated more as an objective deriving from economic growth, rather than a question of social justice (Mósesdóttir 2005 and 2006). Hudson and Rönnblom (2007) illustrate the depolitization of Swedish regional policy where women often hold the subject position of 'The Other' in need for support. They also show that this is less appearant in Northern Sweden where women have formed networks and resource centres claiming interest in 'gender equality' rather than 'women's interest'.

In Swedish regional development policy, the hegemonic discourse has revolved around concepts such as growth, competition and business, where knowledge-intensive and high-tech businesses have replaced traditional industry. Regional business advisors use gender stereotypes when discussing the motives and skills of men and women seeking assistance to start a new business, where women show most interest in starting firms in service and handicrafts (Scholten 2003).

Gender differentiation in activities among entrepreneurs has been found to mirror the general pattern of gender segregation in the labour market (Regeringskansliet 2001), which is high in the Nordic countries.

Pajala – At the Border

Pajala is the name of a small town as well as a municipality.[2] The municipality had approximately 6,700 inhabitants spread over more than 80 villages in the Swedish Torne Valley in 2006. Before industrialization most people in the Torne Valley made their living from Sámi reindeer herding and farm-based activities. When Sweden and Russia made peace in 1809, the border between Sweden and Finland was drawn along the Torne and Muonio rivers and the main population became a Finnish-speaking minority within Sweden. A variation of Finnish developed, called Meänkieli, meaning 'our language'. During the first half of the 20th century there were strong movements to make 'real Swedes' of the Torne Valley people and it was forbidden to speak Meänkieli in schools.

For over a century, forest and mining industrial development led to a substantial increase in population in these places. The rationalization of this industry, together with a marked decrease in public employment in the 1990s, led to increased unemployment. Paradoxically, the closing of mines in Kiruna at the beginning of the 1980s counteracted the depopulation because people who had left Pajala moved back. This caused a number of years of relative optimism, but since then Pajala has faced a population decline.

The education level is lower than the national average, though the schools have shown very good results in national ranking in recent years. Male unemployment is more than double compared to female, and more families are supported by women than by men. There is a clear gender division in both working life and leisure time, expressed by one woman saying: 'We sometimes call this the Taliban Valley'. Recently a new mining reef has been investigated and a Canadian mining company plans to open a mine before 2010. They hope to create 1,500 jobs in the region (Norrbottenskuriren 29 May 2007). Already the high unemployment of almost 10 per cent has been halved in 2007.

Becoming a 'cultural municipality'

The municipal Internet page announces 'Pajala – the cultural municipality in the middle of Nordkalotten'.[3] In around 1990 a woman who was at that time a member

---

2   Sources include www.pajala.se (18 May 2008) and Berglund, A.-K., Johansson, S. and Molina, I. (eds) (2005), *Med periferien i sentrum*. Rapport 2005:14 (Norut NIBR Finnmark).

3   'Nordkalotten' is the Arctic area of Scandinavia.

of the municipal council wrote a proposal suggesting that Pajala should be labelled a cultural municipality. She recalls her argumentation:

> Partly because we should challenge our thoughts. We need new ways of thinking ... and culture is a forerunner to open doors and open up thoughts. So that was one reason. But also because our culture has been oppressed for such a long time. There is so much to get from there. We have a base that we never use. [Giving an example of traditional food.] That is something in our culture that we can make use of and develop and make new products from, that we can live from. So that was also a thought and there are certainly more to be found. And then culture as such, that's good for our individual well-being. It was for those three reasons that I wrote the proposition. I wrote it during a meeting and it was approved at once. (Female former politician)

'Cultural' in the designation 'cultural municipality' is interpreted by most people as a local identity manifested first and foremost in the language, Meänkieli. The dominant narrative is that the Torne Valley people used to be oppressed and that cultural commitment is a way of strengthening local identity. The interviewees bear witness to the low self esteem that people from the Torne Valley experienced during the 1960s and 1970s.

The cultural sector has grown and several authors of national renown come from Pajala. The most recently well known is Mikael Niemi who in 2000 wrote *Popular Music from Vittula* (*Populär musik från Vittula*), a novel about life in Pajala during the 1960s and 1970s. One important step in the cultural revival was the establishment of a national organization for people from the Torne Valley in 1980. New opportunities opened up when Sweden joined the EU and when Meänkieli, together with Sámi, achieved the status of a minority language. The Torne Valley theatre, Tote, established in 1986, has played an important role in the revival of Meänkieli. This has brought a new self-confidence, which is important in the face of today's adverse developments. Tote now receive subsidies from the Swedish National Council for Cultural Affairs and the county administration, with the requirement to perform partly in Meänkieli and to co-operate with schools. One dilemma is whether they should stage plays in Meänkieli or in Swedish. Either tourists and new inhabitants will feel excluded or most of the native inhabitants will not be interested. The solution has been to mix them. Not everyone agrees on the importance of Meänkieli. Some people think that it is a poor language that should not be taught in school, and that creating a grammar is 'too fundamentalist'. Many young people find it more important to learn a language that will be useful outside Pajala. The language question is certainly something that evokes strong feelings.

Apart from different opinions concerning the role of Meänkieli, there is a consensus about the importance of strengthening the local identity. The proclamation of a cultural municipality is a contested issue, since culture is also interpreted as fine arts. The politicians interviewed are all men in their late middle ages, and those in opposition to the leading social democratic party are sceptical of culture as a way out of the problematic situation in Pajala. They view culture as 'snobbish' and 'opium for the people' and ask, 'Who has time for theatre when there is wood to be cut?'

> I was born with dirt under my nails and I care about the Tornedalen culture. The kind of culture promoted by Mikael Niemi ... I am not convinced that cultural commitment is the right thing. I was raised believing that it is production you should live from. Sure, it is an experience to see someone dancing with a sheet by the river, but how is it going to be in the long run? (male politician)

Into public–private partnerships

In Pajala a new emphasis was brought to the cultural label, reinforced by a change of mayor in 2002, when tourism and the image of Pajala based on natural and cultural resources came into focus. A local journalist says, jokingly: 'As soon as he [the mayor] sees a tourist he calls for a press conference'. Apart from the uniqueness of being a border region, the mayor mentions the unregulated five rivers and the salmon fishing when explaining cultural aspects of the municipality, a view with which other politicians agree. He also stresses the importance of a new airport as 'the solution' for Pajala.

The change in emphasis from culture as local identity to culture as a resource for the tourism business is mirrored in a reorganization of the local administration. In 1996 a municipal business company (PUAB) was established to stimulate diversification. The municipal committee for culture and education had a female manager with close connections to Tote. She encouraged a cultural profile in schools, including classes in Meänkieli, music, theatre and projects about the local heritage in accordance with the proclamation of Pajala as a cultural municipality. When PUAB reorganized in 2004, most cultural issues was assigned to it instead of with the municipal committee, and the female manager left.

The three middle-aged men at the PUAB office are guided by a board composed of six men; aside from the mayor these represent different companies.[4] At the PUAB office, culture is said to include 'almost everything', which is similar to what Lysgård and Tveiten (2005, 496) found in a Norwegian small town: 'Culture ranging from fine arts to leisure activities'. In a PowerPoint presentation of Pajala, language and culture are placed under the headline 'Infrastructure'. They stress the possibility of benefitting from the unique combination of nature and culture in the tourist business. They also point out the need of culture, as 'wood for the fire', that culture can both be used to 'tie us together' and to gain money from all the events that take place. Besides culture and nature, they stress high-technology as being a characteristic of Pajala. There are different opinions concerning the

---

4   In 2008 two men and one woman worked at the PUAB office, but the board still consists of men only.

reorganization and one of the women employed in the municipal administration summons the situation:

> Should we engage in culture for ourselves or should we engage in culture that draws an external audience? ... Should we spend money on voluntary associations offering theatre plays to those who return home, or should we spend our money on entrepreneurs? (Female municipal administration manager)

According to PUAB many people, especially middle-aged men, hold the same sceptical views about culture as some of the politicians. Some male and female entrepreneurs interviewed agree: 'Culture is positive, but there has to be jobs'. One man says that 'it is really *knappsu* [feminine]',[5] while two women oppose it by arguing that it is mostly men who are engaged in this. They all suggest that culture should be tied to traditional handicrafts such as tanning, knitting gloves in the village of Lovikka or making coffee cheese. A man who, amongst other things, offers hunting as a form of tourism, views moose hunting as culture. From their perspective, the political emphasis has shifted from theatre towards nature tourism, and they also mention a project about the 19th-century local religious leader Læstadius (funded by the EU), which attracts another type of tourist.

Gendered experiences of cultural economy

In 2004 the 'Vittula Project' in Pajala took place, involving the local authorities and actors from the cultural and business sectors, supported by PUAB. This project emanated from Mikael Niemi's book. The project lasted a year culminating when a film based on the book had its first performance in Pajala, and a range of events took place connected with literature, theatre, film and Niemi's book. The vision of ten thousand visitors was an overestimation, but it attracted international attention.

In an interview the Vittula Project is criticized by a female municipal employee for being invented by a group of men in the sauna, driven by two men, and most of all because of the provocative name that gained exposure in different situations. Vittula is a Meänkieli term meaning 'the female genitals', by the same token that Pajala means 'the place of the smithy'. A man reminds her that many women have gained from initiatives in the cultural sphere: 'So I don't think there have been any problems with this'.

The Vittula Project made media headings about the bussing of women in for the annual festival Römppäviikko during the 1980s. Since 1987, when Pajala celebrated its 400th anniversary, the tradition of Römppäviikko has been renewed. The name refers to the last week in September, when people celebrate the end of

---

5 *Knappsu* is a Meänkieli term meaning female in a derogatory sense with reference to a man. The expression has recently been incorporated into the Swedish language, thanks to Mikael Niemi.

the harvest. One year the anniversary was overshadowed by the idea of chartering a bus from Stockholm to invite women to Pajala with the aim of compensating for the shortage of women. This became an international media event and during the journey the women left the bus and the media gaze one by one, so when it reached its destination only three journalists remained. The event was both exaggerated and misunderstood and it gave Pajala a bad reputation, according to some of the municipal administration managers. They all agree that Pajala is well known, though sometimes in a negative way, as a male-dominated community. The young people enjoyed the activities in the Vittula Project, but they think the local politicians made a big fuss about it and they do not approve of the idea of renaming parts of Pajala as Vittula.

Though the people at PUAB see a problem with the image of Pajala being pervaded by a macho culture, they still have not engaged in assisting women's enterprises or networks. One of the men says, without further explanation: 'You have to creep when it comes to projects addressing women'. PUAB lacks the resources to be proactive and the strategy is to listen to those who contact them; these are seldom women, since 'women are bad at networking'. In 2008 a municipality department started a project directed to women entrepreneurs offering a coaching programme (www.pajala.se 18 May 2008).

The shift from culture as strengthening local identity to cultural economy, together with the male dominance, makes support from PUAB a bit random from the point of view of enterprises and village groups. A group of female entrepreneurs engaged in food production based on local traditions arrange tourist visits and sell their products. Within the framework of an EU project they have gained competence by means of several courses associated with food production and business leadership, with the aim of expanding their activities, and at least one enterprise has been established. Their plan is to create a Food house in their village offering local food and tourist packages including housing, food and guided tours. They have neither received economic nor marketing support from PUAB for this next step. They express disappointment that a well-established entrepreneurial project based on local heritage and involving women has not received any support.

Egilsstaðir – At the Cross-roads

Egilsstaðir, a service centre at a crossroads in an agricultural region, celebrated its 50th anniversary in 2007. The town is an important transport node, with the region's main airport. After recent merging of municipalities the town is an administrative centre, with almost 2,700 inhabitants in 2008, in the Fljótsdalshérað municipality. Public and private services have been the main sources of employment for both women and men. Jobs in industry have mainly been in agricultural processing, construction, kitchen interiors and textiles. The textile industry was part of a large wool industry in Iceland which, in second half of the 1980s, closed most factories in the wake of a global relocation of the textile industry. In Egilsstaðir 40 people lost their jobs, the majority women. Over the decades the town has grown steadily, but according to some of the local informants a transient population is characteristic of the town, mainly due to people moving in and out of public service jobs. Since 1979 an upper secondary school for the region has been in Egilsstaðir and in development visions for the 21st century, establishing centres of higher education and research is emphasized (Iðnaðar- og viðskiptaráðuneytið 2006).

Climbing on the 'cultural economy wagon'

In 2001 East Iceland was the first region in the country to sign a cultural contract with the government ministry of education and culture, with the larger share of financing coming from the government in the initial phase. The main content of the contract was a new cultural fund allocating yearly grants based on applications[6] and the establishment of the post of a cultural administrator. The municipalities intended to develop four cultural centres in the region specializing in different cultural fields: creative arts and exhibitions, music, literature and performing arts. When the contract was renewed in 2005 the ministry of transport was joined to support heritage tourism and crafts were added to one of the cultural centres. The performing arts were allocated to the cultural centre in Egilsstaðir, which in a government statement on regional development in 1999 was declared the lucky recipient of a 'culture house' (*menningarhús*) in East Iceland. The plan is to start building this house for theatre and opera performances in 2009. Following the cultural contract three posts in cultural administration have been established in Egilsstaðir, all filled by women. One administrates the regional cultural fund and two work for the municipality combining administration of cultural events and youth activities. In 2007 the former slaughterhouse in the centre of Egilsstaðir was reopened as a youth and culture centre after much debate where opponents claimed public money was wasted on a house that should be bulldozed. The third round of the cultural contract was signed in January 2008 and now the municipalities aim at putting into the contract five times as much as the government (Menningaráð Austurlands 2008). Both parties have increased substantially the allocation to the cultural funding since 2001, especially the municipalities.

The Business and Regional Development Centre (BRDC)[7] in East Iceland, located at Egilsstaðir urged the municipalities to unite in the proposal for the cultural contract in 2001. According to a man working on the project, culture was

---

6   In February 2008 around 28 million Icelandic kronas were granted to 85 cultural projects in the region. Main selection criterias for grants, defined in the cultural contract, are strengthening of: employment; tourist attractions; co-operation between municipalities; cultural diversity and access for all; cultural activities of young and old people; efficient use of finance; and international co-operation.

7   The English version of the name is now the Development Association of East Iceland (DAEI), which resembles more closely the Icelandic name (see www.east-iceland. is and www.austur.is).

'in the air' at that time in discussions on future directions in regional development in Iceland and he was interested in developing that further. The main pro-argument used was to increase the satisfaction of inhabitants with the supply and quality of cultural activities, with special attention focussed on the needs of young people. Reference was made to a study showing that only half of the respondents in East Iceland, the lowest level in the country, were satisfied with culture and leisure activities in the region (Ólafsson 1997). It was also stressed that cultural activities create employment and have direct impact on sectors like tourism and commerce (Þróunarstofa Austurlands 2000). In these formulations cultural activities are an important ingredient in perceptions of quality of life in certain places and hence a factor in migration decisions.

Recent developments in cultural activities have put Egilsstaðir on the map of international networks in contemporary art. In April 2006 the first international experimental film and video festival held in Iceland, named 700IS Reindeerland, took place in Egilsstaðir. Kristín, the young artist initiating the festival, moved from England to Egilsstaðir in 2005 to take up a position at the newly established cultural centre at the municipality. According to her there has been a large interest in participating in the festival, with over three hundred films/videos sent in each year from more than 30 countries. Kristín related the keen interest in the festival to the novelty of participating in a festival in Iceland, as artists were always going to the same places in the USA, Germany or Japan. Despite use of the word 'experimental' the festival was well received by locals, especially young people. The municipial authorities welcome it as an event that puts Egilsstaðir more firmly on the map, nationally and in international art circles and attracts people at a low season in tourism. Eiðar, a former boarding school outside Egilsstaðir, is also becoming known internationally through plans to develop an art centre and a sculpture garden. A network of 20 well known international artists is working on the plan with the new owner, an Icelandic film producer and a businessman who lived in the USA for many years. The attraction of works by internationally known artists, to a growing segment of the tourist market, is used as an argument in bids for funding for the sculpture garden to the Regional Growth Agreement (see Júlíusdóttir and Gunnarsdotter 2007).

Into public–private partnerships

In the local political sphere in Egilsstaðir the trend has been increased participation of women in policy making[8] and drafting of future visions for the municipality, in

---

8   After the elections in May 2006 the gender balance in municipality committees and the council, which is headed by a woman, is quite good with women being 40 per cent of general members of the whole local political structure. A commonly found gender division emerges in main areas of responsibility, with women being the majority in committees under the heading 'Family and leisure', which includes a cultural committee. Men are in majority in the 'Planning and environment' committees (www.fljotsdalsherad.is).

line with democratic procedures suggested in the implementation of Agenda 21 at the local level. At the same time new actors and forms of governance are increasingly shaping (economic) development policy for the whole region. One actor is the BRDC/DAEI, who initiated the cultural contract, as previously discussed. BRDC is a product of decentralization in regional development and a public–private partnership exercise, with much of the financing coming from government funds while the board is made up of members from private firms and municipalities. Only one woman was found among the nine board members in 2008. A similar gender imbalance was in the taskforce committee preparing a recent proposal to the government for a regional growth contract. The taskforce had representatives from the municipalities and businesses (Iðnaðar- og viðskiptaráðuneytið 2006), including one from the new multinational giant at the local scene (in a nearby costal village), the Alcan aluminium corporation. The only woman on the BRDC's board lives in Egilsstaðir. She also chairs the board of the recently established Network of Women in the Eastern Region, which has empowerment of women and their increased participation in public life as one of its main goals (Tengslanet Austfirskra kvenna 2006). This new network might be a sign of resistance to the marginalization women experience in the new private–public policy-making forums.

Private firms in the region are increasingly drawn into developments in the cultural field as sponsors of events. Through its community funding programme the Alcoa corporation is giving strong support to funding cultural events, along with local bank branches. Alcoa is now among the main sponsors of the experimental film and video festival as well as the yearly international jazz festival. The privatization of land and housing of the former public school at Eiðar, supported by arguments about grand visions of developing an international cultural centre, can be conceptualized as a private takeover of a public cultural institution, rather than a public–private partnership in cultural economy developments. Irrespective of the term used the contract is a sign of increased belief in the potential of cultural developments in economic reinvention of peripheral places.

Gendered experiences of cultural economy

In East Iceland reindeers have recently been discovered as markers of uniqueness and are now used systematically in marketing the area, especially for tourists. In the BRDC's report, *Reindeer as a resource*, it is claimed that there are many unutilized opportunities regarding wild reindeers (originating from Norway in 1787), which can be used to strengthen image, settlement, culture and employment in East Iceland (Þróunarfélag Austurlands 2005). Although both handicrafts and food culture get discussed in the report, the main emphasis is on activities related to hunting. In 1992 the government established a reindeer committee with administration at Egilsstaðir and in 2000 an open market for hunting licences, with around 900 licences now sold yearly to sport hunters. Most of the revenue goes to landowners and employment is mainly for compulsory local hunting guides, all men. The majority of the hunters are men from the capital area, belonging to a growing group of relatively well off sport hunters. In a place promotion campaign in 2006, aiming at attracting new inhabitants to Egilsstaðir/Fljótsdalshérað, the dominant place image given in television advertisements[9] was of wilderness and a masculine hunting culture.

According to the BRDC's report there was no tradition of using the reindeer furs, but in recent years designers and handicrafts people are making use of this 'by-product' by making high fashion clothes, hats and handbags. Not mentioned is that in the 1980s a local farmer took the initiative to process the reindeer furs and the aim was to establish a small industry for local farmwomen. The project resulted in a network of women sewing clothes and bags at home and selling at an outdoor market. Today only one of them is still producing from reindeer skin but, as one woman commented, only 'as much as she can with kitchen work'. Recalling this project and another failed project in sewing clothes one of the interviewed women commented:

> I think women are not good enough in getting finance for projects. It is energetic men that get money and start the projects. But these are specialized products they [the men] are not particularly interested in. What was lacking was professional knowledge in both production and marketing.

Another women's enterprise partly based on the reindeer resource closed down in 2003 after operating for four years in the centre of Egilsstaðir. The *House of the Hands* was a combination of a workshop and shop run by three professional artist and designers, one of them specializing in model dresses from reindeer skin and another in items for the home from natural material. The women hired the old dairy, thereby realizing a dream of a central and visible location for women in arts/design/handicrafts production. Their ambition was to make a living from this work and being more visible in the centre of town was one strategy towards that goal. The four years this firm operated it attracted locals, tourists and national media and enhanced the image of cultural creativity and innovative use of local resources. This was given little value until a flagship project in construction, energy production and the aluminium industry was agreed on in 2003 between the multinational Alcoa, local and national authorities (see Chapter 2). Suddenly the centrally-located house became valuable to firms wanting to reap some profit from the mega project and the house was sold to a local engineering firm wanting to move to the centre. Other small firms, mainly in service and run by women, were also hit by a sudden increase in housing costs.

---

9   It is possible to see the television advertisements on the municipality web page (www.fljotsdalsherad.is). Women are invisible in these presentations and it is hard to see what would attract them to migrate to this place, represented as male adventure landscapes (Pritchard and Morgan 2000).

The sale of the old house and failed attempts to buy another centrally-located house[10] was the end of the *House of the Hands*. According to one of the women they just lost ground and the project was over. In her view the issue was not only the women losing the place, but also the cultural value of the house as the oldest industrial house in Egilsstaðir. She claimed the house had a soul, a good atmosphere which fascinated visitors coming to the old dairy turned into a living workshop. Instead of giving the house some cultural value linked with the kind of activity they were running and the attention they drew to the town, the only thing considered was how much rent they could pay. They never applied formally to the municipality for support when the house was put up for sale, but the situation was discussed informally. The main argument for not intervening was that it is difficult to assist one kind of a private company but not some other, according to both the women and a municipal employee:

> But we were not pleased, as we had been, like a 'show-up case' for the municipality. I don't know how many visitors we received on behalf of the municipality, bank directors, foreign visitors, committees from the parliament and so on ... we were like pretty dolls who one could talk about at festive moments.

The woman making designer clothes from reindeer skin was pessimistic about the future supply of skins as the only factory processing them in Iceland closed down in March 2006. For years she had needed to buy the skins herself from hunters and she was wondering if she should bother to continue with so little support in accessing the material needed to produce from this unique local resource. In a recent proposal for a regional growth contract between the region and the government (Iðnaðar- og viðskiptaráðuneytið 2006) support is sought for establishing a firm processing reindeer meat as a service to hunters; processing of furs is not mentioned.

According to a business and gender equality advisor, positioned at the BRDC in 2003–2005 to assist potential women entrepreneurs, they were mainly interested in starting firms in service, retail and handicrafts. Frequently the women's applications and ideas were turned down with the argument that assistance would interfere with free market competition. At the same time some men could get much assistance with developing products that would be put on a competitive market. In her view 'this obstacle women face in business and employment has no face, but still it has so many faces'.

10　A group of women, including those in the *House of the Hands*, tried to buy another centrally-located house with much empty shopping and office space. The idea was to create a lively mixture of shops, workshops, services and tourist information run by women in the centre. Despite the possibility of some financial back-up from the Institute of Regional Development, the big companies owning the house were demanding far too high price.

Weaving Together Culture and Economy in Pajala and Egilsstaðir

In the contemporary regional policy environment, referred to in the introduction as the new 'economic approach to cultural policy' (Mitchell 2003) and 'the normative cultural economy approach' (Gibson and Kong 2005), claiming the intrinsic value of culture in terms of local identity and individual fulfilment does not seem to be enough to gain financial and political support. Although people working in cultural fields may be driven by motives other than economic ones, they strategically adapt their arguments for economic support to cultural activities to the dominant neoliberal discourse in both Sweden and Iceland. The main content of the discourse is that each region should find and develop its economic growth potential in a competitive global marketplace by attracting investment, money-spending tourists and migrating human capital (Gibson and Kong 2005). In Pajala this search for new economic possibilities is explained by a need to find ways out of an economic and demographic decline. Although Egilsstaðir has not experienced a downturn on a similar scale, culture as a leisure activity is understood in the regional cultural contract with the government as an important component in migration decisions, especially among young people. Attracting young and better-educated people is perceived as vital for the future development of the region (Iðnaðar- og viðskiptaráðuneytið 2006). Although the concept of a 'creative class' is not used, the argument may be interpreted as a vague expression of that theme.

From instrinsic value towards market value

In analysis of changes in cultural policy in the Nordic countries, Duelund (2003, 19–20) uses as a framework a well established categorization of three main lines of meaning given to culture in academic writings. The first, culture as art, reflects the ideal of the cultivated individual. Second, culture can be interpreted as *Volkgeist* – the soul of the people. The third is the anthropological understanding of culture condensed into the 'whole way of life'. In contemporary anthropology culture is basically viewed as something that gives meaning to practice, either perceived as the meaning-making itself or the manifestation/expression of meaning. From our case studies of the use of culture in reinvention processes in Pajala and Egilsstaðir, we find similarities in an increased emphasis on cultural heritage (culture as *Volkgeist*) and artistic activities (culture as art). In Pajala both forms are present when cultural heritage gives material to theatre plays, exemplifying what Ray (1998) identifies as an emphasis placed on raising the self-confidence of local people by (re-)creating a new territorial identity. According to Ray (ibid.), cultural economy may have a normative capacity, such as when inhabitants choose alternative development paths stressing local self-reliance in the use of physical resources. The original thought concerning cultural commitment in Pajala is an illustration of this normative capacity. The idea was to integrate the cultural revival into the municipal domain, with Meänkieli as the most important manifestation, but also to utilize the local heritage to create products to be marketed. In Egilsstaðir the film and art events were said to entertain and educate (cultivate) especially young people and to make the place more attractive to live in. In both cases culture was perceived as having an intrinsic value. Gradually local cultural resources are also marketed as products or as experiences (Ray 1998). This is achieved, for example, by the revaluing of old cultural events, as in the case of the Römppäviikko festival in Pajala, or by creating or inventing a new territorial identity, like the reindeer image in Eastern Iceland.

The symmetry made between the development of cultural activities and attracting potential visitors to these places leaves an impression that the economic potential of the cultural economy in these small towns in the Northern periphery is primarily linked to income from tourists with varying interests, for instance as sports hunters and fishermen, festival attenders or those interested in specific art forms and historic events. In Egilsstaðir, interestingly, the tourist attraction argument was used both in seeking support for contemporary art of global origin and for a centre for craft products based on local resources. The increased weight given to tourism may also be seen in the special support granted to heritage tourism when the cultural contract with the government was renewed in 2005. In Pajala a cultural revival, with an emphasis on strengthening territorial identity, turned into support for local tourist enterprises based on natural resources.

Gender coding and support in the cultural economy

In Pajala in Sweden and in Egilsstaðir in Eastern Iceland, PUAB and BRDC, respectively, are new forms of governance where the local business community and municipalities work out strategies for future economic developments, including the selection of projects for funding. In both cases men are leading these private–public partnership organizations. Similar developments in England (Little and Jones 2000) and Australia (Pini 2006) have been found to have gendered implications, strengthening male leadership in defining development paths, with masculine values dominating the course adopted. Pini claims that the dominance of a discourse on business and entrepreneurship in regional development marginalizes women, who are seen primarily as carers and community builders. Similar ideas of gender division of responsibilities are found in Sweden (Forsberg 1997). Although the women in the Australian case study were very active in small enterprises, such as shops and personal service, the cultural construction of 'businessman' and 'leader' is tied to men and masculine identities.

In our case studies we can see more interest and institutional support being given to the development of local hunting resources than to projects and enterprises using those same local resources to produce food, clothes or other artefacts. In both places the hunting/fishing is culturally coded as a male leisure activity, while food production and clothing/handicrafts are common female activities, in accordance with the understanding of culture as giving meaning to practice. Following Johnson's (2006) use of Bourdieu's disaggregated typology of cultural capital as embodied, objectified and institutionalized, the making of clothes and food is embodied female cultural capital, objectified in reindeer-skin dresses or coffee cheese – to take examples from our cases – but not institutionalized in the same way as hunting and fishing activities.

In Egilsstaðir there has been little formal support for utilizing the skin of the reindeer resource proclaimed as unique. This has been irrespective of the enterprises being established to create extra income by farm women or by women with professional training, creating fashionable products aimed at better-off life-style consumers, which are an important target group for cultural economic products. In Pajala the female entreprenurs with plans to create a food house have faced the same problems, with a lack of municipal support in spite of their project qualifying for EU funding. Gendered practices with a segregation of activities, relating to both production and consumption, and gendered ideology about businessmen and entrepreneurs (Pini 2006; Scholten 2003) may help to explain the indifference shown to women's projects and enterprises. This indifference is found in implementation of policy at the local level, as well as in funding priorities in labour market support at the national level, despite one of the main themes in national regional development policy both in Iceland and Sweden being to encourage women to become entrepreneurs; in other words to create their own income-generating work. What women are doing as entrepreneurs is clearly not valued as having the same growth potential as men's activities and interest in economic reinvention, hence it does not gain the same level of financial and institutional support.

Despite the fact that cultural economic developments are increasingly advocated as the way forward for places with a diminished economic base following global restructuring or depletion of natural resources, strong forces at both the national and local level still seem to prioritize revival of more traditional forms of industry. Many men in Pajala perceived the cultural manifestation as female (*knappsu*) and without economic potential. That opinion was dominant within the municipal domain in Pajala. In Egilsstaðir the men in construction-related occupations got a mega-project going via the government, through the construction of a hydropower station and an aluminium factory. In Pajala a number of male informants seem to be hoping for similar forms of revitalization through traditional, male-coded occupations. Their wish looks as though it will be fulfilled with the plans to open a new mine.

Binding more threads and contrasting trends

As analysed in the context of our case studies, the integration of cultural economy as an instrument in regional reinvention is taking place in a socio-spatial context of gendered power relations. As both Hudson and Rönnblom (2007) and Simonsen (2001) point out depolitization is part of the now dominant discourse in regional development policy and writings on the 'new regionalism'. Power relations between groups and struggles over meaning and resources are ignored. It is in line with mainstream ideas in the neo-liberal source of the idea of competitive regions, that individuals and places define and capitalize on their comparative advantages in a global marketplace. Increasingly the municipal public–private partnerships are representing places, defining goals and priorities in economic reinvention, including the cultural economy. The results of our studies support the claims by Little and Jones (2000) and Pini (2006) that this trend works against increasing participation of women, and other traditionally excluded groups, from both funds and policy making. The growing involvement of business leaders (mostly male) in regional and local development bodies, like PUAB and BRDC, not only reproduces traditional gender imbalance in economic access and control, but also strengthens or reinvents male dominance in defining community development.

The above trend is gaining ground in regional development praxis, parallel with a contrasting discourse and practice of constructing vision for sustainable local development. The Agenda 21 programme, worked on in municipalities in both countries, encourages democratic participation of all groups in planning for a sustainable future. Gender mainstreaming in EU and national policies is another parallel framework, claiming equal access to resources and decision-making to be a central goal.

Apart from gendered meanings and power relations, we find contests and negotiations concerning cultural developments, as art forms or leisure activities, in both Pajala and Egilsstaðir, between groups with different attachment to the places, for example between generations. Paradoxically, fine arts and cultural heritage emphasis in reinvention as cultural identity or as tourist-oriented cultural economy is prominent in our case studies, at the same time as the younger generation seems to place more emphasis on outward connections and popular youth culture in their visions. In Pajala young people seem to view the struggle to establish Meänkieli as a form of rehabilitation for those who experienced oppression at school. The young people themselves are more interested in learning English, Russian or 'real Finnish'. A challenge facing policy makers jumping on to the 'cultural economy wagon', that is now also stopping at remote towns, is how to accommodate both the wishes of nostalgic centre-dwellers and different segments of the local population, as well as balancing the parallel demands of democratic aspects of social sustainability, on the one hand, and economic growth on the other.

References

Amin, A. and Thrift, N. (2004), *Cultural Economy Reader*, MA, (Oxford: Blackwell).

Austur-Hérað (2001), *Á nýrri öld. Stefna Austur-Héraðs. Staðardagsskrá 21, 2001–2006* (report available at: www.egilsstadir.is/egilsstadir/files/anyrriold. pdf).

Berglund, A.-K., Johansson, S. and Molina, I. (eds) (2005) *Med periferien i sentrum*, Rapport 2005:14 (Norut NIBR Finnmark).

Bock, B. (2004), 'Fitting in and multi-tasking: Dutch farm women's strategies in rural entrepreneurship', *Sociologia Ruralis*, 44(3), 245–60.

Duelund, P. (ed.) (2003), *The Nordic Cultural Model* (Copenhagen: Nordic Cultural Institute).

Florida, R. (2002), *The Rise of the Creative Class – And How it's Transforming Work, Leisure, Community and Everyday Life* (New York: Basic Books).

Forsberg, G. (1997), Rulltrapperegioner och social infrastruktur, in Sundin, E. (ed.), *Om makt och kön – I spåren av offentliga organisationers omvandling*. pp. 31–68. SOU:1997:83 (Arbetsmarknadsdepartementet: Stockholm).

Gibson, C. and Kong, L. (2005), 'Cultural economy: A critical review', *Progress in Human Geography*, 29(5), 541–61.

Harvey, D. (1989), *The Condition of Postmodernity* (Oxford: Basil Blackwell).

Houston, D., Findlay, A., Harrison, R. and Mason, C. (2008), 'Will attracting the "Creative class" boost economic growth in old industrial regions? A case study of Scotland', *Geografiska Annaler: Series B, Human Geography*, 90(2), 133–49.

Hudson, C. and Rönnblom, M. (2007), 'Regional development and the constructions of gender equality: The Swedish case', *European Journal of Political Research* 46(47), 68.

Iðnaðar- og viðskiptaráðuneytið (2006) *Vaxtarsamningur Austurlands. Tillögur verkefnisstjórnar að vaxtarsamningi Austurlands, til aukinnar samkeppni og sóknar*. Reykjavík: Iðnaðar- og viðskiptaráðuneytið (report available at: www. idnadarraduneyti.is/media/rafraen_afgreidsla/austurlandLowRes.pdf).

Johnson, L. (2006), 'Valuing the arts: Theorising and realising cultural capital in an Australian city', *Geographical Research*, 44(3), 296–309.

Júlíusdóttir, M and Gunnarsdotter, Y. (2007), 'Culture, cultural economy and gender in processes of place reinvention', in Nyseth, T. and Granås, B. (eds), *Place Reinvention in the North. Dynamics and Governance Perspectives. Nordic Research Programme 2005–2008*. Report 1, pp. 39–53 (Nordregio: Stockholm).

Kneafsey, M. (2001), 'Rural cultural economy. Tourism and social relations', *Annals of Tourism Research*, 28(3), 762–83.

Lash, S. and Urry, J. (1994), *Economies of Signs and Space* (London: Sage).

Little, J. (2002), *Gender and Rural Geography* (Harlow: Prentice Hall).

Little, J. and Jones, O. (2000), 'Masculinity, gender and rural policy', *Rural Sociology*, 65(4), 621–39.

Lysgård, H.K. and Tveiten, O. (2005), 'Cultural economy at work in the city of Kristiansand: Cultural policy as incentive for urban innovation', *AI & Society*, 19(4) 485–99.

Massey, D. (1994), *Space, Place and Gender* (Cambridge: Polity Press).

Menningaráð Austurlands (2008). Um Menningarráð – *Samningar* (web page: www.menningarrad.is)

Mitchell, R. (2003), 'Nordic and European cultural policies', in Duelund, P. (ed.), *The Nordic Cultural Model* (Copenhagen: Nordic Cultural Institute).

Mósesdóttir, L. (ed.) (2005), *Policies and Performances. The Case of Austria, Denmark, Finland, the Netherlands, Spain, Hungary and Iceland,* Wellknow project, Report no. 4. (www.bifrost.is/wellknow/Files/Skra_00077700.pdf).

Mósesdóttir, L. (2006) *Final Report.* Wellknow project (www.bifrost.is/wellknow/Files/Skra_0014164.pdf).

Norrbottenskuriren (2007) Gruvjätte tror på gruvsatsningar i länet, 29 May 2007.

Ólafsson, S. (1997), *Búseta á Íslandi. Rannsókn á orsökum búferlaflutninga. Sauðárkrókur: Byggðastofnun* (report available at: www.byggdastofnun.is/media/skyrslur/byggd.doc).

Pajala Municipality (web page: http://www.pajala.se/mun/pajala/www.nsf/About/about.html).

Pini, B. (2006), 'A critique of "new" rural local governance: The case of gender in a rural Australian setting', *Journal of Rural Studies*, 22(4), 396–408.

Pritchard, A. and Morgan, N. (2000), 'Privileging the male gaze. Gendered tourism landscapes', *Annals of Tourism Research*, 27(4), 884–905.

Ray, C. (1998), 'Culture, intellectual property and territorial rural development', *Sociologia Ruralis*, 38(1), 3–20.

Regeringskansliet (2001), *Women as entrepreneurs in Sweden and the UK (Kvinnor som företagare i Storbritannien och Sverige)* (London: The Women's Unit Cabinet Office) (report available at: www.regeringen.se/content/1/c4/18/90/6a1f84e5.pdf).

Scholten, C. (2003), *Kvinnors Försörjningsrum. Hegemonins förvaltare och murbräckor* (Lund: Institutionen för kulturgeografi och ekonomisk geografi, Lunds universitet).

Shorthall, S. (2002), 'Gendered agricultural and rural restructuring: A case study of Northern Ireland', *Sociologia Ruralis*, 42(2), 160–75.

Simonsen, K. (2001), 'Space, culture and economy – a question of practice', *Geografiska Annaler*, Series B, 83, 41–52.

Tengslanet austfirskra kvenna (2006), *Stjórn.* (www.tengslanet.is).

Zukin, S. (1995), *The Cultures of Cities* (Oxford: Blackwell).

Þróunarstofa Austurlands (2000), *Stefna í menningarmálum á Austurlandi* (Egilsstaðir: Þróunarstofa Austurlands).

Þróunarfélag Austurlands (2005), *Auðlindin hreindýr. Skýrsla starfshóps* (Egilsstaðir: Þróunarfélag Austurlands) (report available at: www.austur.is/images/stories/skjol/audlindin_hreindyr.pdf).

Chapter 6

Creating 'The Land of the Big Fish': A Study of Rural Tourism Innovation

Anniken Førde

Introduction

This chapter tells the story of how Sørøya, an island on the harsh coast of Finnmark in Northern Norway, has created itself as 'The Land of the Big Fish'. Heavily based on the fishing industry, the community found itself in a critical situation when their three processing plants all were closed down in 2002. Searching for a new means of living, a working group of local women teamed up to investigate the possibilities for tourism. A collective strategy of local tourism enterprises was formed, focusing on deep-sea rod fishing. Under the slogan 'Sørøya – the Land of the Big Fish', the enterprises mainly promote trophy fishing, or what they call 'fish-porn'. The result has been a considerable upswing for existing and new tourism enterprises. Sørøya has transformed itself into a tourist destination.

By examining the process whereby 'The Land of the Big Fish' was created, this chapter addresses the complex relations involved with innovation processes of rural tourism. Focusing on the practices of the actors involved in a specific local tourism project and entering into their relations, I seek to identify conditions that limit and create agency for tourism innovation. How are new identities negotiated, and what discourses do they make use of? The empirical case of the tourism network at Sørøya shows the complexity of such innovative processes. It shows how entrepreneurial tourism projects can be created through the production of new place images. The process involves new alliances and new connections between tradition and invention, nature and culture, the local and the global.

Within the field of entrepreneurship, it is increasingly recognized that there is a need for stories of innovative processes (Gartner 2007; Hjort and Steyaert 2004; Steyaert and Bouwen 1997). As tourism and production of place images have become an important aspect of modern societies, there is a need for empirical studies of how culture and people are involved in such processes (Burns and Novelli 2006). Based on the narratives of local tourism entrepreneurs at Sørøya, as they are told and interpreted, this chapter addresses the discourse on tourism innovation – especially in rural areas. It also addresses the more general methodological and theoretical discourse on entrepreneurship and innovative processes, and how these are connected to creative practices within the particular contexts of particular places.

A Relational Perspective on Entrepreneurship

This chapter applies a relational perspective on entrepreneurship. A relational perspective implies a more dynamic approach to entrepreneurship analyses than is often seen in entrepreneurship research. The focus is on social processes rather than measurable variables and aggregates. Entrepreneurship is seen as social creativity, and cultural aspects are included in the entrepreneurship analyses. Such an approach requires qualitative empirical studies of innovative processes.

The case study of Sørøya is part of the research project Innovative Communities – Community entrepreneurship in a rural community context,[1] which aims at broadening the concept of entrepreneurship. Perspectives from entrepreneurship studies of innovation are combined with practice-oriented perspectives of social transformation and cultural invention. Innovative processes in rural communities are explored, within and in between the fields of cultural work, voluntary work and politics, as well as business life. Community entrepreneurship is understood as the social process of creating and exploring opportunities and mobilizing resources that form new ventures in the form of activities, services and institutions for the common good of a community (Borch et al. 2008; Austin et al., 2006; Morris and Jones 1999). Studying community entrepreneurship involves a broad understanding of entrepreneurial processes. It involves studying innovative processes not only within the economic field, but also within the whole variety of social fields that community actors are involved in. These fields vary in scale and involve complex connections through human practices.

As the performative turn has reached entrepreneurship studies, there is an increased emphasis on the cultural context and complexity of entrepreneurial processes (Hjort and Steyaert 2004; Lindh de Montoya 2000). It has become more accepted that entrepreneurship relies on cultural interpretation. Lavoie (1991) argues that the discovery of opportunities is a question of reading selected aspects of complex situations. Culture is what enables the entrepreneur's reading. Successful entrepreneurs, Lavoie argues, are actors especially well 'plugged into the culture' – actors who can read and contribute to different conversations of their fellows within culture. Many recent studies have contributed further to enrich the entrepreneurial approach with concepts of cultural interpretation. Lindh de Montoya (2000) demonstrates that entrepreneurship is not simply a matter of 'discovering opportunities', but more a matter of creating opportunities along the way in the battle for making a living. Understanding entrepreneurship as social creativity implies focusing on changes in people's daily practices. But still, the social processes of everyday life are rarely addressed in entrepreneurship studies.

---

1 The project is funded by the Norwegian Research Council and the county agricultural administration of the Northern Norwegian counties. The project is conducted by Nordland Research Institute and The University of Tromsø, with user involvement of local participants of business, voluntary work and public support systems.

As Steyaert (2004) argues, there is a need for an approach to entrepreneurship that situates social processes of entrepreneurship within everyday social interaction.

Applying a relational perspective implies focusing on social processes, cultural creativity and networks at work. Based on a practice-oriented approach, processes of change are understood as the interplay between cultural dispositions and structural contexts, shaping and shaped through everyday life practices (Bourdieu 1977). To grasp the innovative aspects of people's practices, I employ Rudie's concept of *creative practices.* Rudie (1994) combines the concept of practice with creativity. Referring to Wagner (1981), she argues that cultural invention is created in interaction between conventions and innovations. Individuals hold up new experience against their baggage of experience, and integrate it into their reservoir of knowledge – which can be called upon in different situations. Experiences lacking culturally conventional ways of coping with them require cultural creativity.

A study of creative practices must imply not only what actors do, but also their perception of their own and others' actions. We must at the same time describe their understanding of practice and their practising of understanding. This perspective provides insight into the repertoire of knowledge and relations community entrepreneurs bring with them, and how they can place these into new projects. And it helps us understand how places are both changed and maintained by studying how actors bring together traditional and new practices.

Focusing on creative practices of community entrepreneurs implies a focus on their subjective rationality and their own experience of coherence. It is a question of their knowledge and skills, their way of categorizing and the mental dispositions they use as guidance for their thoughts and actions. It is also a question of how they use experiences and skills from different social fields in their strategies. And it is a question of negotiation with their surroundings, as this combination is not achieved by freely choosing roles, identities and fields of transaction. These negotiations become more difficult in rapidly transforming societies (Rudie 1994). In the case of Søroya, the society is undergoing great transformations. We can thus expect the norms of what is acceptable to be in a state of flux and therefore subject to negotiation. Seeking to reveal negotiations of norms and normalities implies addressing the discursive aspects of local communities. By using a discursive approach, the constituting processes that are usually implicit and mute in discourses of community development can be made explicit. By unearthing locked discourses it becomes possible to offer alternative narratives of innovative communities. To use Foucault's (1972) terms, the object is to identify what possible choices these discourses open up, how these strategic possibilities appear, how they are distributed and how they are connected to each other. I seek to explore how actors can make use of discursive frameworks to create more space for manoeuvre within their community.

Through the case study of 'The Land of the Big Fish', I will demonstrate how entrepreneurship is socially situated, relying on a variety of social relations. Establishing tourist enterprises involves producing tourist places. And tourist places are produced in complex relations involving multiple types of dynamic networking practices (Bærenholdt et al. 2004). Bærenholdt et al. further argue that tourism should be investigated as complex networks, both place-bound and mobile, producing places as material natures, social relations and discursive conceptions. Relations, here, are not to be understood as abstract aggregates, but as the interaction of specific actors situated in specific contexts. Rather than measuring networks and social capital, we need to describe and analyse the relations of the actors involved, and how these are worked out in creative practices.

In the next section the case of 'The Land of the Big Fish' will be situated in the context of a vanishing fishing industry and an increasing interest in rural tourism. Then the methodology of the project is discussed, emphasizing narration and interpretation. The section examining the analyses centres on the creation of 'The Land of the Big Fish', focusing on different events and aspects defined by the actors involved as crucial to the process. Then I discuss how they make use of new discursive frameworks. Finally, in the conclusion, I summarize and discuss how such narratives can contribute to the understanding of innovative processes within rural tourism.

Reinvention of a Fishing Community

Tourism is a question of 'going places' (Feifer 1985); it takes place through encounters with distinct places and place images (Bærenholdt et al. 2004). Today there is an increasing interest in modelling place identities and images, especially within tourism (Burns and Novelli 2006). We shall look into some specific aspects of the transformation process of Sørøya, and how place narratives are manifested within these processes. Changing practices implies changing understandings of place – it implies place reinvention (Nyseth and Granås 2007).

Sørøya is an island in the northernmost part of Norway. The island is divided between two municipalities: Hasvik and Hammerfest. There are about a thousand inhabitants, mainly situated in three small communities in Hasvik, on the west side of the island. The climate is harsh, but the island is known for its rich fisheries. All three communities have been based on the fishing industry: the prawn industry, salt fish and filleting. With the collapse of the fishing industry more than a hundred people lost their jobs. Since then many have left the island, and the population is steadily decreasing.[2] As a response to this critical situation, Hasvik was defined by the national authorities as a stagnating municipality with an urgent need to reform its industrial or economic structure,[3] and was given extraordinary allocations. A development company, HUT, was formed, to develop new job opportunities. HUT

---

2   The population has declined from 1,200 in 2002, to 998 in 2008. According to the population projections of Statistics Norway, the population will continue to decrease. The estimate for 2025 is about 750 inhabitants (source: www.ssb.no).

3   In Norwegian: *omstillingskommune*.

is an abbreviation for *Hasvik i utvikling*, which literally translates to *Hasvik in development* or *progress*. The name is not accidental; the local actors involved stressed that they did not want to present themselves and be presented as a stagnating community to be 'restructured'. They rather wanted to use concepts that for them had more positive and dynamic connotations. HUT is owned by the municipality, but the majority of the board members represent private businesses. It is somewhat of a hybrid organization, combining functions such as an administrative agency controlling allocations from the municipality and the state, and as a consulting company for local entrepreneurs. As Andersen (2004) argues, such organizational hybrids open up new channels for local participation and mobilization. The aim is to find new ways of encouraging new business activities in the community. Since the formation of HUT in 2002 many new activities have been created, even if the numbers of work vacancies available are far from compensating the ones lost with the fishing industry break up. The new activities vary: there is a knitting factory, new enterprises of fish tourism have been established and, an Arctic centre of Slow Food, marketing local stock fish, is under development – to name but a few.

In spite of the break up, condemnation of fishing boats and sale of fish quotas, Sørøya remains a fishing community. With 60 boats, mostly coastal smacks, and two minor fish plants, the fisheries employ about 20 per cent of the workforce. It is claimed that the best fish stock in Norway is to be found at the coast of Sørøya, and the island is known for its big fish. During the first period of rebuilding the community after the crisis, the municipality stated that fishing will still be the main industry. Tourism was defined as the second most important industry. But there were few local tourism enterprises on the island, and the crisis in the fishing industry had also affected these. Through a tough process a new network of tourism enterprises was established, to face the challenges and find new strategies. This process resulted in a common profiling and the creation of Sørøya as 'The Land of the Big Fish'. Tourism in Sørøya is mainly fishing-related tourism, or more specifically, deep-sea rod fishing. Tourists, from Norway and abroad, come to Sørøya to catch big fish. Tourism is not a new phenomenon in the community, but the tourism enterprises have experienced an enormous turnaround in the last few years, and the establishment of the tourism cooperation seems to be one of the most important community entrepreneurship processes in Hasvik in the aftermath of the crisis.

These processes involve dramatic transformation of society. It involves changing modes of production, restructuring of the local economy and hence changing practices. Social and economical transformations also influence the meaning of place; how Sørøya is understood by inhabitants, tourists and others. The character of the community has changed in such a way that it has reinvented its identity. Place perceptions and narratives are a crucial part of such place development processes.

Methodology

The analyses are based on a qualitative case study on Sørøya, comprised of in-depth interviews of actors who, in different ways, have been involved in the process of creating 'The Land of The Big Fish'. These are representatives from HUT, the political and administrative management of the municipality, tourism enterprises, voluntary associations and investors.

Interviewing differently positioned actors, focusing on their experiences and interpretations, I sought to grasp the complexity of the entrepreneurial process. Through dialogue, the actors formulated their own perceptions of their world. As researchers we attempt to make sense of phenomena in terms of the meaning people bring to them. The fundamental material of such an approach is the interpretation of meaningful relations (Kvale and Brinkmann 2008). In the following analyses, I will present some narratives of the process of creating Sørøya as 'The Land of the Big Fish'. Narration emphasizes the stories of our lives and our way of making sense. A narrative approach allows the storyteller to interweave their own interpretations into our analyses (Hjort and Steyaert 2004). Analysing selective accounts of selective events, the aim is not to elucidate objective truths of tourism innovation, but rather to create new stories of such innovative processes based on the situated knowledge of different actors at Sørøya.

Analyses: Creating 'The Land of the Big Fish'

The fishing festival – the spearhead

> It all started in 1986. I was having a beer at the local pub, we were sitting there, a few guys, it was summer and quiet, not a soul. Then one of the guys, he was from here, I think, asked: 'Why doesn't anyone do something to make something in Hasvik?' I was newly employed as Principal for the Office of Cultural Affairs. I found this an important question, and thought a lot about it: Why doesn't anyone do something to attract tourists to Hasvik? And I thought: what do we have? Well, we have fisheries, a lot of boats, clever fishermen, people that want something, a living coastal culture. And we have a lot of big fish ...

> An uncle of mine told me about the Deep-sea Fishing Association. They (Andøya, a coastal community further south) arranged a festival, and a lot of foreigners came. I thought this could be something for us ...

> The leader of the Norwegian Deep-sea Fishing Association came all the way up here to look at it. ... He was in a small smack, got a lot of fish. But they were small, I threw them out. 'You throw them out?', he asked. 'Yes', I said, 'it's too small'. 'No, this is excellent fish', he said. Then we knew that this would work

out. He recommended us to apply for the right to arrange a festival the next year. That's how it started.

Geir Iversen, the former Principal for the Office of Cultural Affairs, later also elected as mayor, tells how the deep-sea fishing festival at Søroya started 20 years ago. The fishing festival is seen as the spearhead of the tourism industry on the island. The festival attracts sport fishermen from all over Europe, and has given the island a reputation within the world of sport fishing. Sørvær, the small village where the festival is arranged, is known as 'The Mecca of Deep-sea Fishing', as the festival holds the record both, of quantity, and of the size of fish caught by rod.[4] The festival is arranged every summer, and is now at the culmination of a week-long cultural festival.

As the initiator's story indicates, this entrepreneurial process is situated within a specific context of complex relations. The idea was created by an actor new in the community, linking knowledge and experiences from different fields. Experiences of deep-sea fishing from his home community were combined with local challenges to breathe new life into Søroya. Making use of his family relations, the community was linked to the national Deep-sea Fishing Association and created their own association. The festival created new relations as it involves a variety of local actors: fishermen, the local sports club and other community associations. It also involves collaboration with local tourism enterprises, shopkeepers, artists and so on. The festival is mostly supported by voluntary work. In the beginning it was arranged by the Deep-sea Fishing Association in close collaboration with the municipal administration. In later years the deep-sea fishing festival has become part of a larger festival, organized by HUT. The national and international network of deep-sea fishing associations are also vital collaboration partners.

At first, the idea of a deep-sea fishing festival at Søroya was met with scepticism. People here at the time were not familiar with sport fishing and fish tourism, and these practices challenged their idea of fishing. They were fishing to make a living, not for the excitement. The debate of fishing techniques and equipment illustrates the negotiation of meaning involved in this process; at Søroya, many didn't understand why you needed to fish with rods in the sea, as they had more efficient equipment. The debate resulted in a compromise; unlike all other deep-sea fishing festivals, the festival at Søroya in its first year included fishing with hand line as well as rods. But even if the festival challenged local perceptions of fishing, it was also founded on the local fishermen's traditional knowledge and skills – of how to handle the boats and the harsh climate, and where to find the big fish. Many emphasize that the festival made people on the island proud of their community. It gained a lot of publicity at the local, national and even international level.

The way the festival 'placed Søroya on the map' seems crucial for the growth of fishing tourism. When the new profile of 'The Land of the Big Fish' was created,

---

4   The record of the biggest fish is a cod of 37.5 kg! (source: http://www.hasvik. kommune.no/soeroeyfestivalen).

it was based on the identity of Sørøya that had been developed through the festival. But today there are no direct links between the festival organizers and the tourism network. The tourism entrepreneurs argue that even if the festival constitutes a support for the fishing tourism, the tourism network has now created a brand of their own, independent of the festival. This separation might be part of the explanation of why the Deep-sea Fishing Association today has great difficulties in recruiting young people. Representatives of the association express fears for the future of the festival. They find people less willing to assist in voluntary community work. As the old members are getting older, they talk of the need to professionalize the festival administration, maybe by employing a project administrator. The change of local norms of voluntary work illustrates a more general trend of complex societies. It is also a result of local negotiations of positions and identities.

The story of how the festival came into being is a complex story of cultural creativity; of how some actors, drawing on a range of relations, found new ways of making use of the natural advantages of Sørøya. Traditional knowledge, like the skills of local fishermen, was combined with new knowledge of marine sport fishing and festival management. Existing networks, like the various voluntary organizations within the community were combined in new ways, and voluntary and public actors worked together to make the festival a reality. In addition, new national and international alliances were created through the deep-sea fishing world. As argued by Bærenholdt et al. (2004), producing places of experience requires a combination of mobile and territorial networks. The story of creating an inventive event is also a story of changing practices and perceptions of place. The festival involved negotiation of norms and values in the community. As demonstrated by Borch (2004), 'fishing for fun' is often met with scepticism as it challenges norms established in commercial fisheries and fishing communities. Today the festival has become an institution. The festival has, by giving Sørvær a reputation as the Mecca for sport fishing, created an identity of the community – based mainly on big fish, voluntary work and an inclusive community. This identity holds promise for the ongoing process of tourism development on the island.

The crisis as a driving force – forced collaboration

> Then came the big bankruptcy in the fishing industry, and it was dramatic to us as we were living of occupational travellers. And they disappeared overnight – a night in February. And there we were … I wanted to gather together all our keys in a bag, hand them in to the bank and say goodbye. Thinking back makes me … ahhhh … it was really terrible! … The first thing that happened afterwards was that we had a conference, arranged by the municipality. The most important thing was that we stated that we had no choice; we could either collect our keys in a bag and leave, or we had to find absolutely all the guts and creativity we had and *do* something. … We agreed on fishery being the girder. Then we discussed what could be the second most important industry. And after we had analysed

all possibilities, we concluded that tourism might be the industry of greatest possibilities ...

Then we had a meeting, all the tourism agents. It was hot here. The people living here didn't go out, they had no money, they had no jobs. They were depressed and reticent. It was critical. The meeting was really emotional. We felt that here we were, all together, on the edge of the cliff, just millimetres from falling over. If we were to survive, we had to find something together. A project with immediate effect! And we agreed on working together, make a brochure, marketing ourselves at a fair.

Mona Saab, the owner and director of the only hotel at Sørøya, tells how the local accommodation enterprises faced a great market collapse as the fishing industry was downsized. And she tells how the shared experience of crisis made them cooperate. The cooperation was initiated by the municipality, and later administered by HUT, as a part of the process of the turnaround of the community. After the crisis, conferences were arranged where people in Sørøya discussed and made strategies for the future. As tourism was defined as a priority industry, HUT initiated a meeting where all the actors involved in tourism on the island were invited. These actors – seven altogether – were competitors and the process of coming to agreement on a common strategy was hard. The first meeting is described by many as a 'meeting of Hell', as the actors involved were frustrated and 'backbiting'. But the critical situation made them realize the importance of collaboration. A project was established to develop tourism and create a network of local tourism enterprises. Two local women involved in tourism – the hotel director and a restaurant owner – were employed. As a start, the tourism network agreed on establishing a common web-site and brochures. But developing a common profile was difficult. After many tough discussions, they agreed on the slogan 'Sørøya – the Land of the Big Fish'. They decided on fishing to be at the heart of their profile. This project has had considerable success and the tourism industry attracted more guests and improved their incomes. HUT reports an incredible increase from 2,000 overnight stays in 2002 to 12,674 in 2007.[5] The turnaround is explained by the new profile and collective strategies of marketing and upgrading of skills. Today, the initiating project has finished, but the cooperation within the network continues with good results for the tourism industry on the island.

The project is a result of the municipality and HUT's initiative to force people to come together in purposeful networks, and was financed through the extraordinary allocations for economic restructuring. In this process, the local authority's' perception of their role as facilitators has played a crucial part. As the former manager of HUT puts it: 'Our role is to make people cooperate. Without cooperation we won't survive!' HUT insisted on involving all local tourism actors, and hand-picked the project team. The process has not only created local networks

---

5   Occupational travellers not included.

of local tourism enterprises, but also networks including government support systems, political institutions and national and international tour operators. HUT stresses their overview of local actors' knowledge and skills, and their ability to link actors of different resources together, as their main advantage. But this way of creating networks is not unproblematic. HUT's involvement with private business actors has been greeted with much scepticism in the community. The women they engaged to lead the project tell stories of a tough experience, dealing not only with battles to agree on the profile, but also with negative attitudes from the surroundings. As this way of combining roles challenged established norms of local administration and development work they, constantly, had to negotiate their position in the community. At the same time, the non-traditional composition is celebrated in various formal institutions. As there is an increasing interest in collaboration, it has been possible to gain financial support to develop the network.

Another major condition for this successful cooperation project seems to be the common perceptions of crisis. Sitting at the same 'edge of the cliff', the actors from the different tourism enterprises had little to lose in cooperating. Old dissension and competition was put aside. Even if they had divergent understandings of how to solve their problems, they shared the understanding that they had no choice but to cooperate and find new strategies together. This shared reading of the situation formed the basis for new relations and the negotiation of a common profile.

The establishment of the tourism collaboration is largely based on existing local resources, put together in new networks. It involves a close cooperation of municipal agents and commercial actors, and strong connections to the public support systems. Again, we see the importance of combining place-bound and more extensive networks, in this case including international tour operators. By forcing different actors together in new combinations, new relations were created. And within these relations new ideas were conceived. The project group says that 'creative heads were put together'. The project profited by the complementary knowledge and skills of the commercial actors and HUT's manager's experience from educational and political work. These actors also possessed a considerable knowledge of local relations; they seem, using Lavoie's (1991) term, well plugged into culture. The project also profited from the strong social commitment of these actors. Together they have invested a lot of effort to bring about cooperation, create a new profile and build networks and alliances. The aim of these agents has been to make their own enterprises, as well as the community, viable. Their double role is illustrative of community entrepreneurs – collective strategies for the best of the community are combined with the struggle for a living on their own (cf. Borch et al. 2008). This process implies radical changes in a community described as traditional concerning politics and industry. The crisis has forced people to be creative. But, as Rudie (1994) argues, the creative practices involve social dramas and negotiation.

Pursuing local heroes

> We agreed on working against the German market. We were advised to employ
> a German lady, working as a consultant here in Norway. We had a meeting
> with her. She started by saying we were amateurs. We were quite young. She
> said we couldn't act like we do, we were too spontaneous and open, German
> tourists would back off. We discussed it, we found that we couldn't change the
> character of [naming local tourism hosts]. This is us, the way we are! We fired
> the consultant the following day. It's the smartest thing we've done. We took the
> control ourselves, and employed two local women with competence in tourism
> and marketing to manage the project.

Eva Husby, the former manager of HUT, explains how they decided to develop
the tourism project based on local actors' competences. The story of 'the German
consultant' has become legendary in Sørøya, illustrating their understanding of
the importance of trusting their own qualities. A professional German consultant,
hired to tailor their activities to the German tourism market, advised them to
change their behaviour towards the guests. They were told that Germans would
not appreciate their spontaneous and open attitude. They then decided to search for
other markets and focussed on The Netherlands and Sweden.

Besides the hotel director and the restaurant manager, another young local
woman, laid off from the fishing industry, was employed to create and develop
the web-site. And they used local graphical designers. As the project group puts
it: 'We chose to use local heroes'. They emphasize the difference in approach of
local and external agents: 'We don't work here, we live here. This is not just our
job, it's our lives! That's why we can't let others dictate how to carry it out'. HUT
prefers local actors, even if they lack competence. They want to enable gifted
persons in the community to become qualified. They also stress the importance of
local knowledge in the establishment of development projects: by knowing people
– who is good at what – they can more easily benefit from people's manifold
competences. And local actors know 'where the shoe pinches'. In this process, the
local actors insist on a community approach to business development. Developing
the tourism industry is not just a question of creating profitable business; it's a
question of creating their future at Sørøya.

When asking people at Sørøya of the advantages of their community, they often
respond 'the natural environment and the people'. In addition to a 'fascinating,
wild and rugged natural environment', they argue that Sørøya has especially
strong, determined, inhabitants. This has to be understood in relation to the crisis,
when many left the island. Those who did not are seen to be strongly committed to
the community. Arguments like 'We have the will to succeed' are often heard. At
HUT they talk about Mondays as 'the day of creativity'; on Mondays people come
to them with ideas they have figured out during the weekend. An investor from a
bigger town, involved in several projects in Hasvik, claims that 'People here know
how to inflect the verb *stubborn*'. It seems as people at Sørøya have made stubborn

a verb, as they have constructed a collective identity where stubbornness is seen as an important part of their practices.

These are dominating narratives of Sørøya. From the start of the rebuilding process, after the close-down of the fishing industry, central actors have insisted on defining Sørøya as an innovative community of determined people willing to walk new paths to fight for their community. This was demonstrated by their resistance towards being defined by the government as a marginalized community in need of restructuring. Local entrepreneurs, from the voluntary sector, business enterprises and public administration, have succeeded in communicating the narrative of a community in development and in progress through media and a number of formal and informal channels within and outside the island. Through processes like the establishment of the tourism network and a common profile, Sørøya is constructed as an innovative community. The narrators make use of the discursive focus on innovation in community development. In the creation of place images and narratives some actors are empowered while others are excluded. As Foucault (1972) argues, discourses both make possible and limit people's choices. But strong narratives are often opposed, and the narrative of Sørøya as an inventive community also includes stories of contrary winds. The community entrepreneurs have met much scepticism and opposition. Within this discourse, opposing narratives are often seen as reactionary and other voices seen as 'opposing innovation'. The competing voices could also be understood as negotiation of values, norms and place constructions. Edging out conflicting narratives, 'The Land of the Big Fish' is a result of successful collective narration, modelled by actors talented in 'reading culture'.

Targeting 'fish porn'

> It was a long process [making the profile]. We have so much; we have beaches, we have grouse, we have midnight sun and this and that. But really, you don't travel all the way to Sørøya to see a nice beach or the midnight sun. To make people understand what they should come all the way here for, we have to sell experiences. It had to be deep-sea fishing ...

> What do deep-sea fishermen care about? They don't care about how hotels look like, or about green lawns. They care about fish, fish and fish. Big fish, different fish. So that's what we did ... The men became all exhilarated. It was like 'porn.'

Bjørg Alvestad from the project groups tells about the process of creating the profile, and the invention of the concept 'fish-porn'. In this process, the negotiation of place meaning was quite explicit. To begin with all the actors brought with them different images and narratives of Sørøya. The project group tells how proud they were of their first web-page. It was filled with all kinds of information and nice photos. Then a deep-sea fisherman asked: 'Where is the fish?' They realized they had to sharpen the profile.

Figure 6.1 'Sørøya – The Land of the Big Fish' (www.hasvik.com)
Source: © Hasvik Development, permission given by the manager, Grethe Jacobsen.

Today a photo of a woman holding a huge cod decorates the first page of the web-site and brochures of 'Sørøya – The Land of the Big Fish' (see Figure 6.1). The woman is the leader of the Norwegian Deep-sea Fishing Association. This picture is followed by a number of similar photos, except the woman being replaced by men. The advertising shows ecstatic fishermen with their trophies: giant fishes of different kinds. All the advertising materials are about fish. Some of the tourism enterprises at Sørøya offer other activities, like horse riding, dog sledging, hunting, kayaking, diving and freshwater fishing but the main tourism activity is deep-sea fishing. The different actors offer different facilities: some have invested in speedboats and fishing equipment, others in accommodation, collaborating with local fishermen. They have specialized in attracting different markets: some mainly attracting Swedes, others Dutch and Belgians. But the profile is common. The tourism agents stress the importance of combining development of their own individual networks with the collective strategy. By focusing on deep-sea fishing, they have managed to create their niche in this tourism market. Most tourist facilities at the island are fully-booked from March to September/October. The tourists are almost only men.

In Norway there has been in recent years a large debate about fish tourism and fishing rights. Fish tourism is a growing industry, competing with commercial fisheries over vulnerable fish resources. Thus, the marine fish tourism industry is often seen as a threat to commercial fishing (Borch 2004). As a result of the conflict, the Norwegian government has introduced a quota for tourists: they can each only bring 15 kilogrammes of fish out of the country. This discourse of conflicting interests is also present at Sørøya, as the tourism agents are met with criticism from fellow villagers of their guests 'stealing' local resources. But, as one of the officials at HUT explains it, the question of quotas is less debated at Sørøya: 'Those [fish tourists] coming here, come by plane with their visa cards in the pocket. So we avoid the problem of tourists taking with them lots of fish when they leave … It's not adapted to "filling-the-freezer-tourism" here.' At Sørøya, there is also some collaboration between fish tourism and commercial fisheries as several local fishermen are involved in the tourism activities. Their knowledge of the waters is crucial for tourism as fishing in this area with rough weather conditions is an activity of great risk. Through establishing 'The Land of the Big Fish' as a common image of, and identity for, Sørøya, based on traditional as well as new knowledge and values, the conflicts between traditional and new activities diminish.

The process of defining the niche for tourism enterprises involves creation, or reinvention, of place. New images of Sørøya are produced, involving negotiations of practices, values and identities. But the new images of a place for extreme fishing experiences are to a great extent a continuation of traditional images. They sell 'fish porn', but also the clichés of the authentic fisherman and the idyllic small fishing community. 'Extreme fishing' has always been a part of local practices. In this process, aspects of local culture are exploited in new ways. They take advantage of modern people's continuous search for both the authentic and exotic, and the increased focus on extreme experiences. At the same time they continue the close connection of nature and culture in their practices. The entrepreneurial activity is both individual and collective, and based on connecting traditions and inventions.

Making Use of New Discursive Frameworks

By exploring the specific relations and contexts of the creative practices at Sørøya, I have tried to identify the main conditions creating and limiting the actors' agency. And I have tried to identify what discourses they make use of in the innovation process of rural tourism. One key element of the process seems to be the strong narrative produced of an innovative community. Facing a critical situation resulting from the close-down of the fishing industry, and realizing that the era of the filleting-industry is over, people were mobilized to find new strategies. The extraordinary allocations for economic restructuring, in addition to private investors, made flexible financial support of new projects possible. Establishing a common interpretation of the challenges, cooperation was made possible. And insisting on the innovative focus in their development strategies, the scene was set to create new activities. In discourses of community development there is an increasing emphasis on entrepreneurship and innovation. As argued by Thrift (2008), places are put under an innovative imperative. At Sørøya they have made use of this discursive focus, employing entrepreneurial perspectives on community development.

Another important discursive framework is the increased focus on networking and cooperation in discourses of community development. The strategic work of creating purposeful networks has been crucial in creating 'The Land of the Big Fish'. By forcing people together in networks with specific tasks, new relations were formed generating new ideas. The close links between voluntary groups, tourism enterprises and the local authority made new combinations of multiple experiences and knowledge possible. And so did the many external relations. Being well skilled in the political discourses of community development the community entrepreneurs at Sørøya have managed to fit their collaborative strategies perfectly to the new trends in regional policy. This way, they have profited from financial, advisory and symbolic support in their work on establishing new networks.

Further, discourses of community development increasingly emphasize the need for place branding: to invent new and unique images. In creating 'The Land of the Big Fish', local actors at Sørøya made use of this discursive focus. In a process of defining their future possibilities and strategies, significant local resources were identified. The tourism network project is mainly based on what they regard as their most important advantage – big fish. In the process they have also emphasized cultural and social qualities of the community, such as knowledge, skills and values. As demonstrated, the process of creating Sørøya as a destination involves negotiation of place images and local identities.

Finally, the tourism network project at Sørøya is based on the increased focus on experiences. Tourism is encouraged by most Norwegian municipalities. It is seen as a growth sector which can replace jobs lost through economic restructuring – especially in coastal communities facing decline in commercial fisheries (Saeter 1998; Borch 2004). As they expect tourists to search for both the authentic and extreme experiences, the tourism entrepreneurs at Sørøya have created a concept tailored for sport fishing tourists seeking the most spectacular catches within the framework of an idyllic fishing village. Making use of new discursive frameworks, they have created novel space for manoeuvre.

Conclusions

Through selective accounts of selective events, I have examined the process of establishing a common tourism strategy in a rural community in Northern Norway. The process of creating Sørøya as 'The Land of the Big Fish' demonstrates how entrepreneurial tourism projects can be created through new alliances and new combinations of tradition and invention, nature and culture, the local and the global. It demonstrates the complexity of such processes, involving creative practices, new relations, negotiation and place reinvention.

The tourism network project at Sørøya demonstrates how new constructions of place images involve renegotiation of identities. As Burns and Novelli (2006) state, the complex making of tourist places involves different actors drawing into the product different histories, values and lifestyles. In this process of negotiation, some voices are included and others excluded. Emphasizing what discourses they make use of in the innovation process, I have tried to show how the creation of 'The Land of the Big Fish' is based on vigorous narrators making use of new discursive frameworks. Insisting on defining their own strategies within these frameworks, they have created unconventional liaisons and working methods of community development. Involving new local alliances as well as extended networks, the local and global are interwoven in these complex processes of place reinvention.

I have tried to elaborate a relational perspective on entrepreneurship, arguing that innovations should be investigated as social processes. As demonstrated in the analyses, the innovation processes are not only results of strategic actions, but also of the people's fight for their everyday life. The entrepreneurial practices are socially situated, shaped and reshaped through interplay of cultural dispositions and structural contexts. Integrating new experience and knowledge in their practices, the actors bring with them elements of traditional practices. Applying Rudie's (1994) concept of creative practices in entrepreneurship research, it is possible to grasp the interaction between conventions and innovation. Such a perspective also brings social creativity and cultural interpretation into the analyses.

Like all entrepreneurial processes, the narratives produced in this chapter are situated in specific contexts. The narratives are produced by narrators from various positions, emphasizing their perception of the processes. I argue that we need to base research on entrepreneurship and innovative processes on the experience and categorization of different positioned actors. And we need to enter into discourses of entrepreneurship, community development and place reinvention, to tell stories of complex processes and challenge established narratives. Hopefully, the analyses of creative practices at Sørøya will inspire new stories of innovative processes in rural tourism.

References

Andersen, O.J. (2004), 'Public–Private Partnerships: Organisational hybrids as channels for local mobilisation and participation?', *Scandinavian Political Studies* 27(1), 1–21.

Austin, J., Stevenson, H. and Wei-Skillern, J. (2006), 'Social and commercial entrepreneurship: Same, different or both?', *Entrepreneurship Theory and Practice* 30(1), 1–22.

Bourdieu, P. (1977:1977), *Outline of a Theory of Practice* (Cambridge: Cambridge University Press).

Burns, P.M. and Novelli, M. (2006), 'Tourism and social identities; Introduction', in: Burns and Novelli (eds), *Tourism and Social Identities. Global Frameworks and Local Realities* (Oxford: Elsevier).

Borch, O.J., Førde, A., Rønningen, L., Vestrum, I. and Alsos, G. (2008), 'Resource configuration and creative practices of community entrepreneurs', *Journal of*

Enterprising Communities: People and Places in the Global Economy, 2(2), 100–103.

Borch, T. (2004), 'Sustainable management of marine fishing tourism. Some lessons from Norway', *Tourism in Marine Environments* 1(1), 49–57.

Bærenholdt, J.O., Haldrup, M., Larsen, J. and Urry, J. (2004), *Performing Tourist Places* (Aldershot: Ashgate).

Feifer, M. (1985), *Going Places* (London: Macmillan).

Foucault, M. (1972), *The Archaeology of Knowledge and the Discourse on Language* (New York: Pantheon).

Gartner, W.B. (2007), 'Entrepreneurial narrative and a science of the imagination', *Journal of Business Venturing*, 22(5), 613–27.

Granås, B. and Nyseth, T. (2007), 'Dimensions of place reinvention', in: Nyseth and Granås (eds), *Place Reinvention in the North – Dynamics and Governance Perspectives*, pp. 9–25 (Stockholm: Nordregio, Nordic Research Programme Report 1).

Hjort, D. and Steyaert, C. (2004), 'Introduction', in: Hjort, D. and Steyaert, C. (eds), *Narrative and Discursive Approaches in Entrepreneurship: A Second Movements in Entrepreneurship* (Cheltenham: Edward Elgar Publishing).

Kvale, S. and Brinkmann, S. (2008), *Interviews: An Introduction to Qualitative Research Interviewing* (London: Sage).

Lavoie, D. (1991), 'The discovery and interpretation of profit opportunities: Culture and Kirznerian entrepreneur', in: Berger (ed.), *The Culture of Entrepreneurship* (San Francisco: ICS Press).

Lindh de Montoya, M. (2000), 'Entrepreneurship and culture; The case of Freddy, the strawberry man', in: Swedberg (ed.), *Entrepreneurship. The Social Science View* (New York: Oxford University Press).

Morris, M.H. and Jones, F.F. (1999), 'Entrepreneurship in established organizations: the case of the public sector', *Entrepreneurship Theory and Practice* 24, 71–91.

Rudie, I. (1994), 'Making sense of new experience', in: Hastrup and Hervik (eds), *Social Experience and Anthropological Knowledge* (London: Routledge).

Saeter, J.A. (1998), 'The significance of tourism and economic development in rural areas: a Norwegian case study', in: Butler, Hall and Jenkins (eds), *Tourism and Recreation in Rural Areas* (West Sussex: J. Wiley & Sons Ltd).

Steyaert, C. and Bouwen, R. (1997), 'Telling stories of entrepreneurship – Towards a narrative-contextual epistemology for entrepreneurial studies', in: Donckels and Miettinnen (eds), *Entrepreneurship and SME Research: On its Way to the Next Millennium* (Aldershot: Ashgate).

Steyaert, C. (2004), 'The prosaics of entrepreneurship', in: Hjort and Steyaert (eds), *Narrative and Discursive Approaches in Entrepreneurship: A Second Movements in Entrepreneurship* (Cheltenham: Edward Elgar Publishing).

Thrift, N. (2008), *Non-representational Theory. Space, Politics, Affect* (Oxon: Routledge).

Wagner, R. (1981), *The Invention of Culture* (Chicago: University of Chicago Press).

Chapter 7

Constructing the Unique – Communicating the Extreme Dynamics of Place Marketing

Brynhild Granås

What is special about a particular place? Recently, many seem eager to pursue this topic in different ways within Western cities, towns and villages: aesthetic as well as more pragmatic forces or advantages of places are given attention and shown in concerns for physical, cultural or social aspects of place identities. Work to define and nurture the particularity of the place includes displaying it in varying ways, ranging from local festivals to processes of physical regeneration. The propensity to engage in place representations is interpreted by social scientists within a discussion concerning globalization (Harvey 1989, 2000; Giddens 1991; Lash and Friedman 1992) and underscores that place still matters. With globalization, places do not lose impact or meaning (Beck 2002); rather, the topic of place may be formulated in new ways (Massey 2005).

Over time, place representations have taken ever new forms and are institutionally embedded in new ways. This chapter identifies place marketing as part of this institutionally embedded field. The analysis investigates the symbolic representations in marketing of the Norwegian town Narvik. This is done by looking at the relation between such representations and cultural, social and political contexts.

Together, this chapter[1] aims at throwing light on how marketing of Narvik these days has come to represent the town as 'ordinary' as well as 'unique' in particular ways. Ordinariness is accentuated by explicitly emphasizing 'civilized' characteristics while uniqueness is communicated with reference to a 'natural wilderness'. In notable ways, the natural surroundings of the town is communicated as providing for highly modern lifestyles, disassociating the landscape from the 'uncivilized' or 'traditional' that otherwise is common for place representation in these areas of Northern Europe (Eder 2006; Olsen 2003; Granås and Gunnarsdotter 2007).

---

1   This chapter is a further development of the text 'The unique and the ordinary: Reinventing place through symbolic communication', published by Brynhild Granås and Yvonne Gunnarsdotter in 2007, part of the Nordregio funded project *Place Reinvention in the North* (Nyseth and Granås 2007). This previously published text contained a comparison of place marketing in Övertorneå (Sweden) and Narvik (Norway).

Through a contextualized analysis, this chapter explores ways of communicating the place. The focus is on how production of place representations in marketing material is framed by institutional interaction and specific situations that concerns economic and social development as well as cultural scripts and symbolic positions available. Hence, this case study also exemplifies how the ascription of meaning to the place is regulated by the positioning of the place within extensive symbolic relations of 'north and south' as well as 'centre and periphery'.

At several points, the discussion also provides insight into wider processes of place reinvention in Narvik town, and the dynamics of place marketing within such processes. The concept of place reinvention refers to a comprehensive concern for the meaning of place within place production, a concern that also constitutes the task for place marketing. Hence, place marketing is here approached as one practice among others that engage in ascribing place meanings.

Narvik – From 'Iron Ore Town' to 'Post-industrial Space'

The recent history of the town of Narvik tells of how a more unambiguous place image has broken down through a process of economic recession. The town, with its 14,000 inhabitants,[2] is located at the head of the deep Ofoten Fjord, 68° north on the Norwegian coast. At the turn of the 19th century, the town popped up on the small Narvik peninsula. Topographically, the settlement was strictly framed by a fjord and surrounded by steep mountains. Four small farms became a town with a population of several thousand over a period of less than ten years (Aas 2001); Narvik was chosen as the transhipment port by Swedish interested parties who required a transport line to start industrial production of iron ore in Northern Sweden. A 42-km railway track was constructed through the challenging mountain landscape to the Swedish border. The railway was completed in 1902, the same year that the town was formally established.

Ever since, iron ore has flowed in by rail and out via Narvik harbour on iron ore ships. Throughout the 20th century, Narvik became known as the richest town in North Norway. A key to this era of wealth was a lucrative municipal tax agreement with the iron ore company LKAB (Aas 2001), which sustained the municipal economy for more than twenty years after the Second World War (Svendsen 2002). The Norwegian State Railways (NSB) and LKAB were the main employers, around which the rest of town life circled. A crisis occurred when the scope and importance of both declined from the late 1960s onwards, though mainly during the 1980s and 1990s (Svendsen 2002). In 2006, LKAB still employed 226 people in Narvik, while NSB had withdrawn. Narvik was no longer solely an 'iron ore town'. Rather, a multitude of economic activities now gradually made up the town life.

Population numbers were surprisingly stable and the degree of unemployment was never critical, but during the recession inhabitants experienced feelings of loss

---

2   The entire municipality of Narvik has approx. 18,500 inhabitants.

and of facing an uncertain future. In the wake of the economic decline, the social democratic traditions and rich popular cultural life that had created a strong town pride were challenged. From decade to decade, the recession called forth a series of initiatives to establish new sources of employment. Today, the town is marked by the diverse qualities of the 'post-industrial space', as described by Lash and Urry (1994, 216–17), including pronounced engagements in reassigning place meanings.

Place Reinvention, Place Marketing, and the Social Progressive Place

This chapter will refer to place reinvention as continuous processes within which meanings are ascribed to the place. Such processes run within and between, on the one hand, informal, unintentional and quiet development processes, and on the other hand, outspoken intentional processes of politics and entrepreneurialism (Granås and Nyseth 2007). They imply continuities as well as shifts in regard to what place meanings are advanced. Place reinvention concerns all aspects of place production, ranging from the way it is practised and experienced by the average inhabitant, lived and symbolically imagined through everyday lives, and conceptualized by marketers, politicians or planners (cf. Lefebvre 1991). As such, place reinvention will be understood here as providing a perspective for intercepting within place studies the variety of modes and ways through which 'the typical' features of places are pointed out and represented.

Further, place marketing is identified as a more strategic aspect of place reinvention, performed within institutional networks of strategic actors. Nevertheless, as the analysis will show, strategic processes of marketing also includes contingencies; place representations in marketing are outcomes of development processes that intersect in unintended ways, they express time specific power constellations, and they tap into cultural scripts that are at hand, by exploiting as well as by confronting them. In line with this perspective, place marketing will be analysed as social relational practices, part of place production. Hence, marketing is separated from the field of economics, where the concept originates, as the embeddedness of place marketing representations in diverse social processes is in focus.

The analysis is based on an understanding of place as a social process, produced within social interaction and articulated in specific ways at specific times through history (Massey 1994, 2005; Simonsen 2005). This approach sees place as progressive in the sense that it is open and always becoming, implying also that the place is practised within relations that often reach far beyond the physical borders of place:

> Instead … of thinking of places as areas with boundaries around, they can be imagined as articulated moments in networks of social relations and understandings, but where a larger proportion of those relations, experiences and understandings are constructed on a far larger scale than what we happen to define for that moment as the place itself (Massey 1994, 154).

This contrasts with a tradition of community studies that has tended to approach matters of place through notions of homogeneity and stasis; such approaches have perceived places as closed holistic systems (Barth 1992) and have failed to see them as loci within larger processes (Friedman 2007, 110). A social progressive approach to place is integrated in the following by comprising within the contextualized analysis also relations that exceed the physically demarcated town. Additionally, the analysis aims at going beyond homogeneous accounts of place by integrating sensitivity towards the antagonisms and tensions involved in the formation of marketing's representations of the place.

Methodology

While the concept of place reinvention opens for a variety of thematic and analytical approaches, the following discussion approaches topics concerning production of place representations in marketing in ways that are analytically inspired by an interactionist and social constructivist methodological position accounted for by Järvinen and Mik-Meyer (2005). The outline starts with an investigation of place marketing through a more specific study of three brochures created between 2000 and 2005; knowledge about the embeddedness of these brochures provides insight into common themes in place marketing practices in this period and the role marketing has taken within processes of place reinvention.

The principal point taken from the 'post-structuralist constructivist interactionist' position of Mik-Meyer and Järvinen (2005, 9) is that textual articulations should be viewed as representations, and interpreted as part of an intersubjective process. This ensuring of aspects of representation and context is contiguous to the theme for this chapter. The analysis does not, however, commit to the ontological position Mik-Meyer and Järvinen sets up, including for example their demarcation of phenomenology as a 'naturalistic' approach.

More specifically, the analysis is organized by drawing on several of Mik-Meyer's (2005) suggestions for how to study documents from this methodological position. On a general level, Mik-Meyer (2005) argues that documents should be perceived as obtaining meaning from diverse sets of external conditions or contexts that frames the production process (Mik-Meyer 2005, 194). More specifically, she suggests that, to ensure this contextualization, documents should be approached through three concepts, covering three contextual and representational aspects – institution/context, interaction/process, and standardization/facts. Derived from these concepts, the following analysis will contextualize the production of place representations by looking at the following aspects: First, the investigation focuses on the local institutional terrain and interactions and specific situations that has framed representations made by these actors. Second, place representations in marketing are analysed within a wider geographical context that concerns the town's symbolic relations to other places.[3]

The three brochures examined more closely, identified here by their front page title and target groups, are: *Narvik – a town with potential* (possible new inhabitants and investors), *Narvik – world class excitement* (winter tourists), and *Make the right decision – choose Narvik* (college students). They were produced between 2000 and 2005 by respectively the local development company Futurum, the local tourism company Destination Narvik, and Narvik University College.

The Unique and Ordinary Town of Narvik

The analysis will start out with a short presentation of place representations found in these three brochures, before we turn to a contextualized analysis of how they have been formed. All three communicate the town as both unique and ordinary (see also Granås and Gunnarsdotter 2007). Uniqueness regards the way the town's natural surroundings provides for outdoor extreme sports activities. The steep mountains that surround the town, and partly also the fjord, are key elements in these representations. This landscape is framed as one that provides for modern high adrenaline extreme sports experiences of different kinds: in particular, winter sports like Telemark skiing, slalom and snow board – off-piste and on regulated slopes – are promoted, but also activities like mountain biking, climbing, hang gliding and diving. An often used composition in pictures is the extreme sports performer running down a steep mountainside; the angle of the picture gives you the feeling that the athlete runs into the fjord that waits at the foot of the mountain.

This place representation has over the last few years been accompanied by the town slogan 'Narvik – sterke opplevelser' that is made use of in the tourist brochure. Literally translated into English it says 'Narvik – strong experiences', but a common translation in Narvik has been 'Narvik – world class excitement'. It has its source in a representation of Narvik as a town for a 'rough and tough' lifestyle associated with extreme sports performances and the excitement, danger and adrenaline such experiences can give. The message of uniqueness all together underscores that Narvik is not necessarily a place for 'anybody'.

---

3 Method: The discussion is based on a previous fieldwork undertaken in the town of Narvik in 2006 (Nyseth and Granås 2007). The main section of data consisted of semi-structured individual and focus group interviews with a variety of local leaders as well as inhabitants outside of such positions. This empirical work was continued by studies of place marketing. An extensive study was performed of brochures and Internet pages that represented the place. Texts and illustrations were systematically examined before three printed brochures were selected for further analysis. The selection was based on the comprehensive and stable format of brochures as compared to Internet pages and on their centrality within networks of marketing material. Participants in the production of each brochure were interviewed to shed light on the process of production.

Another representation found in these brochures, though weakly represented in the winter tourist brochure, is that of the 'ordinary' town of Narvik. This ordinariness is constituted by a range of expressions: its climate (warmer than you think), its communication (more central than you think), its service sector (generally exceptionally well developed, including recreation, night life and shopping as well as kindergartens, schools and health services), its primacy as a place for raising children and its possibilities for enjoying popular culture and recreational outdoor life, including traditional Norwegian cabin life. This communication indicates a message of the 'normal' or 'highly civilized' place. Partly, it can be interpreted as a balancing of the representation of the town as unique in regard to extreme sports possibilities. Additionally, it supports this representation's communication of Narvik as a modern town.

Local Institutional Framing, Interactions and Situations

The period from 2000 to 2005, within which these three brochures were produced, is one of a late- and post-recession Narvik marked by a search for a new identity basis and a struggle for new businesses to arise. Part of the restructuring that then took place was also that local development activities were organized in new ways and a new urban governance regime evolved (Nyseth and Waldenström 2007).

Within this regime, people with new competences took positions and identified new topics and ideas in development work, including that of place marketing. A key institution within the new institutional terrain was Futurum. This semi-public shareholder company was established by Narvik municipality to nurture entrepreneurial activities. Futurum defined as their task to promote the new priority area of tourism as well as to enhance immigration and entrepreneurial activities more generally. Through these engagements, they intercepted needs for place marketing. Three target groups were identified: tourists, potential inhabitants and investors.

The brochure, *Narvik – a town with potential*, exemplifies an early place marketing initiative by Futurum, directed towards the latter audience of inhabitants and investors. The representation of Narvik as ordinary became dominant in this brochure. This can be interpreted as simply reflecting the particular target groups in focus; new inhabitants or investors are supposed to engage in a long-term relationship with the town, and hence to communicate the 'spectacular' characteristics of the town may have been perceived as less relevant. However, Futurum informants claim that, already at this stage, they wanted a stronger profiling of uniqueness; their argument for not emphasizing it more was that they lacked financing to perform such a process in what they thought would be a professionally satisfying way. The emphasis on ordinariness in this brochure may also reflect that its production involved all together 14 local companies and organizations; many interests were to be managed and this complicated the designation of any uniqueness for the town. Illustrations throughout the brochure however indicate what such uniqueness should involve, such as the front page picture of a hang glider flying above the town centre.

Soon after the production of this brochure, Futurum initiated the establishment of the tourism company Destination Narvik. Together, these two run an overarching development plan for tourism called the 'Masterplan' (Futurum 2006), financed by Statens Nærings- og Distriktutviklingsfond (SND, a national public development institution) who designated it as a pilot project. The winter tourist brochure, *Narvik – world class excitement*, that strongly emphasizes the uniqueness of the town, is marked by this process; the Masterplan involved a stronger profiling for place marketing purposes and supplied the town with the slogan that is made use of in this brochure. Hence, a stronger profiling and enhancement of uniqueness was done within a situation where the tourism sector was strongly addressed by new local development institutions, and also supported by national public financial subsidy schemes. It should also be added that this brochure was produced within a very limited budget; hence, a strong prioritization lay behind Destination Narvik's designation of extreme sports audiences as a main target group – this brochure was produced at the expense of a general Narvik tourism brochure. This consideration taps into a broad discussion about tourism development: some have suggested de-emphasizing the extreme sports element and giving priority to a more 'common' tourist market. Others have claimed that such adjustments would erode the town's 'uniqueness' and 'exclusiveness', constituted by extreme sports facilities. As we shall see, this conflict of interest has later been intercepted in a town branding process.

The new slogan reflected a strong milieu for extreme sports performance in the town, in particular for Telemark skiing and slalom, of which people who held positions in politics, business and the new terrain of development companies were part. This milieu has been nurtured by Narvik Slalom Club, an institution that is referred to by inhabitants as influential. The club has managed the ski slope in the town centre through considerable public funding over the years. Telemark skiing, slalom and snowboard are practices that distinguish the 'Narvik lad' (Narvikguten), a figure narrated by inhabitants that encapsulates the perception of an iconic Narvik inhabitant, who moreover is regarded as both 'proud' and 'arrogant'. This symbolic relatedness of the town slogan also indicates its gendered connotations: as with the Narvik lad, the slogan is constructed in accordance with a masculine norm. Also, the network of actors mentioned here is dominated by men.

At the beginning of the 21st century, Narvik University College's involvement in marketing has been enforced by an economic restructuring of Norwegian higher education and a subsequent intensified recruitment competition. Part of their marketing task has been to promote the student town of Narvik. This work has been carried out in a close dialogue and relation with the work of Futurum and Destination Narvik, as expressed in the college's emphasizing of extreme sports opportunities in Narvik. The brochure, *Make the right decision – choose Narvik*, gives priority to a representation of extreme sports, and this aspect of the college's marketing emphasis is underlined when looking at the network of other documents within which this brochure stands. There, the slogan 'Narvik – sterke opplevelser' is also made use of. In this particular brochure, the college however also represents the ordinariness of Narvik as a 'civilized' place, highlighting its high level services, good night life, comfortable climate, centrality, and so on. Together, this constitutes a representation of a highly modern town, towards a presumably young audience.

The college frames and supports this representation by profiling Narvik as a town for high technology, as engineering is its special field. Narvik University College is a central institution within a late-recession Narvik where technological industries receive considerable attention within the local discourse on place development. This reflects a long historical line of technological competence management in the town, starting with the construction of the iron ore railway. The history of the railway construction period is celebrated every year during the very popular Winter Feast Week in Narvik. This strong and well known narrative is, however, not given any central position in place marketing. Nevertheless, the representation of Narvik as unique in regard to extreme sports can be understood as comprising this narrative in a transformed, modernized and communicable way. Like the extreme sports athletes, the railway construction workers were men with courage, strength and adventurousness mastering the challenging mountains. The construction of the railway and the use of new technology brought modernity to the area and constituted Narvik as a highly modern town. Today, the image of being modern can be seen as transformed into the framework of highly modern lifestyles associated with extreme sports. By assigning the place also with meanings of ordinariness and as highly civilized, this featuring of Narvik as modern is further strengthened.

At the time when the empirical work of this research project was performed, a town branding process was run in Narvik, aiming to form a more thorough platform for marketing representations than the Masterplan had provided. This process was initiated by Futurum in a close dialogue with Narvikgården Ltd. This semi-municipal real estate development company took over and ran the project with support from external consultants in Oslo. Participants said that this shift was made because of the economic strength of Narvikgården Ltd, who could implement a costly and comprehensive process. Again, close ties between development companies in the town appear and the process exemplifies once more how new institutional actors have translated new management ideas into local development work. The result this time was a branding package that contained the elements of 'visions', 'values', 'promises' and 'visual design'. The town slogan, 'Narvik – sterke opplevelser', reappears as the 'vision' in this package. Part of the outcome was that other components of the branding package moderated the focus of this slogan as compared to previous interpretations; this was done by including a range of excitement that Narvik town is said to offer. One important framing that has made this adjustment relevant is the development within the tourism sector; even though the 'Narvik lad' may feel comfortable with assigning the place with meanings as a town for highly modern adventures of extreme sports, the tourism sector aims at addressing a broader tourist market; after all, the ski bums do not spend that much money.

Place marketing in Narvik these days continue to assign the place with ordinary as well as unique qualities. The uniqueness in regard to the 'rough and tough' and extreme sports symbols are still central in this image formation, even though the possibilities for 'excitements' are wider than extreme sports.

Symbolic Position: Relations with Other Places

Place marketing in Narvik has ascribed the town with particular meanings of being unique and ordinary. As the discussion this far has shown, these meanings have depended on a range of conditions that have framed marketing practices, ranging from local institutional contexts and interactions, to specific situations concerning economic and social life as well as narratives and symbols available within the town. All along, place marketing representations also reflect interest management among local actors (cf. Mik-Meyer 2005).

The promotion of the ordinary and unique place in these representations is, however, also directed by additional contextual aspects that will now be addressed. Despite the local focus this far, the investigation has at several points addressed relations that also exceed the physically demarcated place. In the following, this focus will be more emphasized as we shall explore the symbolic position this particular town holds within a wider geography. The analysis brings in new dimensions as to how place reinvention processes run, and the dynamics of place marketing within such processes. As a whole, the following discussion illuminates further, not only the fruitfulness, but also the necessity of exploring the place as constituted within a wider geography, as expressed through Massey's (1994, 2005) conceptualization of a social progressive place.

Centre and periphery

Even though the place representations of marketing come out of and imprint on the local context (Mik-Meyer 2005), they are still about communicating the meaning of the place towards an 'outside'. Place marketing therefore in particular ways articulates relational aspects of place, in the sense of connections that reach beyond its physical borders. One such characteristic when discussing places is the symbolic relation constituted by the centre–periphery dichotomy. Paulgaard (2006, 13) refers to this dichotomy as one that '... forms a kind of basic foundation for other constructions'. To put it another way, centre–periphery can be seen as a hegemonic discourse that frames place marketing; it directs place marketing and is addressed by place marketing. The following step of the analysis suggests that articulations of the place as ordinary and unique can be better understood when related to the context of centre–periphery, and after that also the context of north–south, that actors in Narvik operate within.

A place is always a centre or a periphery for somebody or something, and hence the meaning a place may have as 'centre' or 'periphery' is a matter of relations and constructions; it is negotiated and reverted depending on perspective and situation. However, this construction is imprinted by the power aspects of relations within which the place is situated. The town of Narvik is located in what is perceived as a peripheral region in Norway. This reflects power aspects of relations between a small town of a small country and political and economic centres. At the same time, Narvik is a municipal centre and a centre of the region Ofoten.

The social science discourse on globalization describes places in the centre as continuous crossing-points of intensive flows of people, goods, services, money and ideas. The places of the periphery are at the same time described as points where such flows are weaker and more vulnerable. The people of the periphery tend to have to struggle with distances to markets and power centres. This discourse may express a process of centre–periphery polarization (Bauman 1999), where those who stay behind in the periphery are considered 'the waste products of modernity' (Bauman 1999). As such, a periphery position not only represents a 'practical' challenge of distance, but also a symbolic one that can come to light within place reinvention processes that are marked exactly by concerns for the meaning of the place.

The category of centre–periphery contains a hierarchical symbolic relation where the 'progressive' or 'more civilized' centre holds a dominant position in relation to the 'remote' and 'less civilized' periphery. This power relation has been widely discussed and elaborated as problematic through notions of exoticization in relation to periphery and ethnicity. However, this hierarchical ordering of centre versus periphery can be disturbed; if the symbolic relation becomes one between 'the normal' centre in its prosaic sense and 'the exceptional' periphery in its exotic sense, the periphery label can make up a positive potential for marketing of places. To sum up, the centre–periphery construct constitutes symbolic restraints as well as potentials that contextualize any efforts made to direct the flow of resources to places.

As a periphery position is a matter of construction, it is similarly a matter of negotiation and change. However, efforts that aim at changing the meaning of the place are restricted by the power relations that the place is located within, as expressed through categories of centre and periphery. These are conceptual frames that, with reference to Foucault's concept of discourse (1972), one cannot exceed.

North and south

Not only is the caring for the meaning of Narvik town regulated by the periphery position of the town within a wider power geometry; additionally, this periphery is that of a 'northern' kind. Klaus Eder (2006) identifies a Europe where the former barbaric North versus a cultivated South turned into the natural North and the artificial South. Eder's analysis points to the (changing) roles of European borders and how, within this context, the northern border today '… represents the natural past, a kind of primordial reference of a people struggling with nature' (Eder

2006, 265). In his analysis of the north of England, Shields (1991) has shown how inhabitants of this area have been associated with values that are highly appreciated such as honesty, straightforwardness and endurance as well as with unsophisticated behaviour and a low educational level. Within a Norwegian context, the discourse on the north versus the south contains similar representations as those presented by Eder and Shields.

Making the northern periphery ordinary

With the symbolic relations of centre–periphery and north–south as a backdrop, place representations made of Narvik through marketing initiatives can be investigated in other ways. The explicit attention towards the ordinary qualities of Narvik can be interpreted as moves to counter the restraints set by these hegemonic discourses. Such place perceptions are articulated in the brochures *Narvik – a town with potential* and *Make the right decision – choose Narvik*, emphasizing the centrality, climate, urbanity and (welfare and other) services of the town. The message contains more specific descriptions of how this town is not that isolated, not that cold, and not that rural and restricted in regard to services as one would expect. This pinpointing of ordinariness directs attention to qualities of the place that can be interpreted as objections towards a hegemonic discourse that regards the periphery place as uncivilized and inferior. A consideration of the north–south distinction as a discursive framing, associating the north with that of the 'past' and the 'primordial', elucidates further how the marketing of Narvik as ordinary conditions to comprehensive discourses.

Constructing the unique – communicating the extreme

Similarly, place marketing represents Narvik as unique based on perceptions of nature and an emphasis of how the nature of Narvik prepares for 'spectacular' modern lifestyles. As with the 'ordinariness' of the town, this construction of the unique and communication of the 'extreme' deals with restrictions as well as potentialities that the centre–periphery and north–south discourse provides for. The step from the positive connotations of the 'natural north' to the ambivalent epithet of the 'wild north' is rather small. Many northern place representations seem to have fallen into the 'wild north' trap of this distinction (Olsen 2003; Granås and Gunnarsdotter 2007).

The marketing of Narvik has not made use of the 'natural north' in place representations but has, in a remarkable way, given the 'wild north' a twist that turns its meaning away from an epithet and towards something very modern and widely appreciated. The exoticism of nature is fully displayed through strong illustrations and textual descriptions. But this 'spectacular' is directly connected to the lifestyle of extreme sports and hence something very modern and 'civilized'. The extreme sports culture is a global one, displayed through international TV channels and Internet sites and the sports icons of, for example, snowboarding stars. The modern is only one symbolic aspect of the anti-periphery statements made here. Another is that of a playful, speedy, powerful and dangerous nature-based excitement. These are representations that confront the periphery as relaxing, dull and quiet. 'Playing' with the myths of the periphery like this is not necessarily to deny a position as peripheral. If seen in relation to Foucault (1972), the juggling with symbolic representations seen here necessarily takes place within the discourse that provides the northern periphery position, but it constitutes a disturbing of this discourse from within. At this point, the hierarchical relation between centre and periphery is challenged.

Dynamics of Place Marketing within Place Reinvention

This analysis has now contextualized the analysis of place representations in marketing through, first, the institutional context and the situational context of the late recession in Narvik and then, aspects of wider relations. Both discussions may provide insight into the dynamics of place marketing within place reinvention.

This analysis has told how, since the beginning of the 21st century, the meaning of the place Narvik has been cared for and managed through a specific way of representing the place. When the recession slowly started to phase out, place representations became a matter for interlinked and gradually more professionalized marketing processes. This engagement made by actors within a new governance regime of the town displays these actors' potency for intercepting and implementing new management ideas, including ideas of marketing and branding the place.

Specific places may be represented in different ways, and place representations may thus be seen as part of a struggle to control places and people living there (Lefebvre 1991; Holloway and Hubbard 2001). In Narvik, institutional networks have enhanced the idea that this town is one for 'excitement', but more so, for the 'excitement of extreme sports'. While some place meanings have been supported, others have been neglected through the interest management (Mik-Meyer 2005) inherent in place marketing activities. This underlines the point that images made within place marketing must be, as has been done in this chapter, studied '... in a process and in their development at a local level, and not as disembedded representations ...' (Olsen 2003).

A pronounced aim with place marketing is to enhance attractiveness for the purpose of drawing resources to the place. Hence, place representations defined as marketing exemplify an intentional caring for the meaning of the place. This way of working with perceptions of place may lead the attending of place meanings in particular directions. The logic inherent in place marketing pushes the determination of the meaning of the place towards the communicable, made up of the 'unique' (to stand out) and that which is recognized and appreciated (to stand out in a positive sense). This consideration of communicability directs place meanings handled within place marketing towards the clean cut and homogeneous, at the expense of the complex and ambiguous diversity involved in the production of place.

This element of simplification reflects a relationship between place marketing and identity politics, as performed by, for example, politicians or cultural institutions. This analysis' contextual approach frames place marketing practices as part of an identity-political field. Identity politics implies strategic handling of place meanings that are communicable to inhabitants as well as towards external audiences. Such politics also involve the promotion of meaning categories that are embodied with power and have homogenizing effects on place discourses, where some voices are silenced and others are emphasized. It is within this terrain of intentional and strategic place reinvention that place marketing operates. Place marketing is often framed as an outspoken intentional practice, run to enhance the 'attractiveness' and 'market value' of the place. But the task of place marketing is not only that of selling the place (Philo and Kearns 1993); it includes imprinting on identity formations in a wider sense: to sell a place is also to be involved in the formation of the product that is put on the market, as the institutional actors within this analysis do.

To understand the logic of place marketing it is important also to be aware that the meaning of a place may, however, also be changed and processed unintentionally. Hence, place reinvention is also about that which is 'out of control' (Granås and Nyseth 2007) or in other ways out of sight of actors in their intentionally framed approach to place meanings. Narvik town lost its meaning as 'a rich iron ore town' without anyone intending this to happen. It is within an epoch also of a general search for new place identities (Granås and Gunnarsdotter 2007; Granås and Nyseth 2008) that the place marketing activities analysed here have taken place and constituted a force and an assertion of interests.

Additionally, the analysis has described how contextual analysis of place marketing can gain from bringing in the wider geographies of place (Barth 1992; Friedman 2007; Massey 1994, 2005). By not restricting the contextual to that which takes place within the physical borders of the place, the attending of place meanings and representations of the place can be interpreted as part of broader discourses, such as that of north–south and centre–periphery. Within this particular analysis, the attention to such symbolic relations tells how the place representations within marketing deal with power relations towards actors and institutions located elsewhere. Such relations are therefore part of what makes up the place (Massey 1994, 2005). In this case, place marketing relates to an enduring political struggle against the political and cultural marginalization of a northern town. Within a late- and post-recession Narvik, where the townspeople had lost their former pride based on the iron ore transport industry, place marketing initiatives have contributed to the reassertion of the cultural dignity of inhabitants, including their identities as northerners and proud inhabitants of a town that 'still is modern'.

References

Aas, S. (2001), *Narviks historie, bind 1. Byen, banen og bolaget* (Narvik: Stiftelsen Narviks historieverk).

Altern, I. (ed.) (1996), *Lokalsamfunn og lokalsamfunnsforskning i endring* (Universitetet i Tromsø: Institutt for samfunnsvitenskap).

Barth, F. (1992), 'Towards Greater Naturalism in Conceptualizing Societies', in Kuper (ed.).

Bauman, Z. (1999), *In Search of Politics* (Cambridge, MA: Polity Press).

Beck, U. (2002), *Globalisering og individualisering* (Oslo: Abstrakt forlag).

Bærenholdt, J.O. and Granås, B. (eds) (2008), *Mobility and Place. Enacting Northern European Peripheries* (Aldershot: Ashgate).

Eder, K. (2006), 'Europe's Borders. The Narrative Construction of the Boundaries of Europe', *European Journal of Social Theory*, 9(2), 255–71.

Foucault, M. (1972), *Archaeology of Knowledge* (New York: Pantheon).

Friedman, J. (2007), 'Global Systems, Globalization and Anthropological Theory', in Rossi (ed.).

Futurum (2006), Narvik Masterplan (htttp://www.masterplan.futurum.no (home page), accessed 19 October 2006).

Giddens, A. (1991), *Modernity and Self-Identity: Self and Society in the Late Modern Age* (Cambridge: Polity Press).

Granås, B. and Gunnarsdotter, Y. (2007), 'The Unique and the Ordinary – Reinventing Place Through Symbolic Communication', in Nyseth, T. and Granås, B. (eds).

Granås, B. and Nyseth, T. (2007), 'Dimensions of Place Reinvention', in Nyseth, T. and Granås, B. (eds).

Granås, B. and Nyseth, T. (2008), 'Place and Transports. Particularities of a Place and its Mobilities', in Bærenholdt, J.O. and Granås, B. (eds).

Harvey, D. (1989), *The Condition of Postmodernity* (Oxford: Blackwell Publishers).

Harvey, D. (2000), 'From Managerialism to Entrepreneurialism. The Transformation in Urban Governance in Late Capitalism', in Miles, M., Hall, T. and Borden, I. (eds).

Holloway, L. and Hubbard, P. (2001), *People and Place: The Extraordinary Geographies of Everyday Life* (Harlow: Prentice Hall).

Järvinen, M. and Mik-Meyer, N. (eds) (2005), *Kvalitative metoder i et interaktionistisk perspektiv. Interview, observationer og dokumenter* (Købehavn: Hans Reitzels Forlag).

Kearns, G. and Philo, C. (eds) (1993), *Selling Places. The City as Cultural Capital, Past and Present* (Oxford: Pergamon Press).

Kuper, A. (ed.) (1992), *Conceptualizing Society* (London: Routledge).

Lash, S. and Friedman, J. (eds) (1992), *Modernity and Identity* (Oxford: Blackwell Publishers).

Lash, S. and Friedman, J. (1992), 'Introduction: Subjectivity and Modernity's Other', in Lash, S. and Friedman, J. (eds).

Lash, S. and Urry, J. (1994), *Economies of Signs and Space* (London: Sage Publications).

Lefebvre, H. (1991), *The Production of Space* (Oxford: Blackwell).

Massey, D. (1994), *Space, Place and Gender* (Cambridge: Polity Press).

Massey, D. (2005), *For Space* (London: Sage Publications).

Mik-Meyer, N. and Järvinen, M. (2005), 'Indledning: Kvalitative metoder i et interaktionistisk perspektiv', in Järvinen and Mik-Meyer (eds).

Mik-Meyer, N. (2005), 'Dokumenter i en interaktionistisk begrepsramme', in Järvinen and Mik-Meyer (eds).

Miles, M., Hall, T. and Borden, I. (eds) (2000), *The City Cultures Reader* (London: Routledge).

Nyseth, T. and Waldenström, C. (2007), 'Governing Place Reinvention: Obstacles and Challenges', in Nyseth, T. and Granås, B. (eds).

Nyseth, T. and Granås, B. (eds) (2007), *Place Reinvention in the North. Dynamics and Governance Perspectives* (Stockholm: Nordregio).

Olsen, K. (2003), 'Making differences in a changing world: The Norwegian Sámi in the tourist industry', conference paper: *Taking Tourism to the Limits*, Hamilton, New Zealand 8-11 December 2003.

Paulgaard, G. (2006), 'Constructing Uniqueness in a Global World. Young People in a Northern Setting', *Tidsskrift for ungdomsforskning*, 1.

Philo, C. and Kearns, G. (1993), 'Culture, History, Capital: A Critical Introduction to the Selling of Places', in Kearns, G. and Philo, C. (eds).

Rossi, I. (ed.), *Frontiers of Globalization Research: Theoretical and Methodological Approaches* (New York: Springer-Verlag).

Shields, R. (1991), *Places on the Margin: Alternative Geographies of Modernity* (London: Routledge).

Simonsen, K. (2005), *Byens mange ansigter. Konstruksjon av byen i praksis og fortælling* (Roskilde: Roskilde Universitetsforlag).

Svendsen, O. (2002), *Narviks historie, bind 2. Storhetstid, brytningstid, framtidshåp* (Narvik: Stiftelsen Narviks historieverk).

Chapter 8

City Marketing:
The Role of the Citizens

Krister Olsson and Elin Berglund

Introduction

The transformation from an industrial society to a knowledge society has in substantial ways altered the conditions for urban planning and management. The last few decades have seen a societal development increasingly structured by economic and cultural globalization, European integration, increased mobility, de-industrialization and a growing importance of service sectors and the experience industry. The development has altered the nature of urban and regional economies and resulted in an increased competition between cities. It has also resulted in an urban planning occupied with the question of reinvention of place, including issues concerning economic development, city attractiveness and competitiveness.

In particular, city marketing has emerged as a concept associated with place reinvention. However, the concept is often used in an unclear way, both in practice and in much of the literature, and there is a great deal of confusion of what city marketing actually is. City marketing is often understood as a supply oriented and outward-looking practice aiming at selling cities to external markets, for example new inhabitants, visitors and investments. However, drawing on marketing theory city marketing could be understood as a demand oriented practice, aiming at satisfying the needs and wants of both external markets and internal markets, for example those that already live and work in a city. The one-sided occupation with attracting external markets has resulted in an unclear role for local citizens in contemporary urban development planning. In general there is lack of knowledge on how local citizens experience and value various measures of place reinvention. In this chapter we discuss questions concerning how to obtain and utilize such knowledge in urban planning.

Thus, the issues raised in this chapter are, from a Swedish perspective, *why* and *how* to take local citizens, and their interests and attitudes, into account in urban planning and development. In particular, the chapter addresses the question of how to involve large groups of citizens that are directly as well as indirectly affected by various urban development planning measures. The point of departure is taken from city marketing literature and marketing theory. In the chapter we discuss the concept of city marketing, from a perspective of practice and theory, and we identify challenges concerning the role of citizens in contemporary urban development planning. Through empirical findings from a survey in the small Swedish town of Arboga, we discuss a quantitative approach for evaluating urban planning and place reinvention measures from a perspective of local citizens.

City Marketing in Practice and Theory

City marketing in practice

Since the 1980s, city marketing has emerged as a key concept within urban development planning and urban management. In practice, city marketing has come to denote politics and planning conducive to city attractiveness and competitiveness. Generally, city marketing is understood as an outward-looking practice and has come to signify a wide range of spatial (for example water front housing), promotional (for example catchy slogans) and organizational (for example public–private partnerships) arrangements, strategies and activities.

Accordingly, the concept of city marketing is often associated with various kinds of urban development projects in which local authorities, most often in cooperation with private sector actors, devote great resources to reinvent their cities in order to be perceived as attractive places to live, work, visit and invest in. A central component of the reinvention is the construction of spectacular and often expensive amenities for entertainment, culture and consumption, for example concert halls, museums, shopping malls and professional sports stadiums. Other components are the staging of events, for example local and regional festivals and sports events at various levels, and designations such as the European Capital of Culture. In general, the process of reinvention also includes upgrading of public space, most often city centre makeovers including everything from squares to pedestrian walks and green spaces.

Both in practice and in the prescriptive city marketing literature, a positive image and a brand communicating the distinctive qualities of place are seen as crucial in order to sell cities to various groups on external markets (see Kotler et al. 1999; Judd 1999; Hall and Hubbard 1998; Holcomb 1994). Empirical studies show that many Western cities promote themselves as unique, vibrant and dynamic and that they, among other things, give prominence to their central location, their good business climate, their quality of life, and their culture and built heritage (see for example Berglund 2006; Murray 2001; Ward 1998).

The practice denoted as city marketing has been subjected to a large amount of critique, especially within the urban geography literature. The critique concerns commodification of urban amenities, discrepancies between promoted images and reality, and standardization making cities more alike. It also concerns the allocation of scarce public resources away from public welfare to signature projects, transformation of public goods into private or club goods leading to social polarization in cities, and that external markets (that is visitors, future inhabitants and business firms) are being prioritized at the expense of internal markets (that is those that live, work or run a business in the city) (see for example Sandercock 2003; Eisinger 2000; Fainstein and Judd 1999; Zukin 1995).

City marketing in theory

In much of the academic literature, city marketing is described with reference to the 'city' component of the concept and has, as discussed above, come to denote politics and planning conducive to city attractiveness and competitiveness. There is, as it now stands, only a handful of writings that conceptualize city marketing with reference to the 'marketing' side of the concept. These writings are descriptive in character and date back to the late 1980s and the 1990s (see Ashworth and Voogd 1988; 1990; 1994). With reference to social marketing, marketing in non-profit organizations and image marketing, city marketing is described as both a managerial principle and a set of accompanying planning techniques (Millington 2002; van den Berg and Braun 1999; Borchert 1994; Ashworth and Voogd 1990). This conception of city marketing draws extensively on the marketing concept and the interlinked science of marketing management (see for example Kotler 1972).

When it comes to the marketing concept, city marketing is seen as a demand-oriented planning process in which urban functions and physical space (the supply) are adjusted according to the needs and wants of targeted consumer groups (the demand). At the core of the marketing concept is, in other words, that urban products are defined by the demand made upon them by the consumers and not by the qualities of the urban products themselves. It should be noted that demand in this context does not only include explicitly stated demand but also a large portion of latent and option demand. Moreover, demand should not be equated with the demand of the external markets, which is often the case in much of the academic literature and in practice. Demand foremost refers to the needs and wants of the existing consumers, primarily on internal markets (Ashworth and Voogd 1990; 1994).

From a marketing perspective, urban products are complex and multifaceted. Being used and valued in different ways by the same or different consumers in the same or different times, they are difficult to define and delimit. Since urban products and the demand made upon them are neither static nor given, the products and the demand should be subjected to iterated analysis (Ashworth and Voogd 1990). Market analysis is a key activity in the descriptive theory of city marketing and draws extensively on the normative science of marketing management. Kotler (1986) describe marketing management as a kind of demand management that seeks to influence the level, timing and nature of demand in a way that helps to attain the objectives that has been set for the marketing effort. Ashworth and Voogd (1990) speak of marketing management in terms of market planning and suggest that it, in an urban context, includes four ensuing phases: analysis of markets; establishment of marketing goals and strategies; determination of a geographical marketing mix; and, elaboration and evaluation. However, although analysis of the consumers and their demand, interests and values are described as the most central element of the market planning process (see also Kotler et al. 1999), the descriptive theory of city marketing lacks in detail on the issue of how to perform such demand analysis in practice.

Challenges in city marketing practice and theory

There are several problems, or challenges, related to the practice and theory of city marketing. The first concerns the issue of wording, and how to denote activities referred to as 'city marketing' in practice and in much of the academic literature. In practice, a group of local elites more or less define the urban product and its image and thereafter seek to create a market (a demand) for it. This way of structuring the urban development planning and measures aiming at city attractiveness and competitiveness can be described as *supply-oriented* and stand in sharp contrast to the way city marketing is defined in the descriptive literature. The latter draws, as discussed above, from marketing theory and sees city marketing as a *demand-oriented* process in which the urban product not only is defined by the consumers but also adjusted according to their demand. Using the vocabulary of marketing theory (see for example Kotler 1986), one can say that contemporary urban development planning and measures aiming at city attractiveness and competitiveness are oriented towards *selling*, while the descriptive literature deals with the very essence of *marketing* (see Figure 8.1). The practice referred to as 'city marketing' in much of the academic literature is hence a practice of 'city selling' and it should, correctly, be denoted as such.

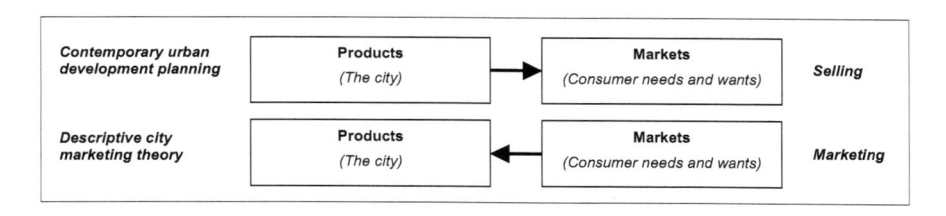

Figure 8.1 The difference between selling and marketing a city
Source: © Krister Olsson (chapter author).

The second challenge concerns the issue of targeting, and that the practice generally referred to as 'city marketing' is understood as an outward-looking activity with the objective of attracting external markets to the city. When internal markets, for example local citizens, are considered it is generally in terms of 'good ambassadors'. To a great extent, one can say that local citizens are regarded as indirect producers rather than 'end consumers'. The problem with this approach is that internal markets are always directly or indirectly affected by efforts undertaken to attract, for example, visitors, future inhabitants and business firms. This calls for a need to explicitly acknowledge the demand, interests and values of the internal markets, not only because conflicts may arise between external and internal markets but because the internal markets are likely to be much larger, and in this sense, more important than the external ones. There is, as it now stands, a lack of knowledge on how local citizens experience and value the current practice of place reinvention and urban development planning measures (see for example Hall and Hubbard 1998). On one hand, there is a political rhetoric extolling the necessities and virtues of reinventing cities and their images. On the other hand, extensive critique is directed towards these activities, stressing that they benefit external rather than internal markets. In the end, in-depth knowledge on how local citizens actually experience and value the practice of city selling and its manifestations is limited.

Based on the above reasoning our conclusion is that there is a great deal of confusion and misunderstanding of what city marketing is and how it can be applied in practice. This is true both in contemporary urban development planning and in much of the academic literature. So far, we have argued that city marketing is the opposite of city selling and that it is important to consider not only the demand of the external markets, but also the demand of the internal markets. A main point is that city marketing shouldn't be equated with place reinvention measures such as discrete signature projects, upgrading of public space and branding campaigns. In this chapter, city marketing is seen as a way of thinking about urban planning that equally can be applied to, for example, public transport, cultural heritage management and education. A main point is that traditional motives for urban planning, that is promoting public goods, considering externalities, improving information for decision making and considering distributional effects (Klosterman 2003), are relevant both for the evaluation of the current practice of 'city selling' as well as the descriptive city marketing theory. In this chapter, we derive from the descriptive city marketing theory and consider city marketing as a demand-oriented approach to urban planning. Our main interest, as discussed above, is the demand, interests and values of local citizens, and how to analyse and utilize these in urban development planning processes. The problem, as mentioned in the previous subsection, is that the descriptive city marketing theory lacks in detail on the issue of how to perform such demand analysis in practice.

Urban Planning and Citizen Participation

Citizen participation has been a central question in planning debate and development since the late 1960s, taking its starting point in a critique of the performance of public planning. In particular, contemporary planning theory has come to defy the traditional view on planning as an instrumental rational activity, that is an expert activity based on neutral and objective judgements, and citizen representation by politicians and collective organizations (Allmendinger 2002; Khakee 2006). Much of the debate has concerned the issues of *why* and *how* to engage the general public in the planning and decision-making process.

On a general level public participation in planning could be described as an activity that involves all affected interests through direct interaction:

> Public participation in planning means involvement in the planning process of all the affected individuals and parties, to influence planning decisions and outcomes. It implies direct interaction in the planning system between the planning 'establishment' and interested non-governmental participants rather than only through elected representatives in political or administrative processes. (Alexander 2008, 58)

However, building on this general statement participation can take many different forms and expressions, and, thus, public participation is 'something rather vague' (Alexander 2008, 58). To put it simply, the purpose of citizen participation in urban planning could be described from two different perspectives. First, it could be described as an activity with the main purpose being to favour social cohesion and local identity. Second, participation could be described as an activity primarily aiming at utilizing citizens' attitudes and interests in order to improve the outcome of planning (Nilsson 2005; Khakee 2006).

Following the latter view citizen input is essential in the planning and decision-making process. Input from a wide group of citizens in planning is by definition only relevant when it comes to public goods. In contemporary planning theory there is a strong ideal, in which all interests should be acknowledged and given the opportunity to participate in the decision-making process on the same terms (see for example Healey 1997; Innes and Booher 2003). Experiences from planning practice, however, tell us that it is often, in mainstream planning, difficult to engage citizens to take part in planning considerations, with the exception of those who are directly and, in their own view, negatively affected by planning propositions, that is neighbours. Thus, it can be discussed whether a wide group of citizens can be expected to participate in a direct way in urban planning (Olsson 2008).

One problem is that there are no incentives for individuals to provide for public goods. The paradox is that, the larger the group of people concerned, the fewer will, proportionally, act in order to provide a good in question (Olsson 2003). Consequently, there is an expectation that the provision shall be organized within public planning and management. The question, then, is how to take the interests and attitudes held by large groups of local citizens into account in urban development planning processes?

In general, participatory planning approaches and methods are framed by a qualitative and narrow approach with direct participation by a small number of citizens, often at a neighbourhood level. Taken that contemporary place reinvention and urban development planning measures often include and affect parts and aspects of the urban environment with a strong common interest, and that they aim at affecting large groups of citizens, both directly and indirectly, it is not enough to involve a limited group of people in market analyses. As discussed above, direct involvement is not efficient simply because too many citizens are concerned, and that individuals have no incentives to provide for public goods. Furthermore, direct involvement in planning discussions assumes that all citizens have the ability and time to participate, and hence, a strong interest to be active in concrete discussions. Many citizens, however, do not fulfil these requirements and are consequently excluded from contemporary planning discussions. The reasoning above points to a need to develop new approaches in practice for identifying public good characteristics in the urban environment, and for evaluating urban development planning from a perspective of local citizens. In the following section these issues are further elaborated on through a case study of planning and development in the small Swedish town of Arboga.

City Marketing Practice in Arboga, Sweden – A Citizen Perspective

Arboga was granted town status in the 13th century and is one of the oldest towns in Sweden. The street pattern from the Middle Ages and well preserved 18th- and 19th-century wooden houses gives Arboga town centre a distinct character (see Figure 8.2). In the last few decades the town has been objected to harsh structural change. The population has decreased by almost 1,000 inhabitants in the last decade and currently the population is 13,400 inhabitants. Since the early 1990s the total number of workplaces has decreased by 33 per cent. This change is mainly a result of a strong regression in the manufacturing industry in Arboga, which has decreased from approximately 3,500 workplaces in 1990 to 700 in 2005. Consequently, people commuting out from the municipality have increased since the early 1990s, whereas people commuting in have decreased. In 2005 the net commuting was more than minus 700 persons.

Arboga is located in the western part of the expansive region of Mälardalen, approximately 155 km west of Stockholm. Two European highways and two regional railways converge in Arboga. Thus, the transport infrastructure is regarded as of great importance for future development in Arboga, providing access to the regional labour market and a base for development of the tourist sector. The town council passed comprehensive goals for the future development of Arboga in 2007. One main objective is to increase the population and reach 14,000 inhabitants in 2020. In this undertaking the town's historical and cultural profile is considered as a key asset for the town's attractiveness and for its reinvention. In conjunction with the strategic goal setting a new slogan ('Arboga – a place for inspiration') was launched after a working process including representatives for local businesses, the municipality and local cultural life.

Furthermore, the town council has initiated a process to replace the existing Comprehensive Land Use Plan from 1990. The new plan will be adopted in 2009. In the autumn of 2007 the town planning office arranged three public meetings. Each meeting attracted between four and ten inhabitants. One week in October the town planning office arranged for local citizens to meet responsible planners and politicians in the town centre, resulting in approximately 400 proposals and ideas (varying in detail and relevance) from the inhabitants concerning the future development of Arboga.

Figure 8.2 Wooden houses in Arboga town centre
Source: © Krister Olsson (chapter author).

The survey: a quantitative approach to citizen input in planning

The empirical study presented in subsequent subsections is primarily concerned with how citizens in Arboga experience and value various manifestations of urban planning practice. Of particular interest is how to involve large groups of citizens and how to identify collective claims on the urban environment. As discussed above, it is generally difficult to engage a broad group of citizens to take part in urban planning in a direct and active way. This conclusion is underlined by the observation that only a very limited number of local citizens took part in the public meetings that the town planning office arranged in Arboga as part of the comprehensive planning process. Moreover, it should also be noted that the additional 400 ideas and propositions from local citizens were not collected in a systematic way and, therefore, it is unclear what or who these represent in a more detailed way.

Drawing on the reasoning above, a quantitative approach to citizen input in planning was used in the empirical study in Arboga. The idea is that a survey design including a questionnaire directed towards a random sample of local citizens has some advantages compared to direct and active participation, that is qualitative approaches. In a survey, it is possible to reach large groups of citizens and capture the anticipated diversity in demand on the urban environment. Using random sampling, it is possible to statistically generalize from the results. Moreover, all citizens in a random sample can participate on more or less the same terms. The assumption is not, however, that qualitative methods can be substituted completely with the quantitative approach, but that it will complement other more traditional forms of participation. The implementation of the quantitative approach in Arboga is described in detail in Olsson and Berglund (2008). The survey in Arboga is one of a series of similar surveys in Swedish towns and cities (Olsson 2003; 2006; 2008).

The survey in Arboga was conducted in late 2006, and included an extensive questionnaire that was sent by mail to a random sample of almost 1,000 citizens in Arboga in the age span of 16 to 74. Three reminders were sent out. Altogether, 595 citizens participated in the survey, which gave a response rate of 63 per cent. An analysis of missing values showed that there was no significant difference between the respondents and those that chose not to participate. The respondents are thus taken as representative for the whole sample, and the sample as representative for the whole population in Arboga.

Figure 8.3 Sign by the main country road passing Arboga town
Source: © Krister Olsson (chapter author).

The rationale for the questionnaire was to find ways to identify common interests among the citizens for various aspects of the urban environment, that is the public good characteristics of the urban environment, as well as to identify the demand, interests and attitudes of local citizens concerning various urban development measures. In the survey, the respondents were asked questions about, among other things, the town centre in general, meeting places in the town centre, an annual medieval festival, and preferred ways of participating in urban planning and management.

The town centre

In Arboga, as in many Swedish towns, much focus is directed towards the town centre. In the urban planning in general in Arboga, the historical centre is seen as a major asset contributing substantially to the town's attractiveness. The historical town centre is, for example, announced as a sight worth seeing ('stadskärna') on road signs by the main country road passing the town (see Figure 8.3).

In the survey, the respondents were asked to mark on a map one area in the town that they especially liked. A strong majority pointed out the town centre as the most liked area. In that sense, the historical centre stands out as very important for local citizens in their everyday life, and not only as a product promoted and sold on road signs to travellers passing the town. Moreover, nine out of ten respondents fully or partially agreed with a statement that the physical development of the town centre is a concern for all people living in Arboga, and, thus, not solely a question for developers and decision-makers. In conclusion, the town centre is of great interest to various local citizen groups and the centre can evidently be characterized as a local public good.

Nevertheless, it should be noted that there was also a very strong agreement among the respondents that it is important for future development of Arboga that the town centre is perceived as attractive to visitors. One-fifth agreed with a statement that the town centre, in the urban management, primarily is adjusted to the needs of visitors at the expense of the needs of local citizens. Nevertheless, these empirical findings do not give any substantial support to a notion that there is a conflict between internal and external markets as is often assumed in the critical debate about urban development measures.

Meeting places in the town centre

The respondents were asked to mark on a map a meeting spot in the town centre where they usually meet friends (see Figure 10.4). In total, almost 55 per cent of the respondents expressed an opinion, whereas the rest declared that they where uncertain or did not have an opinion. The results presented in the figure shows a pattern with three distinct clusters of meeting spots. The cluster represented far north on the map points towards the rather new train station which includes a popular café. The cluster in the south refers to the traditional town square, surrounded by cafés and restaurants as well as the town hall and a few shops. The third cluster in the middle of the map points towards the modern commercial part of the town centre.

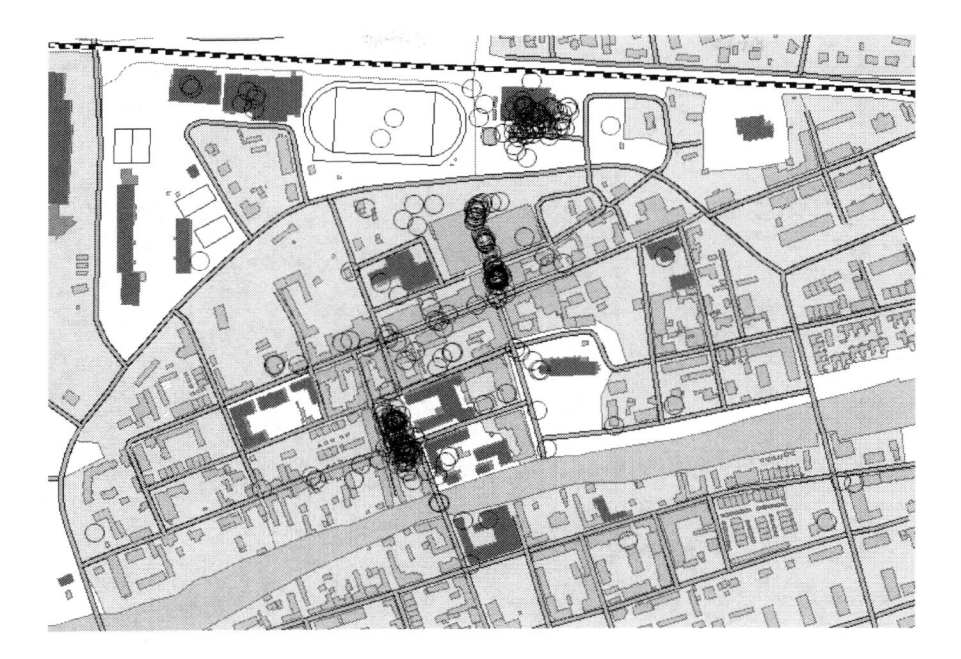

Figure 8.4 Meeting places in Arboga town centre
Source: © Krister Olsson (chapter author).

The representation of clusters in Figure 8.4 shows a pattern that is made up by overlapping individual answers, where each circle represents a meeting spot for one respondent. Thus, overlapping circles make up a pattern of the most important meeting places in the town centre. Consequently, the pattern in the figure can be understood as parts in the town centre in Arboga with a strong common interest among the local citizens.

The medieval festival

In the survey, the respondents were asked about their opinion of the medieval festival, which is the largest event in Arboga (see Figure 8.5). The festival takes place in Arboga town centre for one week every August and attracted, in total, 70,000 visitors in 2006. Drawing on the critical city marketing literature, one could easily come to the conclusion that the festival mainly addresses external markets and creates tensions or conflicts between local citizens and visitors. However, it is evident that such a conclusion would be too hasty. First, the festival is organized by a non-profit organization with the prime motive of furthering knowledge about the history of Arboga to citizens in Arboga as well as to people from the surrounding area of Mälardalen. The festival addresses, in other words, both internal and external markets.

Figure 8.5 Medieval festival in Arboga
Source: © Krister Olsson (chapter author).

Second, and even more important, a strong majority of the respondents in the survey were of the opinion that the medieval festival addresses both internal and external markets. In addition, there is no evidence for a critique that the festival would give rise to substantial tensions or conflicts between local citizens and visitors. For example, less than one in twenty respondents fully or partially agreed with a statement that the festival forces local citizens away from the town centre. As many as nine out of ten were of the opinion that the festival creates a sense of togetherness among those living in Arboga, and as much as 97 per cent agreed that the festival turns Arboga into a lively town. The same number considered the medieval festival to be good advertising for Arboga. In sum, the survey provides strong evidence that citizens in Arboga feel included in and very much appreciate the medieval festival.

The citizens' view on participation

Important to the survey was to study the degree to which citizens in Arboga feel that they are involved in the planning and management of Arboga town centre. The survey shows that only one out of ten felt involved in decisions regarding the town centre. Moreover, one-fifth was of the opinion that they can influence decisions about the town centre if they want to. The survey indicates that the citizens of

Arboga are not entirely content with the present situation. As much as two-thirds wanted to be more involved in decisions regarding the town centre. In fact, only one-fifth declared that it is up to the politicians alone to make decisions about the town centre.

On the rather straightforward question of *Do you want to be involved in and influence urban planning and management in Arboga?* almost three-fifths replied in affirmative. The critical issue, then, is which means of participation they prefer. The respondents were asked to mark one or two predefined alternatives of participation (see Figure 8.6).

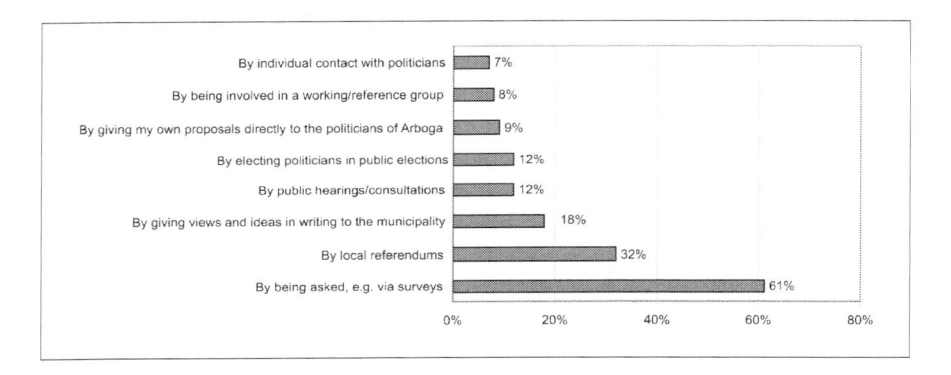

Figure 8.6 Preferred ways of participating in the urban planning and management in Arboga

Source: © Krister Olsson (chapter author).

The result is unambiguous: a great majority of the citizens preferred not to be active and directly involved in the planning and management in Arboga. Traditional means of public participation were thus rejected to the benefit of more distanced forms of participation. Only about one-tenth stated that they wanted to participate by being active in a working/reference group or by attending public hearings/consultations. However, one-third preferred local referendums and as much as two-thirds wanted to participate by being asked, for example via surveys like the one conducted in this study. The latter result strongly supports the main thesis of this study, that is, that a quantitative approach not only is necessary to identify public good characteristics in the urban environment but also suitable and efficient for involving large groups of citizens. However, a critical voice may argue that the result is biased and question it with reference to a research effect. There is, of course, a risk of bias and that the survey method influenced the answers given by the respondents. However, the response rate of 63 per cent speaks on behalf of the trustworthiness of the result. Thus, the number that stated that they wanted to participate by being asked, for example via surveys, equals the number that actually participated in the survey.

Analysis and Discussion

The aim of this chapter has been to discuss why and how the interests and attitudes of local citizens should be taken into account in urban development planning and reinvention processes. The issue of *why* relates to the fact that urban development planning and measures aiming at city attractiveness and competitiveness are mainly oriented towards *selling* cities. Often, a group of local elites more or less define what constitutes 'attractive' urban qualities worth developing and promoting. Moreover, the practice referred to as 'city marketing' in much of the academic literature is generally understood as an outward-looking activity with the objective of attracting external markets to the city. Internal markets are not considered to the same extent. However, internal markets, and local citizens in particular, are always directly or indirectly affected by place reinvention and urban development measures. Furthermore, the internal markets are likely to be much larger and hence much more important than the external ones. Consequently, this is an important reason for taking the interests and attitudes of local citizens into account in the urban development planning processes.

Another reason is that in-depth knowledge on how local citizens experience and value the practice of place reinvention and its manifestations is limited. Drawing on rather general arguments in the literature, either pro-active, prescriptive or critical, there is a risk of ending up with too hasty and incorrect conclusions about the implications of urban development measures. This is exemplified by the survey in which local citizens in Arboga, in sharp contrast to the critique of city selling measures, clearly state that they feel addressed by and very much appreciate the medieval festival. Thus, there is no evidence that the medieval festival benefits external markets, for example visitors, at the expense of internal markets, for example local citizens.

A third reason deriving from the very essence of the descriptive city marketing theory is that all urban planning efforts should begin with market analysis, that is analysis of the interests, attitudes and demand of various consumer groups. Thus, according to the theory, it is the consumers rather than, for example city leaders, politicians and strategic planners, that should define the urban product and what constitutes attractive urban qualities. In contemporary planning theory, there is a strong participatory ideal and an ongoing discussion on how to involve the general public in planning and decision-making processes. However, traditional methods for participation often assume direct involvement and active citizens. Contemporary place reinvention measures includes and affects parts and aspects of the urban environment with a strong common interest, and aims at affecting large groups of citizens. Thus, direct involvement is not realistic and sufficient for evaluating urban development measures from a perspective of local citizens, and for identifying the public good in the urban environment.

When it comes to the issues of *how* to involve citizens, and *how* to understand the public good in the urban environment, it is necessary to acknowledge that the whole is more than the sum of the parts. For example, the pattern of meeting spots in Arboga represent common interests, whereas individual answers, which together make up the pattern, merely represent the private interest of the individual. Hence, this reasoning suggests that the evaluation of city marketing and planning measures and the identification of the public good in the urban environment benefit from quantitative analysis and a systematic mapping of the common interest. Thus, the quantitative approach complements, and adds to, traditional ways of working with public participation, that is citizens taking part in planning in an active and direct way. Furthermore, even though the respondents evidently appreciated various planning measures in Arboga (for example the medieval festival) they were not content with their degree of involvement and the forms of participation. It is clear that the respondents rejected traditional means of participation and preferred more distanced forms, such as the survey in this study.

Surveys directed to large groups of citizens in order to bring out a citizen view on urban development planning measures, and to capture the public good in the environment, have some obvious advantages compared to direct involvement. Through random samples and statistical methods it is possible to reach many citizens in large areas, for example a town. Carefully designed surveys will mean that all respondents have the same opportunity to give input to planning considerations and, in that sense, no-one is excluded from taking part. Thus, the method has, in principle, the potential to involve people that lack the ability and resources to participate in direct ways. However, there are also some obvious problems with surveys, for example questionnaires.

First, not all will respond to surveys, and there are always some missing values. In the survey in Arboga, it was roughly one-third that declined or refused to take part. Thus, it is important to perform a careful analysis of missing values in order to evaluate the quality of the survey, and to ensure that the results are not biased. Second, the use of surveys means that the sender will decide which issues are important to discuss and investigate. Consequently, this puts further demands on the design of the survey, for example, that questions are not biased and are as open-ended as possible. Third, it should be noted that quantitative analysis does not lead to a detailed understanding of the specific meaning that citizens ascribe to various aspects of the urban environment. In that sense, quantitative and qualitative approaches complement each other, rather than that they could be used interchangeably. Thus, the use of questionnaires could, for example, be a starting point in analysis of the demand of urban products, rather than the end product in a dialogue with citizens in city marketing and urban development planning.

Concluding Remarks

The quantitative approach that has been discussed in this chapter is one possibility to involve citizens and strengthen their input in urban development planning. It is also a practical example of how to identify and measure the demand for public goods in the built environment. Building on the marketing concept, that is that urban products are defined by the demand from targeted groups, in this case local citizens, the approach is a concrete contribution to the issue, which is weakly elaborated on in the literature, of how to perform demand analysis in city marketing and urban planning practice. Moreover, following the reasoning in this chapter, a sustainable reinvention of place is hardly a supply-oriented process aiming at selling cities to external markets, but a demand-oriented process in which the input from local citizens has a key role.

References

Alexander, E. (2008), 'Public participation in planning – A multidimensional model: The case of Israel', *Planning Theory & Practice* 9(1), 57–80.

Allmendinger, P. (2002), *Planning Theory* (New York: Palgrave).

Ashworth, J. and Voogd, H. (1988), 'Marketing the city: concepts, processes and Dutch applications', *Town Planning Review* 59(1), 65–79.

Ashworth, J. and Voogd, H. (1990), *Selling the City: Marketing Approaches in Public Sector Urban Planning* (London: Belhaven Press).

Ashworth, J. and Voogd, H. (1994), 'Marketing and place promotion', in Gold and Ward (eds).

Berg van den, L. and Braun, E. (1999), 'Urban competitiveness, marketing and the need for organising capacity', *Urban Studies*, 36(5–6), 987–99.

Berglund, E. (2006), *Stockholm, Restauranger och Marknadsföring* (Stockholm: KTH).

Blücher, G. and Graninger, G. (eds) (2006), *Planering med nya förutsättningar: Ny lagstiftning. Nya värderingar* (Linköping: Linköping University Electronic Press).

Borchert, J.G. (1994), 'Urban marketing: A review. In managing and marketing of urban development and urban life', in Braun (ed.).

Braun, G.O. (ed.) (1994), *Proceedings of the IGU – Commission on 'Urban Development and Urban Life'*, Berlin, 15 to 20 August 1994.

Campbell, S. and Fainstein, S. (eds) (2003), *Readings in Planning Theory* (Oxford: Blackwell).

Eisinger, P. (2000), 'The politics of bread and circuses. Building the city for the visitor class', *Urban Affairs Review* 35(33), 316–33.

Fainstein, S.S. and Judd, D.R. (eds) (1999), *The Tourist City* (New Haven, London: Yale University Press).

Gold, J.R. and Ward, S.V. (eds) (1994), *The Use of Publicity and Marketing to Sell Towns and Regions* (Chichester: Wiley & Sons Ltd.).

Hajer, M.A. and Wagenaar, H. (eds) (2003), *Deliberative Policy Analysis. Understanding Governance in the Network Society* (Cambridge: Cambridge University Press).

Hall, T. and Hubbard, H. (1998), *The Entrepreneurial City: Geographies of Politics, Regime and Representation* (Chichester: Wiley & Sons Ltd.).

Healey, P. (1997), *Collaborative Planning. Shaping Places in Fragmented Societies* (London: Macmillan Press).

Holcomb, B. (1994), 'City make-overs: Marketing in the postindustrial city', in Gold and Ward (eds).

Innes, J.E. and Booher, D.E. (2003), 'Collaborative policymaking: Governance through dialogue', in Hajer and Wagenaar (eds).

Judd, D.R. (1999), 'Constructing the tourist bubble', in Fainstein and Judd (eds).

Khakee, A. (2006), 'Medborgardeltagande i samhällsplanering', in Blücher and Graninger (eds).

Klosterman, R.E. (2003), 'Arguments for and against planning', in Campbell and Fainstein (eds).

Kotler, P. (1972), 'A generic concept of marketing', *Journal of Marketing* 36, 46–54.

Kotler, P. (1986), *Principles of Marketing, The European Edition* (Englewood Cliffs: Prentice Hall Europe).

Kotler, P. et al. (1999), *Marketing Places Europe* (London: Pearson Education Ltd).

Millington, S. (2002), *An Assessment of City Marketing Strategies and Urban Entrepreneurialism in UK Local Authorities* (Manchester: Manchester Metropolitan University).

Murray, C. (2001), *Making Sense of Place: New Approaches to Place Marketing* (Leicester: Comedia).

Nilsson, T. (2005), *Till vilken nytta? Om det lokala politiska deltagandets karaktär, komplexitet och konsekvenser* (Lund: Lunds universitet).

Olsson, K. (2003), *Från bevarande till skapande av värde. Kulturmiljövården i kunskapssamhället* (Stockholm: KTH).

Olsson, K. (2006), *Bilden av Ystad* (Stockholm: KTH).

Olsson, K. (2008), 'Citizen input in urban heritage management and planning. A quantitative approach to citizen participation', *Town Planning Review* 79(4), 25–48. (In press.)

Olsson, K. and Berglund, E. (2008), *Medborgare, kulturmiljö och planering. Ett kvantitativt angreppssätt på medborgardeltagande* (Stockholm: Riksantikvarieämbetet).

Sandercock, L. (2003), *Cosmopolis II: Mongrel Cities in the 21st Century* (London: Continuum).

Ward, S. (1998), *Selling Places: The Marketing and Promotion of Towns and Cities, 1850–2000* (London: E & FN Spon).

Zukin, S. (1995), *The Cultures of Cities* (Oxford: Blackwell).

Chapter 9
Cool & Crazy:
Place Reinvention through Filmmaking

Gry Paulgaard

The fishing port of Berlevåg is about as far as you can get from anywhere, perching on the Barents Sea above the Arctic Circle in Finnmark, Norway's northernmost county. Despite the remote location and frozen terrain, Berlevåg has something to warm hearts across much of Europe – a 30-man amateur choral ensemble starring in a poignant and quirky film called *Heftig & Begeistret*, or *Cool & Crazy*.

(Bird 2002)

Some years ago, a documentary film starring a number of mostly rather elderly men living in a small fishing village in the northern part of Norway, turned out to be one of the greatest successes, nationally and internationally, in the history of Norwegian film (Sørensen 2004). Surprisingly, the film also gained the credit for shooting Berlevåg itself from 'remote obscurity to international acclaim' (Smith 2002).

The film *Heftig & Begeistret* very loosely translated as *Cool & Crazy* for its international release, is a feature-length documentary made by the Norwegian film director Knut Erik Jenssen (2001). After the launching of the film at the Tromsø International Film Festival in January 2001, it became a big hit in Norwegian, Scandinavian as well as other European cinemas and was also shown in the US and Japan. Many national and international film critics expressed surprise that a documentary about a male choir in the most far-flung northern region, in the Norwegian language with subtitles, was lauded at numerous cinemas and film festivals in and outside Europe. Why should anyone want to see a film about the lives of members of a male choir from the proverbial *back of beyond*? One of them posed the question, '[W]ouldn't watching icicles form be more interesting?' and answered herself, '[A]ctually, no', describing the film as so charming, full of warmth, humour, sensitivity, beauty, social commentary and stirring music that it was able to melt any negative preconceptions (Bird 2002). The 'documusical' was said to be aptly dubbed as an Arctic version of Wim Wenders' *Buena Vista Social Club* (1998),[1] even though a very, very depressed one according to *The Guardian* (Bradshaw 8 February 2002).

---

1   Wim Wenders famous film is a documentary about a legendary group of Cuban musicians named after the Buena Vista Social Club, a members club in Havana, Cuba, that held dances and musical activities, a popular location for musicians to meet and play during

Almost overnight the 'actors' in the film, the members of Berlevåg Male Choir, became national icons. Before the film, the tones from this amateur choir had hardly reached beyond their home town. After the film the choir was invited on tour to various places in Norway and beyond, sang at the Norwegian king's 70th birthday celebration, performed at the Roskilde music festival in front of an enthusiastic 40,000-strong audience, visited New York to perform at Ground Zero and sang in Tokyo when the film was launched in Japan. The choir also released a CD with songs and hymns from the film, which outsold many of Norway's most popular artists (Sørensen 2004).

Even though the film, the film director and the choir received international acclaim, it is not obvious that this should affect and even renovate the meaning of the place Berlevåg. The film actually focuses on just a few of the choristers: 'a pair of geriatric brothers, a former drug addict, a communist, a church organist and the chain-smoking, wheelchair-bound conductor' (Smith 2002). Nevertheless, according to several net sites about this place, the film *Cool & Crazy* 'has created a genuine and common interest in all aspects of life in this fishing village'.[2] It is said that the film has made this place, with less than 1,100 inhabitants, visible on a global map by taking not only the choir, but *the place* out into the world, gaining a reputation for the people there as open-minded and culturally inspired.[3] The uniqueness, attractiveness and self-confidence linked to the place seem to be hugely strengthened by the acclaim which the film has received.

As described earlier in this book, the attempt to construct a new 'place image' is seldom limited to the launching of a new advertising campaign (Hubbard 1996, and Chapter 1), '[m]atters of place meaning are also involved in interplays with informal levels of social processes that together put the meaning of place on the agenda, not only in terms of strategic development work, but also in terms of people's everyday life experiences' (Nyseth and Granås 2007,15). Narratives, both cinematic narratives and others, are also a part of people's everyday life experiences, representing a collective experience embedded in a particularistic world of communication. This chapter will focus on how film might play an important role, even though as an unintended event, in the process of place reinvention.

The concept 'place reinvention' addresses changes that have an influence on the meaning of a place, both for the inhabitants and for people in the world outside. Film has the capacity to reach huge audiences across distances and borders. The way a film is received by an external public does not necessarily

---

the 1940s. The success of the film and the album made by the Cuban performers in the film, sparked a revival of international interest in traditional Cuban music and Latin American music in general.

2   Welcome to visit Norway, Berlevåg (http://www.visitnorway.com/templates/ NTRarticle.aspx?id=41776, accessed 4 April 2008).

3   Welcome to Berlevåg an active fishing community (http:www.visitnorway.com/ templates/NTRDestinationArticle.aspx?id=165290, accessed 13 March 2008).

coincide with the way an internal public understands the film. Different audiences might read different meanings into the same narrative. Nevertheless, by making a narrative available in public, the text is given authority and thereby potential influence and validity by others (Moldenæs, Chapter 10). Cinematic narratives as films, especially popular films, have the possibility to attract attention in different media. In order to clarify how film may contribute in the symbolic construction of respectively country and regional image, two other films, very different from *Cool & Crazy*, will also be brought into the discussion: *The Hunters* made by the Swedish director Kjell Sundvall (1996) and *Borat, Cultural Learnings of America for Make Benefit Glorious Nation of Kazakhstan* (2006) made by the Jewish-American director Larry Charles (2006).

The major empirical basis for this chapter is the film *Cool & Crazy*, web reviews about the film and web sites about Berlevåg, together with conversations and interviews with some of the members of the choir and other people in Berlevåg. I have done field studies in the coastal areas of Finnmark for several years, also in Berlevåg, before *Cool & Crazy* was made and after. Part of this empirical material constitutes the background for the discussions in the chapter.

A focal point in this presentation is to discuss how the cinematic narrative in *Cool & Crazy* is organized and put together into 'a narrative sequence providing fidelity and resonance' (Eder 2006). The film was considered to melt any negative preconceptions; a statement indicating the existence of negative images embedded in the knowledge of this northern area. Since the film was received with such a big surprise, and also received fidelity and resonance both abroad and at home, it is important to examine how this cinematic narrative corresponds with other narratives of people and places in this region. This will make it possible to understand how the film *Cool & Crazy* might contribute in the construction and redefining of meaning and identity of Berlevåg.

'The Reality of Images': A Constructivist Perspective on Place Reinvention

Constructivism implies that ideas and images represent a form of reality, not of material but of a discursive nature. Analyses of the 'reality of images' (Eder 2006) can illuminate how various narratives play an important part in the construction of identity. The 'reality of images', in Eder's use of the term, refers to how the narrative construction of European boundaries are encoded in other types of texts indicating a pre-institutional social reality. Images and identities, as well as ideas, are not constructed in a vacuum, or by assuming a tabula rasa (van Ham 2008). Indeed, they are rigorously circumscribed by the webs of understanding of practices, identities and interests of other actors that prevail in particular contexts. Therefore, the assumption that 'there is something behind' constructions of reality is justified (Eder 2006). Places as well as persons are entangled in a web of meanings and expectations. It might be more appropriate to refer to reconstructions rather than constructions (Kjørup 2003). The *reality* of images is defined in relation to 'layers of other constructions that define their relative strength and plausibility' (Aspers 2002). As such, the fidelity and resonance of images and identities are embedded in a discursive universe that makes narrative sense for people.

One crucial point regarding both the possibilities and the constraints for the construction of identities and uniqueness is the meaning of others, both 'real others' and 'virtual others'. This seems to have been omitted by some of the theorists who focus on the endless freedom both people and places in contemporary society have for the creative construction of uniqueness:

> As cultural critics proclaim this postmodern era the age of nomadism, the time when fixed identities and boundaries lose their meaning and everything is in flux, when border crossing is the order of the day, the real truth is that most people find it very difficult to journey away from familiar and fixed boundaries ... (Hooks 1996, 2)

The difficulty of 'journeying away' from familiar and fixed boundaries clarifies the importance of others, as crucial for the construction of self and identity. We need others and others' responses, in order to carry out a reflexive self-formation (Mead 1934). Coley (1956) used the metaphor 'looking-glass-self' to emphasize the meaning of others, referring to the self as a mirror where one sees oneself through others' responses. I understand the concept 'auto-communication', as Turid Moldenæs make use of in Chapter 10 as grounded in some of the same theoretical framework. Moldenæs shows how the concept auto-communication is fruitful in analyses of how one can communicate with oneself through external media in order to confirm and maintain an identity. By using this concept she also clarifies the connection and mutual dependence between 'image regarded as external, superficial and unreal' and 'identity regarded as internal, deep and pure' (Moldenæs, Chapter 10)

Massey (2005) uses the term 'the encounter with difference' describing how space presents us with the existence of others. Identities are created by means of experiencing similarity and differences. Encounters with differences and otherness are important for perception of uniqueness at a personal as well as territorial and cultural levels. This also affects the symbolic construction of place as bounded enclosed spaces defined through difference (Eriksson 2008a). Encounters with difference are not solely based on face to face meetings with others in different social situations. Narratives do also represent possibilities for encounters with difference, so also cinematic narratives:

> In this age of mixing and hybridity, popular culture, particularly the world of movies, constitutes a new frontier providing a sense of movement, of pulling away from the familiar and journeying into and beyond the world of other. ... Movies remain the perfect vehicle for ... the quintessential experience of border crossing for everyone who wants to take a look at difference and the different without having to experientially engage 'the other'. (Hooks 1996, 2)

Film is here considered as a perfect vehicle for experiencing difference and otherness in contemporary societies. By watching films one does not have to move physically to cross the borders into distant worlds very different from one's own. On the other hand, film represents also a media for identification by experiences of familiarity and resemblance. Film is therefore considered as a representative practice which might have a significant role in the construction of national and regional identities (Hooks 1996; Eriksson 2008a). In the following we shall se how differences are confirmed and reinforced through film, but also how such encounters have the capacity to open borders through attraction and identification.

Encounters with Difference through Film

> ... there is no meaning in the film itself ... the meaning of a film lies in a relationship between the implication of the maker and the inference of the audience. (Worth 1981)

Even though the reality of images presented through film, especially documentary films, might be considered as representations of reality, they do not represent a mirror image of an 'objective reality'. Cinematic narratives, either based on fiction or documentary, represent constructions as well as other narratives. The meaning of a particular film cannot be understood isolated from the social reality that define the plausibility and fidelity of the content for a diverse audience. This does not reduce the importance of the way filmmakers are contributing by the construction of cinematic narratives, but the interpretation of audiovisual images may in many respects invite to another kind of recognition than written narratives.

In an analysis of the Swedish film *The Hunters* (*Jägarna* in Swedish), the geographer Madeleine Eriksson (2008a) discusses how this film contributes to the construction of Swedish national identity in relation to stereotypes of the rural North in Sweden. *The Hunters* is a fiction film, a thriller where the subject is illegal hunting. The film portrays a veteran police officer from Stockholm returning to his native village, starting to work in the local police force. After a while he realizes that his old peaceful hometown is becoming the most dangerous place in the world for him.

A main contrast in the film is the clash between modern ideals and an uncivilized, narrow-minded and profoundly traditional society (Eriksson 2008a). The location of the film is not made explicit, but the location is obviously not anywhere:

> The audience is never explicitly informed where the film takes place. Thus, the reindeer, the woods and the mountains appearing in the opening scenes explain in simple terms that *The Hunters* takes place in the north of Sweden. At one occasion is the location narrowed down to a 'small Norrbotnic community'. In spite of this, when writing about the film in articles and reviews, the film comes

> to signify Norrland or 'up there', a geographical generalization that put an end to representations of a differentiated geographic space. (Eriksson 2008a, 9)

By the director's choice of images, signs and symbols, which are inscribed in a universe of meaning that is already structured, 'everybody knows' where the action takes place. Just by watching the opening scene of *The Hunters*, the audience can *see* where this narrative is located. The meaning of the film is not solely based on the construction of images. These images are encoded in other types of texts, narratives and understandings that define the meaning of this film for the audience. By juxtaposing the cinematic narrative with historical accounts and contemporary news in Swedish media, Eriksson demonstrates how the film reinforces and reproduces representations of the rural north as essentially different from other places and regions in Sweden. She shows how film critics and the general audiences use this film as a reference for descriptions of people, culture and character in the north of Sweden as 'the banal evil in the rural north' (Eriksson 2008a). As, such the North becomes a significant other for defining Swedish national identity.

Another film, the 'mockumentary'[4] comedy *Borat, Cultural Learnings of America for Make Benefit Glorious Nation of Kazakhstan* (hereafter *Borat*), might be regarded as a narrative construction of 'we' and 'other' relations based on national differences. The main character in this film is a fictitious Kazakh journalist 'Borat', travelling through the United States, recording real-life interactions with Americans by saying he is making a documentary to bring back findings for 'benefit of the glorious nation of Kazakhstan'. Even if the main goal of the film was to show how easily ordinary Americans went along with the racist, homophobic and sexist jokes performed by the main character Borat, the country of Kazakhstan came across as a boorish, backward and anti-Semitic country, the armpit of the world (van Ham 2008, 142). The film raised major controversies and was actually banned by many Arab countries and the Russian government discouraged cinemas there from showing it.

In American and Western European cinemas the film became a blockbuster and the main actor, the British comedian Sacha Baron Cohen received a Golden Globe reward for his performance.[5] For the country of Kazakhstan the acclamation of the film was not at all appreciated. It was not considered to 'make benefit of the glorious nation of Kazakhstan', rather the opposite. Kazakh officials reacted very negatively to the picture of the country presented through the film. A spokesman from Kazakhstan's Foreign Ministry appeared at a news conference declaring that Cohen's behaviour was deemed utterly unacceptable, being a concoction of

---

4 A 'mockumentary' film is described as a 'mock documentary', a parody often maintaining or exaggerating the structure of a documentary film. A mockumentary is presented as a documentary even if it in fact contains fiction.

5 Sacha Baron Cohen received the 2007 Golden Globe for 'Best Performance of an Actor in a Motion Picture – Musical or Comedy'.

bad taste and ill manner, completely incompatible with the ethics and civilized behaviour of Kazakhstan's people (van Ham 2008).

None of the scenes from the film *Borat* were shot in Kazakhstan, the connection to the country was solely based on fiction. The Kazakh reactions show that even a fiction film might be considered to be so powerful in defining the image of a country, that official representatives from different countries found it necessary to give official reactions on the movie. Kazakhstan also hired PR firms to counter *Borat*'s impressions and ran several campaigns in different US media in order to alter the image presented in the movie (van Ham 2008). Compared to the film *Cool & Crazy*, the positive resonance of the film *Borat* in the world outside Kazakhstan, was certainly not reciprocated in Kazahkstan itself but rather it provoked a very negative reaction. The response to the film *Borat* exemplifies how the broadcasting of images across borders and distances has an unintended, but powerful impact on the construction of place images. Compared to *The Hunters*, where the audience recognized the location of the film by the use of images embedded in other narratives about Norrland, the presentation of Kazakhstan in the film *Borat* was based on the *lack* of information for a Western audience. To most of the Western world Kazakhstan represents an unknown country behind the Eastern borders. There were no other narratives known about Kazakhstan that could compete with and challenge the negative image of the country presented in the movie. The image of this country presented by the film as the backward, weakly developed and racist other to the West seemed to overshadow the intention of giving a critical presentation of ordinary Americans.

These examples show how narratives presented through external media communicates with an internal as well as an external public, although the content of the message is different when it is made relevant internally. Even though both *Borat* and *The Hunters* are fiction films and therefore not 'real' images of people and places, they are given a particular significance in defining regional and national culture and identity. Diverse audiences read different meanings into the same narrative, but the power to define the validity of the interpretations are not equally distributed. In the case with *Borat*, the reactions from Kazakh authorities were considered to be a lose-lose situation: 'not reacting would be complacent, whereas reacting would look very silly' (van Ham 2008, 143). Films, even if they are amusing, do not only represent simply amusements or time-killing exercises, they might also have ideological functions by producing and reconstructing existing values and differences (Hooks 1996; Hatty 2000; Eriksson 2008a). These examples show how encounters with difference through film might reinforce and reproduce stereotypes and differences, whether it is intentional or not.

Authenticity in an 'Otherwordly' Region

> For city people it is an eye-opener to see humble people expressing their deepest thoughts so fluently. And in such a landscape. (Bird 2002)

As shown earlier, the reviews of the film *Cool & Crazy* emphasizes an almost overwhelming surprise by the fact that a film about a men's choir in the far north became a big hit among film critics as well as the general public. Obviously the film represents something unexpected. The statement above comes from one of the members of the jury at the Gothenburg Film Festival that labelled *Cool & Crazy* the year's best Nordic film in 2001. Surely it was meant as a positive expression, even though the underlining of difference between city people and people in the northern landscape indicate some preconceptions that might be considered as negative. However, the film might have crossed some 'borders' considered as 'an eye-opener for city people' and also, as we have seen 'melt any negative preconceptions'.

The quotation above might indicate some similarities between city people and the choir, but this image is not unambiguous. According to a film critic in *Time*, *Cool & Crazy* paints a portrait of men that 'love the simple things that give their lives meaning – family, singing and home in an otherwordly region as far from Oslo as Oslo is from Rome' (Bird 2002). Old men who love the simple things in life, might be considered a rather trivial and boring story, as some critics also have declared. A portrait of old men in an 'otherworldy region' seems to be far more interesting, since most of the review material about the film underlines the positive and unexpected attraction created by this cinematic narrative.

The word 'otherworldy' gives associations to a zone of otherness, not only an out-of-the-way position in strict geographical terms, but more of a supernatural or magical space. Even though the choir performs some religious hymns, the 'otherworldy' image seems not to be used to refer to ordinary religious motifs or unearthly creatures. On the contrary, the subjects in the film might be regarded as quite ordinary men, mostly old men, living their rather ordinary lives in a fishing village in the north of Norway. The average age of the choir seems to be around 70, with ages of the men ranging from around 30 to the choir's oldest member in his mid 90s. They live in a place where the progressive decline of the fisheries has made an important and negative impact on the local community. The population is decreasing. Out-migration of young people has caused an increasing percentage of elderly people in the population. One of the choir members is the chief of the social security office, in the film he says he is 'the employer of the choir'.

The men live in a place where the climate is harsh, cold and windy, except for the beautiful midnight summer period. Many of the scenes show the choir standing outdoors in the freezing winter singing in the windy and bitter cold landscape. Some of the singers are photographed close up, showing they have icicles hanging from their nose and beard. Repeatedly we are offered a close look at the snow-white-capped waves crashing into the stones and the breakwaters in the harbour. It seems as if without the mole the waves would have smashed the whole village to matchwood (Jenssen 2005).

A running theme in the film is 'how the choir offers an escape from the hardships of the real world, while the camaraderie it inspires brings warmth and good humour to this most forbidden outpost' (Smith 2002). The narrative is built up by different sequences showing the choir's preparation to hit the road to perform a concert in the Russian town of Murmansk. A climax at the end of the film is the concert itself in front of an enthusiastic audience. The men in the choir seem to work together very well, except for a furious row about the communist past of Russia on the bus trip to Murmansk. The most politically active singer roars: 'Lenin was the greatest man of the 20th century! You [he says to the others] probably think that Bjørn from the Fishermen's Union was the greatest'. The use of black humour and self irony is an important aspect of the communication throughout the film, alongside other emotional expressions such as sadness, anger, love and friendship.

Travelling through an environment polluted by the former Soviet industry some of the men seem to be brought to tears by the idea of ruining the earth. In contrast to what they see of the landscape on the Russian side of the border, their home town takes on quite another appearance. One of the film critics says that the choir's concert in Murmansk 'swells with pride for a better way of life, even if they may represent the last generations to enjoy it' (Tobias 2002).

There is considered to be a melancholic core in the film, both through the sentimental and patriotic texts performed by the chorus and the members of the choir themselves 'representing a vanishing group – hardy Norwegians who live off the sea and can sing without irony of ancestral "bearded heroes" '(Bird 2002). The melancholic impression is contrasted by the use of humour and self-ironic commentaries. Commenting on his old age, the choir's oldest member says: 'We Strand boys [Strand is his surname] have to be shot, they say we do not die of our own.'

The men's use of humour appears often in flirting suggestions related to sex and gender (Jenssen 2005). The fact that many of the most intimate sequences is filmed by Aslaug Holm,[6] a woman the men considered as extremely competent with the camera, really cheerful and very charming, have contributed strongly to their self expression. One example is a scene where one of the men lies naked in the bathtub singing the Presley song *Can't Help Falling In Love*, saying he used to be quite a Cassanova, but that he finally 'pulled up the anchor' a few years ago. Another man shows the photographer (and the audience) his bedroom, saying 'it used to be a workhouse, but now it is a museum'. A third member of the choir looks straight into the camera and declares with a big smile: 'I really like women, I really do.'

These images show that the men in the choir seem to love women as much as they love singing and fellowship. They appear as charming, honest and comfortable in front of the camera. In an interview with BBC 4 (9 December 2002) the director of the film says: 'These people with old clothes and faces are about as much themselves as you can reach within the media.' From many of the reviews, it seems as if Jenssen has succeeded in communicating an authentic and

---

6 Aslaug Holm is one of Norway's most well known camera women and director of documentaries; she worked as a director of photography and editor on the film. She received the award of the Norwegian Film Association for her work on *Cool & Crazy*.

genuine narrative: 'We get a good idea of what life might be like way north of the Arctic Circle, where the only real livelihood is the town's one remaining fish cannery' (Erickson 2002, 2007).

What we see on the screen goes very well with other images, stereotypes and narratives of northerners as open minded, frivolous, boastful and immodest. As such the reality of images in this film is not representing a break with other types of texts and understanding of people in this area as we shall see. Since the film has been greeted with such a big surprise and is considered to represent an eye-opener for city people, this narrative must also represent something unexpected. In the following this chapter will examine how the film corresponds with other narratives, myths and stereotypes of people in the northern region.

'The Back of Beyond'; The North as the Other Pole

> Nobody, Norwegians or Russian looks the slightest bit alienated, backward, or deprived for living in such a remote corner of the globe. (Erickson 2002, 2007)

The remoteness and the peripheral status of Berlevåg are emphasized in all the critiques and reviews of the film *Cool & Crazy*. Berlevåg, as all the other places in the north of Norway, is far away from all the geographical centres in Europe and the rest of the world. However, the conceptions of this place as 'far away from anywhere', a 'remote obscurity' or 'otherworldly' are not only defined by geographical terms. As indicated in the quotation above the remoteness also refers to particular characteristics of people living here. Understanding of the North as a remote position is embedded in 'layers of other constructions' (Aspers 2002), defining geographical differences in relation to cultural systems and value hierarchies.

Klaus Eder's analysis of 'Europe's Borders. The Narrative Construction of the Boundaries of Europe' (2006) shows how the North is constructed in a European context: 'The North represents the natural past, a kind of primordial reference of a people struggling with nature' (ibid., 265).

Images of the North as 'the natural past' might inhibit both positive and negative connotations, but the coding of the northern periphery as the complete antithesis to the modern, urban civilizations seems to be more or less constant (Paulgaard 2008). This particular hegemonic understanding divides the world both in time and space, space turns into time, geography into history (Massey 2005). Jonathan Friedman (1996, 5) terms this temporalization of space a mistranslation of space into time, including both primitivism and evolutionism: '[T]he difference between them lies in the respectively negative versus positive evaluation of this temporal relation, an imaginary continuum'. Within such a universe of meaning, the North represents an 'otherworldy' region referring to the 'natural past' in relation to modern, urban centres and city people.

At a symbolic level the hegemonic narrative of the northern periphery functions as an encounter with difference (Massey 2005). The North becomes a zone of otherness, fundamentally different to other territories and places in the South – the centre. This core contrast between centre and periphery contributes to the construction of the North as essentially different, whether it is figured as idyllic or troubled, magic or backward, alienated and deprived. The expression of surprise, since the men in the choir don't 'look the slightest bit alienated, backward or deprived by living in such a remote corner of the globe', is rooted in such a hegemonic and stereotypical narrative.

The understanding of the film *The Hunters*, seems also to be based on this core contrast defining the difference between the northern region and the southern region in Sweden (Eriksson 2008a). According to the representation of Norrland as a backward region and Norrlanders as lazy, traditional and largely responsible for their weaker social, economic and political position, the locality of the film was 'recognized'. In that respect the film is considered to contribute to the reproduction of essentially negative images, myths and stereotypes of Norrland (Eriksson 2008).

The reactions to the film *Borat* can also be understood in relation to the core construction defining the difference between centre and periphery, here as the frame of reference for the differences between the East and the West, where the East represents the periphery and the West represents the centre. Such underpinnings defining the contrast between the centre and the periphery are not easily deconstructed. This narrative represents a 'reality of images' embedded within a well established universe of meanings, even though the social reality is much more complex.

For several years there has been a symbolic struggle over narrative projects providing a plausible way of telling the story of the North. The northerners' resistance against the role as 'national underdogs' has been strongly demonstrated in different ways. There have been a lot of intense debates in different media, where myths about people and places in the North have either been rejected and criticized or defended and praised. On different occasions there has practically been a people's mandate for 'Modern tales of the North'. Some years ago there were a lot of seminars with almost exactly the same title saying, 'Modern tales of the North – do they exist?'

Recently central actors and institutions in the north of Norway describe a new dynamism in this region based on technological development, international cooperation and tourism. Trying to get rid of the old negative identity, the North is constructed as a magic wilderness combined with high modernity, a civilization of people living in a close relationship with nature. This is conceptualized as a (re)enchantment of northern identity and landscapes referring to a virtual reversal in the symbolism of the natural (Guneriussen 2008). During the 19th century the conception of nature and wilderness as an ugly, dangerous, and an inhospitable environment unsuitable for civilized humans changed (Cronon 1996, 78). The reversal of the meaning of wilderness is understood as a critique of rationalized and industrialized modernity, transforming the traditional other to a modern category representing 'a voice of Wisdom, a way of life in tune with nature, a culture in harmony, a gemeinschaft, that we have all but lost' (Friedman 1999, 391). As an antidote to 'unnatural' civilization, wilderness is constructed as something exceptional and out of the ordinary life in modern societies, an almost magic space for freedom and authenticity (Alver 1999, 80; Guneriussen 2008, 242).

Within such a frame of reference the interpretation of Berlevåg as a remote 'otherworldy' region might be given more positive connotations, referring to a genuineness and authenticity in contrast to the ordinary life in modern urban societies. From such an angle *Cool & Crazy* still represents an encounter with difference in relation to an external audience, as *The Hunters* and *Borat*, but the differences might seem to be valued more positively in the first film than in the other two. The exotic 'branding' of a place where stereotypes are given a positive or negative value can be seen as a way of 'putting culture on display' and must not be confused with the way people identify themselves and their localities (Olsen 2003). However, the symbolic struggle over narrative projects shows how narratives are taken seriously, representing symbolical material in the construction of both images and identities.

Visual Mediation – Otherness and Identification

> Movies make magic. They change things. They take the real and make it into something else right before our very eyes … They give the reimagined, reinvented version of the real. (Hooks 1996, 1)

Films do not merely offer us the opportunity for reimagining people, places and cultures on the screen, they also have the possibility to transform culture right before our eyes by their capacity to create new awareness about what we are seeing (Hooks 1996, 9). It is not unusual for the images in a cinematic narrative to be constructed by the use of aesthetical aspects manipulating the audience in order to create identification both in fiction films and documentaries (Jenssen 2005). The director of *Cool & Crazy*, Knut Erik Jensen, is known to challenge the limits of a classical documentary (Sørensen 2004). In *Cool & Crazy* he wanted to show the contact between the people and nature:

> I wanted to show that the people belonged to the nature and that they are singing towards the sea. The song at the beginning of the film is emerging from the sea. These people's lives are based on the sea and the songs and the way they behave is directly related to that. That simplicity gives several dimensions to the songs. The contrast between the old men's faces and the context of the songs and the places where they sing means it can be very emotional. (BBC 4 2002)

The manipulation of visual images and sound, by staging attractive tableaux for the songs and the choir, placing special emphasis on the weathered faces of the choir members and the severe beauty and wilderness of the landscape gives an almost surrealistic impression. Scenes showing the choir standing outdoors in the middle of the winter singing in the drifting snow, represent a total break with 'common sense'. Although the songs are almost drowned out by the roaring wind and the waves from the sea, these images create a much stronger emotional effect than recordings of the choir in more natural indoor settings. The patriotic and religious songs are said to ring like an 'indomitable force of nature':

> Braced resolutely against the elements, as the Barents Sea pummels the rocks in the background and a howling blizzard chips more divots into their craggy faces, the roughly 30 members of the Berlevåg Male Choir open Knut Erik Jensen's documentary *Cool and Crazy* in a triumphant march toward the camera. Citizens of a tiny fishing village on the Norwegian coast, within a casting distance from the North Pole, they sing in a thunderous baritone that seems designed to hold sway with the impossible brutal weather. (Tobias 2002)

The constructions and manipulation of rather exotic images using the northern weather and spectacular nature as an extraordinary stage set, represent powerful tools in order to attract the audience. Thus the choir is transformed from an ordinary amateur choir, to an unconquerable force of singers out of nature, giving an almost magic impression. This image corresponds both with narratives of the North 'as the natural past' (cf. Eder 2006) and with new narratives of the magic North. Even though the film gives a reinvented version of reality it also confirms stereotypes of people in this area. One critic characterized the men as 'frost-bedecked ancients' and told the audience to 'prepare to be surprised by the men's resilience and good humour' (Fraser 2001). Another characterized the men as the tough survivors of one of the world's coldest climates, 'fishermen burned and carved by the wind and the sun' (La Croix 2002). The exotic image reinforces the construction of otherness and difference in relation to other areas of the world.

Like other texts and narratives, this film is 'read' within an established universe of meaning that makes sense. This constitutes an important background for what people see and expect to see in the film. The narrative background is also important in order to create a surprising and emotional effect. By showing that the men in the choir are not only frost-bedecked ancient stereotypes, but real humans, expressing their deepest thoughts about the simple things that gives their life meaning, the film manages to create resemblance and identification across borders and distances:

Perhaps the genius of the movie is the fact that anyone can recognize the people in the movie with someone you already know. One of my best friends, a 22-year-old woman, for the time being living in Denmark, said about *Heftig og Begeistret*: 'I feel like they could have made this film in my home place and come to the same result'. (Ronnyb 2001)

The men in the choir do not appear as totally different from other people despite the exotic and 'otherworldy' impression. For an external audience the encounter with familiarity and similarity, behind all the exotic otherness might come as a great surprise. This seems to add an extra glow to the emotional relationship between the film, or the people in the film, and the audience. The influential film critic in the British newspaper, the *Observer*, Phillip French (2002) declared that *Cool & Crazy* had improved his quality of life (Sørensen 2004). Another film critic wrote: 'Some may think it trivializes the lives of the subjects in the film, but I feel it celebrates them. It shows us how all our lives however ordinary they may seem to us, can be inspirational to others' (Miller 2005).

This film both confirms and challenges stereotypes, creates experiences of otherness as well as familiarity and resemblance. Encoded in other types of texts indicating a pre-institutional social reality the North is recognized as a 'space of exception' (Eriksson 2008b), this seems to have strengthened the 'border crossing effect', by revealing the men behind the stereotyped, frost-bedecked old faces in 'this most forbidden outpost', at least for the external public.

The Place and the Film

> Before the film people said the seagulls flew upside down over Berlevåg, they did not want to see the misery below. (choir member 2008)

Seen from Berlevåg the place is neither 'otherworldy', nor 'as far as you can get from anywhere'. It is home for around 1,100 people, young and old, women and men, singers and non-singers. I have spoken with some of these people and all of them say that watching their home town and their neighbours on a wide screen was rather strange. Shortly after the film was released, there were a lot of jokes about the old men in the choir. Some also suggested that the film painted a negative portrait of the place since the film only focused on pensioners and other unemployed people. Both members of the choir and other people in Berlevåg say they had never dreamt that this film could become such a great success nationally and internationally.

The film was released at a time when the place had been under a rather depressive atmosphere for several years. As with many of the other fishing villages in northern Norway, Berlevåg had experienced large periods of progressive decline and closure of fisheries with considerable impact on the local economy and working possibilities. Young people were moving, there was a lack of jobs and the unemployment rate was very high. Compared with the continual stories of success constructed by the people in Båtsfjord, a place in the vicinity (Moldenæs, Chapter 10), the mood in Berlevåg was gloomy where people spoke negatively about the place. Many had hoped the success of *Cool & Crazy* and the choir would stimulate new growth concerning working possibilities and migration to Berlevåg. This has not happened. Even though the members of the choir experienced a dramatic change in their lives, going from anonymity (at least outside this community) to becoming celebrities, this did not affect the way other people in Berlevåg lived their lives.

However, the acclamation of the film and the choir did have an uplifting effect locally. A young woman from Berlevåg says that people started to talk more positively about the place after the film. After the initial surprise of the overwhelming success the film engendered proud feelings of the place, the nature and the history of the area. Suddenly the place was known outside the region. When visiting other places everybody knows about my home town because of *Cool & Crazy*, a girl said. Coming from a small place in Finnmark, the northernmost county in Norway, this kind of knowledge is not to be taken for granted.

The spin-off effect of the film at home is not *only* about placing Berlevåg on the map and making the place visible nationally and internationally, it also has to do with what people see in the film, how it is interpreted in relation to other narratives. When the film received national and international acclaim, the narratives about the film and the place in different media gave quite another image of the place than negative reports about bankruptcies in the fishing industry, lack of work and high out-migration. Watching their home place trough not only the camera lenses, but also the reactions and reviews from film critics and an external public, seems to have confirmed and strengthened the local identity in a positive manner. Berlevåg had something other people appreciated and valued.

The fact that *Cool & Crazy* in many respects reinvents the place as more exotic, confirming traditional myths and stereotypes of otherness, not necessarily coinciding with the discursive universe and daily life in which many of the locals live, does not prevent local identification. The nature, the weather, the choir, the fellowship, the humour and small talk situations, was recognized within this society. The external appreciation of fellowship which the film envisages, promotes local identification (Christensen 2004; Moldenæs Chapter 10). The response from others through different media reflected back, not only to those who made this film and the choir, but towards the public in Berlevåg. They had the opportunity to see their home place in the mirror of others' response in a way that served to reinvigorate the consciousness and place identity within the local context. Thus the experience of positive response and identification from an external public contributes to the reinvention of identity through communication and confirmation from others in different media.

Concluding Remarks

Film represents a powerful media because of the capacity to create engagement, social commitment and attraction as well as uneasiness, horror and aversion. Historically this has been strongly demonstrated through fascist regimes in Italy and Germany that used film as a means of propaganda for their ideology and politics (Jenssen 2005). The power of film can be understood as a kind of 'soft power', defined as: '... the ability to get what you want through attraction rather than coercion or payments' (Nye 2004, 256). The concept of soft power contrasts the subtle effects of culture, values, symbols and ideas with direct coercive measures through hard power, for instance military action and economic incentives in world politics. As a contrast to hard power, soft power is considered a significant asset in influencing others by the ability to attract which goes beyond influence and persuasion.

The films discussed in this chapter – *Borat*, *The Hunters* and *Cool & Crazy* – have influenced others by the ability to attract a large public. The films have also contributed to symbolic constructions of place images even though I will not claim that the directors of *The Hunters* and *Borat* 'got what they wanted' (cf. Nye's (ibid.) definition of soft power) through the audiences response to the films. While *Cool & Crazy* received credibility and resonance by attracting the public at home as well as an external public, the cinematic narratives mediated in *Borat* and *The Hunters* are not appreciated within the areas these films pretended to represent. The three films discussed in this chapter are very different; the only similarity is the way they act as encounters with difference within territorial contexts. *Borat* and *The Hunters* are considered as solely based on stereotypes, perhaps not so strange since they are fiction films. *Cool & Crazy* might also be considered as based on stereotypes, but the audience gets an opportunity to meet the people behind the stereotypical images. This seems to have created attraction, especially from an external public.

In order to attract the audience through film, the filmmaker must be attracted in the first place, as the circular nature of seduction outlined in Moldenæs' account for the concept auto-communication (Chapter 10). The film director Knut Erik Jensen comes from a neighbouring municipality in Finnmark and has made several documentaries, short films and feature films during a period of more than thirty years. With *Cool & Crazy* he is said to bring to screen a world he knows and loves: 'And he does it in a spirit of the people he portrays, with irreverence and wit and highly charged'(Norwegian Film Institute 2003).

Describing how visual media can bring new comprehension in the field of visual anthropology, the Norwegian researcher Toril Jenssen (2005) shows how personal commitment always is necessary in the professional treatment of film work. In order to make the public identify with the subjects in the film, the filmmaker must be able to give them dignity through the (re)presentation on the screen. Referring to Benjamin (1975), Jenssen describes how the audiences who see a film are taking over the eye of the camera. 'The audience identify with the people they see by identifying with the camera' (ibid., 298). The director of *Cool & Crazy* has managed to let the choir members attract the public through the film; they appear with all their charm in front of the camera. This is especially evident in the scenes photographed by Aslaug Holm.

The construction of narratives through film is not independent of the relationship between the 'constructor' and the subjects. Film work is therefore not that different from fieldwork and the construction of knowledge through narratives within social science (Paulgaard 1997). Although interpretations of audiovisual images might invite another kind of recognition than written narratives, the power of a particular film is embedded in a discursive universe that makes sense. Within the context of other narratives of the North, *Cool & Crazy* has managed to surprise the audience by letting them 'journey away from familiar and fixed boundaries' by the encounter of familiarity with people on the northern rim. As a centre for the events in the film Berlevåg is reinvented as a remote 'otherworldly' periphery within the modern world.

References

Alver, B.G. (1999), *Myte, magi og mirakel* (Oslo: Pax).

Aspers, P. (2002), 'Vad skulle det annars vara? Om socialkonstruktivism', *Sosiologi i dag*, 2, 23–39.

BBC 4 Storyville – Knut Erik Jensen Interview, bbc.co.uk (published online 9 December 2002, http://www.bbc.co.uk/print/bbcfour/documentaries/storyville/jensen-interview.shtml).

Bird, M. (2002), 'Singing in the Snow', *Time* in partnership with CNN (11 March) (http://www.time.com/time/printout/0,8816,216364,00.html, accessed 4 March 2008).

Benjamin, W. (1975), *Kunstverket i reproduksjonsalderen* (Oslo: Gyldendal Norsk Forlag).

Bradshaw, P. (2002), '*Cool and Crazy*', *The Guardian* (published online 8 February 2008) (http:/film.guardian.co.uk/News_Story/Critic_Review/Guardian_review/=,4267,646566,00.html, accessed 4 March 2008).

Christensen, L.T. (2004): 'Det forførende medie. Om autokommunikasjon i markedsføringen', *Mediekultur*, 37.

Coley, C.H. (1956), *The Two Major Works of Charles H. Holey: Social Organization; Human Nature and the Social Order* (Glencoe, Free).

Cronon, W. (1996), *Uncommon Ground. Rethinking the Human Place in Nature* (New York: W.W. Norton & Company).

Eder, K. (2006), 'Europe's Borders. The Narrative Construction of the Boundaries of Europe', *European Journal of Social Theory*, 9(2), 255–71.

Erickson, G. (2007), '*Cool & Crazy* DVD Savant Text' (published online 23 January 2002) (http://www.dvdtalk.com/dvdsavant/s505cool.html, accessed 25 May 2008).

Eriksson, M. (2008a), 'Urban and rural imaginaries in Sweden, the intercontextual workings of a film', paper presented at The 'Spatial Justice' International Conference. 12–14 March Paris, France, accepted for publishing in *Journal of Rural Studies*, (Thompson Reuters).

Eriksson, M. (2008b), '(Re)producing a "peripheral" region – northern Sweden in the news', *Geografiska Annaler*, Series B, Human Geography, 90(4), 1–20.

Fraser, N. (2001), *Cool & Crazy*, Storyville Homepage, BBC 4 (published online 19 December 2004) (http://www.bbc.co.uk/bbcfour/documentaries/storyville/cool-and-crazy.shtml, accessed 4 March 2008).

Friedman, J. (1996), *Cultural identity & Global Process* (London: Sage Publications).

Friedman, J. (1999), 'Indigenous struggle and the Discreet Charm of the Bourgeoisie', *Journal of World-System Research*, 2, 391–411.

Guneriussen, W. (2008), 'Modernity Re-enchanted: Making a "Magic" Region', in: Bærenholdt, J.O. and Granås, B. (eds), *Mobility and Place. Enacting Northern European Peripheries* (Aldershot: Ashgate).

Hatty, S.E. (2000), *Masculinities, Violence, and Culture* (London: Sage Publications Inc).

Hooks, B (1996), *Reel to be Reel, Race, Sex and Class at the Movies* (London: Routledge).

Hubbard, P. (1996), *People and Place; The Extraordinary Geographies of Everyday Life* (Harlow: Prentice Hall).

Jenssen, T. (2005), '*Cool & Crazy*: Anthropological Film at the Point of Convergence between Humanities and Social Science', *Visual Anthropology*, 18, 291–308.

Kjørup, S. (2003), *Menneskevidenskaperne. Problemer og traditioner i humanioras Videnskapsteori* (Roskilde Universitets Forlag).

La Croix, J.K. (2002), '*Cool & Crazy* review', *Metro Times*, Detroit (published online 2 December) <http://www.metrotimes.com/editoral/printereview.asp?id=61229, accessed 25 April 2008).

Massey, D. (2005), *For Space* (London: Sage Publications).

Mead, G.H. (1934), *Mind, Self and Society. From the Standpoint of a Social Behaviorist* (Chicago and London: The University of Chicago Press).

Moldenæs, T. (2009), 'Reinventing a place through the myth of creation; the case of Båtsfjord', in: Nyseth, T. and Viken, A. (eds), *Place Reinvention: Northern Perspectives*, (London: Ashgate).

Miller, A. (2005), 'Truth is stranger than fiction', IMDb user comments for *Heftig og Begeistret* (published online 26 June) (http://us.imdb.com/title/tt0276189/usercomments, accessed 25 April 2008).Norwegian Film Institute (2003), *Cool & Crazy*, (http:/www.nfi.no/english/norwegianfilms/show_utskrift.html?id=284, accessed 13 April 2008).

Nye, J.S. Jr (2004), *Soft Power. The Means to Success in World Politics* (New York: Public Affairs).

Nyseth, T. and Granås, B. (2007), *Place Reinvention in the North – Dynamics and Governance Perspectives* (Stockholm: Nordregio report 1).

Olsen, K. (2003), 'The Touristic Construction of the "Emblematic" Sámi', *Acta Borealia, Nordic Journal of Circumpolar Societies*, 20(1), 3–20.

Paulgaard, G. (1997), 'Feltarbeid i egen kultur – innenfra, utenfra eller begge deler?' in: Erik Fossåskaret, Otto Laurits Fuglestad, and Tor Halvdan Aase (eds), *Metodisk feltarbeid, produksjon og tolkning av kvalitative data* (Oslo: Universitetsforlaget).

Paulgaard, G. (2008), 'Re-centering Periphery. Negotiating Identities in Time and Space', in: Granås, B. and Bærenholdt, J.O. (eds), *Mobility and Place* (London: Ashgate).

Ronnyb (2001), Fantastic movie, IMDb user comments for *Heftig og Begeistret* (published online 14 March) (http://us.imdb.com/title/tt0276189/usercomments, accessed 25 April 2008).

Smith, N. (2002), *Cool & Crazy*, BBC – Films – Review (published online 29 January) (http://www.bbc.co.uk/films/2002/01/29/cool_and_crazy_review_2002-review.shtml, accessed 13 March 2008).

Sørensen, B. (2004), 'Den standhaftige finnmarkingen. Knut Erik Jenssen og suksessen "*Heftig og Begeistret*" ', *Ottar*, nr 3.

Tobias, S. (2002), '*Cool & Crazy*', The AV Club (published online 29 March) (http://www.avclub.com/content/node/5554, accessed 25 April 2008).

van Ham, P. (2008), 'Place Branding: The State of the Art', American Academy of Political Social Science, ANNALS, AAPSS, 616, March 2008 (pp.126–49)

Worth, S. (1981), *Studying Visual Communication* (Philadelphia: University of Pennsylvania Press).

Chapter 10

Reinventing a Place through the Origin Myth

Turid Moldenæs

Without story and myth, there is no public dream.

(Bolman and Deal 2001, 149)

I arrived in Båtsfjord, a small fishing village in Finnmark, the northernmost county of Norway, in the autumn of 1997. The previous year had been a good one for the fishing industry as the government had set generous fish quotas, and the market prices for fish were good. In 1997, however, quotas were drastically reduced. In the neighbouring settlement of Vardø, the outlook was pessimistic. Many had already considered moving out of the region. I was not familiar with Båtsfjord at that time, but aware that both settlements were dependent on the fishing industry. I thus assumed that the atmosphere was the same in both places. On arrival, I took a taxi and struck a conversation with the driver and asked: 'How is it in Båtsfjord, have you thought about moving out when the fishing quota is reduced?' To my surprise the driver laughed and answered: 'Move? No! It is Hagbart, Kjell Olaf and Øystein who determine what will happen. It's always been like that.' This response was surprising for two reasons. First, it was unexpected given the prevailing sentiments in the neighbouring fishing community. Second, it indicated confidence in the ability of people within the community to sort out its problems – in stark contrast to general notions about the culture and mentality of the people of North Norway.

The taxi driver's remarks can be understood as an autobiographic act expressing something about the identity of this place (cf. Czarniawska 1997). In a number of subsequent conversations with local residents, the image of a place with a strong faith in its own ability to manage its destiny has been further supported. In addition, the residents have pictured Båtsfjord as a new settlement whose origins commenced at the end of Second World War, in spite of the fact that evidence suggests that the settlement began to flourish around 1900 (Solhaug 1979). It appears as though the community has reinvented itself in the post-war period as an entirely new kind of place characterized by development, innovation and growth, and that it has continually reinvented itself ever since.

Rather than a 'tale of two cities', this chapter is the story of a fishing village to the far north of Norway.[1] As a small settlement, there is nothing special about Båtsfjord. There are several hundred such settlements in Norway with about two

---

1 The expression 'the tale of two cities' is borrowed from the novel *A Tale of Two Cities* written by Charles Dickens.

thousand inhabitants or so, all surviving on industries such as fishing, agriculture, forestry and occasionally mining. What is special about Båtsfjord, are its history and the way its identity has developed. This contrasts with the development of neighbouring settlements. In this chapter I examine Båtsfjord's unique and successful development in a region which is otherwise characterized by out-migration, state subsidies, and the absence of that particular communal spirit which has given Båtsfjord its special identity. I discuss how and why Båtsfjord confirms and reinforces its identity as a successful post-war community. More precisely, this chapter is an analysis of narratives, oral as well as written, which – taken together – provide the autobiography of Båtsfjord; the story of how the identity of this place is created, expressed and confirmed in and through the autobiography itself. Autobiographic acts are often regarded as self-presentations directed towards an external audience. However, they may also be regarded as auto-communication, a manner by which one communicates with oneself in order to confirm and maintain an identity (Christensen 1995). Narrative identity and auto-communication are the two concepts framing the analysis and the subsequent discussion.

Narrative Identity

During the 1990s, there was a narrative turn in the social sciences based on the recognition that narratives are the natural way of communicating (Czarniawska 1997). Narratives of who we are and where we come from are constitutional for society (Christensen and Morsing 2005). Those stories we tell about ourselves are both expressions of and creators of our identity. The narrative approach to identity implies that identity is an on-going story where both the narrator and the listener are joint authors (Czarniawska 1997). A particular literary genre – the autobiography – is closely associated with the study of identity and identity formation. The autobiography which Czarniawska (1997, 53) denotes as 'lives under construction' is based on a retrospective reflection of one's own life course (Anderson 2001, 2004), with a plot providing an account of the development of a specific identity. This occurs, as such, in retrospect when one has a full overview of the story. Moreover, the autobiography often describes a positive development with some complications where the main character experiences difficulties and makes mistakes, finally developing insight and self-recognition. Important events such as birth, crises and successes are consequently normal ingredients in the autobiography. The same applies to individuals such as heroes and villains, friends and enemies, and so on.

Even though many communities have compiled an official 'autobiography' in the form of a contemporary or historical chronicle, it is often the unofficial accounts which express, confirm and eventually redefine the historical development or life-history, and consequently, the character of the place. As such, the identity comprises and is constructed through autobiographic acts, expressions or narratives of what one has undertaken, when and how, and also the context in which such activities took place. The identity of a place is thus created and modified by such events and can be traced in all written documents relating to its history as well as through the day-to-day conversations of the residents (and others). Even though these narratives are produced in both formal and informal settings, it is primarily the more or less spontaneous everyday narratives, written as well as spoken, which establish the basis of a narrative approach to identity.

In this chapter, spoken and written narratives are studied. The spoken narratives have been collected through participation in formal meetings, informal conversations and more than one hundred systematic interviews during the period 1997–2003. The written accounts are local revue scripts and public information documents. In total, these written and oral accounts comprise Båtsfjord's autobiography. Rather than presenting the oral accounts separately as quotes, they are presented as one single, coherent narrative under the title 'The Story of Båtsfjord'. 'The Story of Båtsfjord' is a synthesis of all the oral narratives, and represents what I consider to be the most typical everyday story of the place. As the autobiography is a subjective story told in the first person, related 'from the inside', I have chosen to retain the first person approach in 'The Story of Båtsfjord'.

The revue material covers the period from the late 1980s until the mid 1990s and comprises 33 scripts. Official presentation material (all from the 1990s) includes flyers entitled 'Båtsfjord – An active fishing municipality' (an attempt at recruiting labour from outside), 'Båtsfjord' (a tourist brochure), and 'Båtsfjord. A maritime centre' (information to fishermen about local maritime services). Additional sources include documents describing the largest firms and the local business community, as well as the municipality's web pages.

Narratives as Auto-communication

In the recent literature on marketing and branding, narratives are used as a means of impressing an audience. In such a 'story-telling perspective', the narrative is a strategic, official self-presentation; a symbol without substance. Pertinent here is the distinction between identity and image, where identity is regarded as internal, deep and pure, and image as external, superficial and unreal (Hatch and Schultz 2000). Christensen (2004a) maintains that the general public is far less concerned with the message than the messenger herself. When narratives are considered tools for impression management (cf. Goffman 1959), the communication between the sender and receiver is perceived as a one-way process. According to Christensen, the point is that the circular nature of seduction is neglected. He refers to Baudrillard (1983) who claims that a seducer is only able to seduce if he himself is seduced. Referring to Lotman (1990), Christensen associates the circular nature of seduction with the concept of auto-communication, which comprises 'self-referential acts of communication that organises the sender around its own mental images' (Christensen 2004b, 7). The person communicating is both sender and recipient, simultaneously. In the auto-communication process, culture is defined, rediscovered and reorganized as a self-generating process in much the same way as an individual constitutes his own personality. Auto-communication is therefore essential to the existence and the identity of a community, and an integral part of all cultures. It is primarily directed towards exposing and celebrating common values, codes, and so on, the so-called meta-texts. The meta-texts, or the circumstances related to the message, are thus more important than the message itself. In one sense, communication becomes a constant reminder of the symbols, values and watchwords, which unite a community (Christensen and Cheney 2000). As such, auto-communication is more ritualistic than informative, concerned with meaning and identity (Christensen 2004b).

According to Christensen (2004b), auto-communication occurs every time a sender interprets the message based on her own codes or culture. This also occurs when the sender celebrates and praises herself in the message, while indirectly reminding herself of her own responsibilities and obligations. This can occur through watchwords, visions and strategic plans which are intended to advance internal fellowship and identification, but also through media which are essentially external such as advertising campaigns and autobiographies. Communication through external media frequently has an important message to the internal public, but the message is given a different meaning when it is made internally relevant. A new message is produced at a more general level where the external communication comprises symbols of fellowship, which promote internal identification (Christensen 2004b). When a culture uses its communication with its environments as a mirror where it recognizes its own culture, it is also involved in auto-communication.

Christensen (2004a) maintains that everybody who is confronted with their own texts in external media, experiences that the message is given an aura of seriousness, placing obligations on the sender. This is due to the fact that the text is now available to others in a public and recognized form. External media, irrespective of genre, permit seduction as well as self-seduction. Senders who know that the message will subsequently appear in external media are encouraged in advance to attach particular importance and significance to their own text, irrespective of the status of the particular media chosen. It is then the reflector or 'mirror' which gives authority to the message, and thereby also has potential influence or validity for the sender. To the extent that self-seduction characterizes the presentation, there is a subsequent potential for external seduction (Christensen 2004a). As such, the concept of auto-communication binds together image and identity, and manifests the mutual dependence between them. Identity is thus influenced by image, and the reverse.

From Traditional to Flexible Production

Båtsfjord's origins are usually traced to the years immediately after World War II (Hovgaard 2001). Development then occurred at a rapid pace, both in population growth as well as in the industrial and physical infrastructure. From a population of 200 in 1945 growth commenced at a rapid pace, peaking at 3,000 towards the end of the 1970s. The population increase was mainly due to the need for manpower in the rapidly growing fishing industry. This was originally based on the production of stockfish (dried fish) in the 1950s, but developed into a substantial producer of frozen fish-fillets during the 1960s. The transition from stockfish production to frozen products is partly explained by government initiatives and partly by the crisis in the market for stockfish in the 1960s. Parallel to an increasing population and an expanding fishing industry, the cultural life of the community blossomed – as did the township's infrastructure, including a new social and cultural centre, a new sports hall, an all-year connection to the national state highway, and a local airport.

By the end of the 1980s, the fishing industry was severely hit as the Barents Sea cod stock all but collapsed. This was intensified by increased competition from foreign producers of frozen fillets on international markets – forcing prices down. As the crisis saw young people leaving the township to get an education, population declined. By the 1990s, however, the population had again increased and Båtsfjord became one of the most successful fishing settlements in Norway (Hovgaard 2001). The negative demographic trends had been reversed, largely due to immigration of foreign labour, and a much improved cod fishery. A new soccer field and a new airport served to strengthen the local cultural activities and the infrastructure.

At the turn of the century Båtsfjord had become a household name in Norway. The population had stabilized itself at around 2,400 and the local fishing industry was flourishing. The local volleyball team created headlines nationally by winning the Norwegian Elite League and by playing in the European Cup. According to Hovgaard (2001, 137), the post-war development of Båtsfjord as a 'primus motor' in the region can be partly understood as a result of state-centred 'fordistic modernization', based on large-scale industrialization. Simultaneously, the crisis encouraged local entrepreneurs and strengthened the drive for local ownership, providing the basis for the strong local industrial community which subsequently arose.[2]

This story, built on official statistics and public documents, is one way of narrating Båtsfjord, from the perspective of the outsider and with the voice of the observer, pinpointing objective features such as population growth, industrial development and development of the physical infrastructure. Furthermore, this story has a plot that allows for bringing in, not only the people of Båtsfjord, but also the state as an explanation of Båtsfjord's development after World War II. Another

---

2   In 1981, there was only one locally-owned fishing plant. In 1990, there were four.

way of narrating Båtsfjord is to adopt the perspective of its people, telling the story in their own words. This oral story of how the people of Båtsfjord themselves interpret the place and its development, is an autobiographic act which gives us a story with a different plot, here presented as 'The Story of Båtsfjord'.

'The Story of Båtsfjord'

Båtsfjord is a success! Other fishing communities are now lying on their backs. We have higher employment and more businesses in operation. People do not have to work in plants where they are not happy. Here, all the houses have a new coat of paint. In Vardø, the paint is flaking. Just a few years ago, Båtsfjord was the third richest municipality in the country. In Båtsfjord, people earn 'real money'. The residents believe in investing in their homes and buy expensive houses in a community where there are few, if any, employment opportunities outside fishing. We have managed to generate optimism and faith in our township, not just for the short term, but in the unforeseeable future! Even though some have migrated, we have managed to stabilize the population. We have always wanted to be among the best. We are following a new path!

Båtsfjord is a young community with few traditions. It emerged in the post-war period. The settlement was virtually nothing until the harbour was built and boats got engines. It was then that large numbers of fish-buyers arrived and Båtsfjord became a Klondike-like community which attracted a special type of person: highly creative people who contributed greatly to its development. Most people are in-migrants. Hagbart's father came from Vardø. From outside! As did his brother. They both arrived empty-handed believing that 'we can achieve something here'. Kjell Olaf was also an 'immigrant' – from Lofoten. There aren't many families here whose roots extend back more than two generations. But Øystein is a local lad. This is possibly a good combination. Together, we are dynamite!

In Båtsfjord, there were employment opportunities, which were lacking in Vardø and in Berlevåg. Båtsfjord is a hard-working community. Here, all the women are employed. We do not have the time to sit and moan and groan, like they do in Vardø. Those who are not employed are those who do not want to work. In Båtsfjord, there have been fortune hunters who have worked a lot of overtime. If one did that in Vardø, one would have problems with the union. This created another type of person and other ideals. In Vardø, the women spent the day in cafés. There was also another type of civic organization. A more refined culture. A parlour orchestra with violin and mandolin. And a theatre. We had just the revue. In Vardø, the families go back generations.

When we run into problems, we tackle these ourselves. We don't go running down the corridors of Parliament, shouting for help. The new airport is one example. We called it 'the mini-Gardermoen' after Oslo's main airport. Early in the 1950s, the people of Båtsfjord wanted a road across the mountains. Even though this demand was refused by the authorities, we took pickaxe, spade and barrow and commenced on our own. The local fish buyers were very much involved in this. And take the old airport. What happened was this: in the early 1970s the local residents wanted an airport but the government said no. However, we had this local aero club whose members were determined that we should have an airport. The machine entrepreneurs and the members of the club joined forces. The airport was built! The sports hall was also the result of a joint effort. During the bank and fishery crisis in the 1980s there were 'empty shops' and unemployment. Then the municipality and local business community supported the local volleyball team so that the residents should have something to 'cheer'. And the fish buyers imported cod from Canada to keep the residents employed, even though there was little profit in this. By these means, they ensured that the population would not emigrate.

Coming from Båtsfjord, one is obliged to proclaim that it is the navel of the world. Instead of complaining, we praise ourselves. We don't speak about the negative aspects. They are the same everywhere. Everybody talks negatively about North Norway. We have been good at marketing ourselves positively to the outside world. Outside Båtsfjord they have heard about the fish buyers and the volleyball team. We are also known for having work, being employed. We are not parasites! The fact that Båtsfjord is a success is due to the community spirit. Doing well is typical in Båtsfjord!

Previously, Vardø was the 'big city'. Today Båtsfjord is the big brother. People in Vardø and Berlevåg say: 'You are lucky. You have Hagbart, Kjell Olaf and Øystein!' The three 'big uns' as we refer to them. People have great faith in these guys. But they are not regarded as being above the rest. All three are one of us. Isn't it strange that three such persons should land right here in the middle of Båtsfjord? Without them, the rest of us would be of little use. When something new was in the air, they quickly seized the opportunities. Hagbart was the first one to import fish from Russia; and the one who took up production of frozen fish. The fish buyers have always managed to get hold of fish for processing. The key to the survival of Båtsfjord is local ownership. All three of them have Båtsfjord in their hearts and are willing to invest what they have. They know that we need full-time, round-the-year employment and have managed to achieve this. What has really demonstrated the value of these guys is the fact that the neighbouring communities have come apart at the seams. Our fish buyers have been modern and market-oriented to a much greater degree than those in other fishing settlements along the coast. The local fish buyers have shown the way. They cooperate. So do the fish buyers and the local politicians. In Vardø and Berlevåg the fish buyers have been much more in disagreement. Båtsfjord will survive! As long as we think positively, look to the future and stick to it!

A Modern Identity

'The Story of Båtsfjord' shows that the identity of this community is deeply rooted in fishing and the fishing industry. But in contrast to other comparable fishing communities this is an identity which is associated with being the biggest, the best, the leading and the most modern. The story presented by the inhabitants of Båtsfjord of a promising future is, in other words, partly associated with the negative destinies of the neighbouring communities. The story may be read as an autobiography based on a number of 'stand alone' episodes covering the same theme in an almost never-ending story of success. There is a common theme for all episodes: they are dramatic events, representing turning points in the history of the place (the mountain road, the old and the new airport, the sports hall and the new soccer field, and more). These are stories of conflict and heroism where the same heroes (the residents and their leaders), the same villains (the public officials), the same solutions (community cooperation), and the same successful outcomes are repeated. Båtsfjord is a township established on private initiative, entrepreneurship and joint efforts. It is a place that thrives on its own, and a success accomplished by the inhabitants themselves.

The same place identity is also expressed in official stories and identity expressions. The municipality's coat of arms, for example, is a fish hook, while on the website's the township is referred to as the 'Fishing Capital', 'Norway's largest fishing village', and in the brochure 'Båtsfjord', it is referred to as a 'modern fishing settlement'. Here, the population 'spirit' is also described:

> Characteristic for Båtsfjord's population is the 'keep it up' spirit, the will to make an effort, and the ability for new ideas. The inhabitants are thus the municipality's most important resource.

In 'Båtsfjord – An active fishing municipality', the following is stated:

> Båtsfjord is Norway's largest fishing village and the largest fishing port in Norden. The ocean's resources, a good harbour and plant managers with 'go-ahead spirit', plus the ability to cooperate, have provided the basis for Norway's most modern fishing industry. Båtsfjord is an international settlement with many nationalities.

These examples illustrate that the local residents' picture of themselves and their stories can not be compared with those of the neighbouring settlements, that is, those who are held at a distance by the people of Båtsfjord, but also in relation to those with whom they compare themselves, that is, the first among equals, nationally and, at times, even internationally. In other words, Båtsfjord is not to be compared with some remote rural settlement, but as one which has the same opportunities and faces the same challenges as any urban community – the capital included. In 'The Story of Båtsfjord', this is particularly striking when the new airport is described as 'the new Gardermoen', Gardermoen being the new hyper-modern airport in Oslo. This reference clearly signals Båtsfjord's identity as something special and 'superior' to that of the neighbouring settlements.

The identity of 'the city' can also be found in several revue texts where fun is made of how people from southern Norway regard both 'northerners' in general and people from Båtsfjord who migrate to the South. Among these is a song entitled 'The Fringe'. Here it is maintained that Båtsfjord has 'rich folk by the dozen ..., loads of fast-food outlets ..., heaps of porno ..., nightlife unlimited', and so on. The message of this repertoire is that there is no reason to refer to Båtsfjord as a 'fringe settlement'.

Simultaneously, 'The Story of Båtsfjord' reflects that the identity of the place is closely tied to the 'fact' that it is a new place. More precisely, Båtsfjord is regarded as a post-war settlement, which is a result, as well as an expression of, modernization and industrialization. It is also a place where the population looks to the future rather than to the past. This strong future-orientation, illustrated by the focus on development and belief in the future, together with the importance attached to private initiative and the strong belief that the people themselves are the masters of their destiny, suggests that the settlement's identity can be described as a modern identity (Czarniawska 1997). Additionally, the story of the modern identity is one that is oriented towards the future, concerned with self-respect, efficiency, autonomy and one that values personal opinion. Self-respect, by disregarding the opinions of others, efficiency by considering one's capacity to realize projects, autonomy by not having to rely on others, and flexibility in the sense of being able to keep a distance to one's own viewpoints. The 'self' is thus a project plotted against one's own life story (Czarniawska 1997). In other words, self-respect, autonomy and efficiency are some of the key elements in 'The Story of Båtsfjord'. On the other hand, the traditional identity, which is oriented towards the past, treats the 'self' as a social copy plotted against the society of which it is part (Czarniawska 1997). To the extent that the future comprises a part of Båtsfjord's place-identity, this is evident by the understanding of the settlement as entirely dependent on the sea and the fishery.

The Myth of a New Settlement

Clearly, Båtsfjord is a post-war settlement in the light of the rapid growth in the population from 1945 to 1980. However, as a settlement highly dependent on the fisheries, it is not as new as many residents often describe it. An initial growth occurred around 1900 – owing much to the industrialization of the local economy that took place towards the end of the 19th century when a number of whaling stations were established along the coast. During the so-called 'whaling period' which, for Båtsfjord, lasted from 1884 until 1904, there was considerable local activity and, at the most, there were three whaling stations in the community (Olsen 1994).

Whaling ended in 1905 and was substituted by the traditional fisheries. Several fish-processing plants were established which purchased and processed cod in the spring. During the cod season, the local population grew considerably. In the spring of 1905, substantial activity is reported; three to four thousand people were residing in the community (Olsen 1994). In 1909, several quays were constructed to allow for increased purchase of fish during the season. At the same time a coal depot was established. In 1915, some 300 buyers' ships and 700 fishing boats were reported in the fjord. A combined school and church building was taken into use in 1920, and in the period 1920–40 Båtsfjord had roughly 25–26 fish-processing plants (Olsen 1999). Although activities were mainly seasonal, and most processing plants were foreign-owned, there were several cases of local ownership. Hence, even before World War II, the settlement could not be characterized as entirely transitional.

With the modernization of the fishing fleet in the mid-1930s, the need to live close to the fishing grounds declined. Its excellent harbour made Båtsfjord a natural choice for fishermen and their families, and the permanent population grew in pace with the technological development. As such, a large part of Båtsfjord's population came from previously active, aspiring 'industrious' fishing settlements in the same municipality, who adapted their experiences and a new technology in a new time, to a new place. Thus, these were not 'new' residents, but rather the same people settling permanently in a new place. These were people who had many of the same creative skills and new ideas as those who are described in 'The Story of Båtsfjord'.

Furthermore, Båtsfjord was one of the few places in Finnmark to be spared from the 'scorched earth policy' of the retreating Nazis at the end of World War II. As such, Båtsfjord was not a 'new' settlement as were the neighbouring townships which had been completely destroyed during the German retreat. Due to this situation the township became, as stated in the story, a Klondike-like community, which attracted people from many different places, both for shorter and longer sojourns, and a place where money came easily, and was just as easily spent. But even this was not new. What was happening was pretty similar to what had happened before, albeit on a much larger scale.

The subsequent development provided the basis for a new identity, a place that could no longer be characterized as a temporary or seasonal community. It had developed into a community of permanent 'settlers' who caught and processed fish based on the new post-war technology. The story of an entirely new place growing out of almost nothing could, in many respects, be interpreted as a myth in the traditional meaning of the concept, in other words as a fiction. With the sea and the fish as the core, the population of Båtsfjord has reinvented the place and created a new place-identity based on modernization, industrialization, innovation and growth. In the following, applying the concept of auto-communication, I discuss an alternative interpretation of this myth.

The Origin Myth as Auto-communication

'The Story of Båtsfjord' is a celebration of the place and the people, from start to finish. It contains a number of examples of self-praise that are expressed through the positive accounts of the community and how the population and the leaders take the initiative and stand united, and how this has led to today's success. The infrastructure is sound, with all-year employment, and firms and sports clubs which are in the national league and able to compete internationally. It is this which makes Båtsfjord unique. The negative aspects are associated with the ordinary aspects of life which Båtsfjord shares with other places. Also, in the expressions of identity initially intended for an external public, we find the same elements of self-praise. Examples are the above-mentioned statements in brochures describing Båtsfjord as 'The Fishing Capital', 'Norway's largest fishing village', 'The largest fishing port in Scandinavia', 'Båtsfjord is still the best', and describing the inhabitants of Båtsfjord as people with an 'up-beat' sense of humour, and full of 'new ideas'; a description coupled with the claim that they are the municipality's 'most important resource'.

The stories of the inhabitants and their leaders' achievements have become ingrained as mythical tales, which create order, binding the Båtsfjord community together. Both the local firms and the success of the volley-ball team strengthen and foster this fellowship, establishing a symbolic association between the individual and the community. The leaders and the volley-ball team have not only succeeded in their primary capacities, but also as representatives of the entire community. Like other mythical communities, it presumes a metaphorical kinship and a distinction between peoples (Hylland Erikson 1996). The kinship metaphor is primarily used to indicate a demarcation between peoples or family members as when the concept of 'big brother' is used as a reference to places which Båtsfjord has out-grown, become larger than and independent of. One is also more concerned with how the people in Båtsfjord, 'our people', commenced, rather than where they originally came from, and when.

Casting an eye over the self-praise which is expressed in connection with each successful project, and when the 'The Story of Båtsfjord' is regarded as a narrative complete with a plot, it can be understood as an origin myth; an account of the beginning of the place (cf. Doty 2004). 'The Story of Båtsfjord' is concerned with the origins of Båtsfjord as well as with why its inhabitants are privileged. It can be interpreted as a story about a settlement which was founded on the basis of a communal effort by people with extraordinary qualities and morals, who 'found' each other at a special place. As such, the origin myth works as a meta-text with an internal message of how a person, as an inhabitant of Båtsfjord, should behave – that is, take the initiative and cooperate. The moral is that this is the manner in which one will master all challenges and foes. By understanding 'The Story of Båtsfjord' as an origin myth, the reinvention of Båtsfjord is based on the need to explain its current success as a product of the people's own efforts. As such, the origin myth links personal experiences and personal biographies to those of the community, which points to a central aspect of a myth (Hylland Eriksen 1996). The autobiography, as a reflection of one's own life and as a manner in which to establish one's identity, is in itself an origin myth where the memory is given precedence. The truth of the story can only be determined retrospectively. Only time can determine its meaning (Freeman 1993). As Hylland Eriksen (1996) says, there are many versions of the past, but some are forgotten. In order to comprehend the path from the past to the present and to give it a meaning, a future is created which naturally results in an understanding of the present. The myth becomes a form of illusionary art, which produces a feeling of progress and development, something which again gives the myth legitimacy.

If we look at 'The Story of Båtsfjord' from this perspective, it is only by regarding the settlement as a post-war community that the development from the past to the present has significance. The only way by which the present situation may be explained as a result of a resourceful, creative and cooperative people, is by 'forgetting' the period prior to World War II and to reinvent Båtsfjord as a new settlement. Implicitly, this builds upon the reasoning that if the same people had arrived there earlier, then the development of Båtsfjord would have commenced earlier. Prior to World War II, Båtsfjord was not distinguished in any way. Similarly to the neighbouring communities, Båtsfjord was dependent on the fisheries, and on a fishing port where the number of vessels grew considerably during the seasons. To the extent that Båtsfjord distinguished itself, it was by being a settlement which was smaller than its neighbours. Put another way, this concerns a past which did not logically lead to today's situation.

The myth of a specific beginning creates meaning and order too. This makes it possible for the current inhabitants to understand themselves as one people with common and unique characteristics, but without excluding those whose origins are not local. This then enables them to describe today's successful leaders as 'locals', as belonging to the people of Båtsfjord, even though their origins are in other places. In order to be defined as a community, its people must have something in common. The only thing which the present inhabitants do have in common is that they met in Båtsfjord after World War II, both those who were there already, and those who arrived there subsequently.

Auto-communication as a Ritual and Development Dynamic

Furthermore, 'The Story of Båtsfjord' shows that the inhabitants are more than willing to act as ambassadors for the place. In general, they narrate voluntarily and with considerable enthusiasm about the positive aspects of the place, internally as well as externally. 'The Story of Båtsfjord' could thus be interpreted as an act of self-presentation with an external public as the prime target. However, as a meta-text, 'The Story of Båtsfjord' does not solely communicate the fact that private initiative and cooperation are beneficial, but also that as a local inhabitant one should engage in self-praise. This is an obligation which the local inhabitants regard as being essential to any member of the community, and which can therefore be understood as being anchored in their identity. The formulation in 'The Story of Båtsfjord' that as an inhabitant of Båtsfjord, one has a duty to boast about the settlement, is one example of this. This is also the basis for self-praise, as a way of countering the many negative pictures of North Norway, often presented in the national media. The obligation to boast can be regarded as a strategy by which one distances oneself from this perception; that the inhabitants of the northernmost county are reliant on state transfers and subsidies, and external assistance. The origin myth thus becomes a celebration, reminding Båtsfjord's inhabitants of who they are, how and why they are different, and how their success was achieved. As such this becomes an integrating ritual.

The introductory story on the belief in the local leaders can also be understood in the light of this obligation. In other words, the story is internalized because the inhabitants themselves are, and have been, involved in their creations. In the wake of this, the narratives have been produced and told. Hence, 'The Story of Båtsfjord' is a natural narrative with a material base, which has mushroomed over time. It is based on real events and has arisen as a result of these, as the successful projects, which were commenced with local initiative, have become material for new episodes in an ongoing story of success. New successes have resulted in new stories. As part of this process, the local inhabitants have discovered the external value of 'The Story of Båtsfjord', and used it systematically for external purposes. Indeed, the more the story is used externally, the stronger is its internal effect. This is because it acts as a mirror reflecting the inhabitants' own roles and the significance of their own contributions. The auto-communicative effect is that they are bound even more closely to the place, which they themselves have taken part in creating.

On the other hand, an interpretation of 'The Story of Båtsfjord' as an externally-oriented self-presentation is supported by the content of the revue texts, which to a far greater extent than the story focuses on the negative aspects of the place. Here, the picture of a community in harmony and cooperation is challenged, and internal conflicts between business leaders and local politicians are a regular theme. One example which this monologue takes up is the relationship between 'the big three' and the leader of the local council. The monologue spoken by the councillor is as follows:

> We are all aware of your interest in having permission for such a natural thing as to build in the market square. All of us who know you understand that you are determined to do something, and so – as in this instance – it only remains to instruct the planning department to commence with the development plans. As a permanent reminder, so that you are able to remember the market square before you began to grab it bit by bit, and that in order for you to remember

for always that fight which I lost, I will, on behalf of Hansen, Gundersen and myself, present you with this etching which illustrates the struggle.[3]

The revue text also shows that the Båtsfjord residents are hungry for publicity in as much as they immediately contact the media if they believe they have something important to say. This can be illustrated with the first and last verses from a song 'PR-Hungry Inhabitants', where irony is expressed over the Båtsfjord residents' regular mention in the press:

If I were a blackbird as a bird up in a tree
Then I'd sing a song about fame.
In order to be mentioned in the press, they stop at nothing,
bending the truth as may be necessary.

The journalist in Vadsø must be happy.[4]
A hint of something comes from Båtsfjord now and then.
We are PR-hungry people, both young and old
I don't know – perhaps we are a bit thick.

One theme which is mentioned in one of the revue texts but not included in 'The Story of Båtsfjord', is that several of the firms in Båtsfjord have received government subsidies. In other words, the inhabitants of Båtsfjord are not as self-reliant as 'The Story of Båtsfjord' makes us believe. The text is a sketch, conveying a letter from the Minister of Fisheries at the time. The letter is an invitation to a business lunch held by the local association of business leaders and concludes as follows, notably completely in accordance with the importance attached to private initiative in 'The Story of Båtsfjord':

Now not everything is simply a question of grants and subsidies in your municipality; private initiative appears to be flourishing. I assume that your respectful council leader has gone round with that famous lump in his throat ever since Thursday when rumours began to spread about yet another project was to be tried out in the county, and that it was the people from Båtsfjord who were behind this ... Finally, I will apologise that I, in spite of strong arguments ... on costs, for lunch, and not least on alcohol, have not found a place in the agreement of support for your working lunch.

However, as auto-communication, the revue texts can be seen as a mirror, reflecting an actual situation, and 'The Story of Båtsfjord' as a vision which one

---

3   The etching hung on the wall of the industrial leader's office for a long time. It illustrated the council leader and the entrepreneur, each at his own side of the market square, but where the entrepreneur is walking away in victory.

4   The regional newspaper is published in Vadsø, the regional capital.

is continually striving to meet. The origin myth thus serves as a constant reminder to the inhabitants of Båtsfjord of how they are required to act in order to maintain their position as the biggest, first and best. As such, boasting is not merely a ritual celebrated by the inhabitants themselves. It serves to remind them that it is an obligation to act in accordance with what is being narrated. Consequently, 'The Story of Båtsfjord' becomes the norm and ideal upon which the actual events in the society are evaluated and adjusted, and a vision which the inhabitants continually strive to achieve. The difference between the narrative and the events occurring in the settlement as illustrated in the revue texts, can as such be understood as a (potential) transitional situation (March 1995). A similar point is made by Brunsson (2003) who maintains that if we think our ideals should be higher than those practised today, this inconsistency appears unavoidable. According to Christensen and Morsing (2005), the difference may be understood as a 'lever' for development, as a starting point for self-scrutiny and as a mirror in which one may continually evaluate oneself. They further maintain that if such self-presentations shall be something more than a tribute to previous triumphs, it must contain an element of desire, faith and hope.

In other words, auto-communication is not merely a confirmation of an established identity; it is also a manner by which to communicate a desired self-image. 'The Story of Båtsfjord' can thus be regarded both as a celebration of previous successful projects, and as a presentation of a desired future which the inhabitants of Båtsfjord believe in, and which in itself establishes the basis for future development. Belief is a self-motivating power. When a story is narrated again and again, and is supported by the fact that the situation is functioning well, this motivates similar actions in the future. It is in this manner stories become self-fulfilling prophecies. By communicating with oneself through 'The Story of Båtsfjord', the settlement continuously re-creates the foundation for further development. The story can, however, only function as a 'lever' for development through an origin myth which commenced during the strong population growth after World War II, and the successful projects to which the inhabitants have jointly contributed.

Reinventing from Within and Below

In this chapter I have shown how Båtsfjord reinvented itself after World War II and created a modern place-identity linked to industrialization, development, new ideas and initiatives as well as a vision of the future. This new identity is an example of how change in the economic base of a community – due to the adoption of new technology – can result in a mental realignment. As such this study serves to illustrate how material and symbolic changes are closely linked (cf. Nyseth and Granås 2007). The source of this new identity lies in the fact that people arriving from different places were united in their objective of ensuring a foundation for development and growth, first and foremost a local infrastructure for industrial development, but subsequently also an infrastructure for local cultural activities. This again provided the basis for an epic story, based upon the myth of the origin of the settlement; a story that relates its history to how the people and the local business owners have jointly established this community and become masters of their own fate.

Båtsfjord's new identity is confirmed, amplified and maintained by new and successful projects providing material for new episodes of the same plot. This identity is continually reproduced through the origin myth as an unending story of success. The origin myth, which is an unreserved tribute to the people and the local business owners, is a ritual that continually reminds the people of Båtsfjord of who they are, and how they have become what they are today. It works as auto-communication; a means by which they communicate with themselves.

This study also illustrates that reinventing a place is not necessarily a strategic and planned process. Even though the origin myth is currently used to promote the community, it is not an attempt of conventional marketing. In other words, it is not based on the desire to establish an attractive place-identity for external purposes; an obvious interpretation based on recent literature on place-identity and the construction of place-identities under the label of place branding and place marketing. In this literature, place-identity is described as competitive identity, something which may be planned, built and designed (cf. Anholt 2007). Conversely, Båtsfjord's new identity emerged from the need to unite the population in a common cause; people who originally had nothing in common other than having arrived from different places.

But this origin myth also functions as auto-communication to remind people of what has to be done so that the township shall retain its unique position vis-à-vis the neighbouring communities. As such, this is a 'lever' for development. The difference between the story and the practice, also revealed in this study, is not an attempt at impression management; strategic manipulation of symbols to create a new external image not consistent with what the place claims to be. Instead, there is a challenge and a duty – conveyed by the story – to act in the same manner in the future. The origin myth serves as a model to be followed (cf. Eliade 1963, 1975). It is a 'living myth' in the sense that it supplies the people of Båtsfjord with prescriptions of how to behave. The origin myth thus functions virtually as a self-fulfilling prophecy and as a condition for further growth, as the potential of a place's development lies in its identity.

In summary, the reinvention of Båtsfjord is a project of genuine identity development (cf. Røvik 1998). It is related to the township's self-understanding; the understanding of what it is and will be, as an organic process unfolding from within and from below, in tandem as it were, and in response to the development of other settlements – something which the origin myth serves to emphasize. In brief, the township has continually rediscovered itself through auto-communication; by communicating with itself through the origin myth, the inhabitants of Båtsfjord have created a common meaning and identity, and thereby a foundation for the (further) development of the place.

References

Anderson, L. (2001, 2004), *Autobiography* (London: Routledge).

Anholt, S. (2007), *Competitive Identity. The New Brand Management for Nations, Cities and Regions* (New York: Palgrave Macmillan).

Baudrillard, J. (1983), *In the Shadow of the Silent Majorities* (New York City, NY: Semiotext(e)).

Bolman, L.G. and Deal, T.E. (2001), *Leading with Soul. An Uncommon Journey of Spirit* (San Francisco: Jossey-Bass).

Brunsson, N. (2003), 'Organized Hypocrisy', in Czarniawska, B. and Sevon, G. (eds).

Christensen, L.T. (1995), 'Buffering Organizational Identity in the Marketing Culture', *Organizations Studies*, 16(4), 651–72.

Christensen, L.T. (2004a), 'Det Forførende Medie. Om Auto-Kommunikasjon i Markedsføringen', *Mediekultur* 37, 14–23.

Christensen, L.T. (2004b), 'Marketing as Auto-Communication. Toward a Critique of the Marketing Culture' (unpublished paper).

Christensen, L.T. and Cheney, G. (2000), 'Self-Absorption and Self-Seduction in the Corporate Identity Game', in Schultz, M., Hatch, M.J. and Holten Larsen, M. (eds).

Christensen, L.T. and Morsing, M. (2005), *Bagom Corporate Communication* (Ferdriksberg: Forlaget Samfundslitteratur).

Czarniawska, B. (1997), *Narrating the Organization. Dramas of Institutional Identity* (Chicago: The University of Chicago Press).

Czarniawska, B. (2000), 'Identity Lost or Identity Found? Celebration and Lamentation over the Postmodern View of Identity in Social Science and Fiction', in Schultz, M., Hatch, M.J. and Holten Larsen, M. (eds).

Czarniawska, B. and Sevon, G. (eds) (2003), *Nothern Lights – Organization Theory in Scandinavia* (København: Liber, Abstrakt, Copenhagen Business School).

Doty, W.G. (2004), *Myth. A Handbook* (Tuscaloosa: The University of Alabama Press).

Eliade, M. (1963, 1975), *Myth and Reality* (New York: Harper & Row).

Freeman, M. (1993), *Rewriting the Self. History, Memory, Narrative* (London: Routledge).

Goffman, I. (1959), *The Presentation of Self in Everyday Life* (New York: Doubleday).

Hatch, M.J. and Schultz, M. (2000), 'Scaling the Tower of Babel: Relational Differences between Identity, Image, and Culture in Organizations', in Schultz, M., Hatch, M.J. and Holten Larsen, M. (eds).

Hylland Eriksen, T. (1996), *Kampen om fortiden. Et essay om myter, identitet og politikk* (Oslo: Aschehoug Argument).

Hovgaard, G. (2001), *Globalisation, Embeddeness and Local Coping Strategies. A Comparative and Qualitative Study of Local Dynamics in Contemporary Social Change* (PhD thesis, Roskilde University).

Lotman, Y. (1977), 'Two Models of Communication', in Lucid, D.P. (ed.).

Lotman, Y. (1990), *Universe of the Mind: A Semiotic Theory of Culture* (London: I.B. Tauris).

Lucid, D.P. (ed.) (1977), *Soviet Semiotics: An Anthology* (London: The Johns Hopkins University Press).

March, J.G. (1995), *Fornuft og forandring: Ledelse i en verden beriget med uklarhed* (Fredriksberg: Samfundslitteratur).

Nyseth, T. and Granås, B. (2007), 'Flerfaglig stedsforståelse i analyse av lokale transformasjonsprosesser', in Nyseth, T., Jentoft, S., Førde, A. and Bærenholdt, J.O. (eds).

Nyseth, T., Jentoft, S., Førde, A. and Bærenholdt, J.O. (eds) (2007), *I disiplinenes grenseland. Tverrfaglighet i teori og praksis* (Bergen: Fagbokforlaget).

Olsen, M. (1994), *Beretningen om Syltefjord* (Båtsfjord: Båtsfjord kommune og Lions Club).

Olsen, M. (1996), *Alvor og moro i Syltefjord* (Båtsfjord: Båtsfjord kommune og Lions Club).

Olsen, M. (1999), *Det gamle Vardø herre og Vardø by* (Kirkenes: Dagfinn Hansens Trykkeri AS).

Røvik, K.A. (1998), *Moderne organisasjoner. Trender i organisasjonsforskningen ved tusenårsskiftet* (Bergen: Fagbokforlaget).

Schultz, M., Hatch, M.J. and Holten Larsen, M. (eds) (2000), *The Expressive Organization. Linking Identity, Reputation, and the Corporate Brand* (New York: Oxford University Press).

Solhaug, O. (1979), *Kirke og folk i Båtsfjord kommune* (Syltefjord/Båtsfjord: Båtsfjord kommune og Lions Club).

Solhaug, O. (1985), *Sånn va det. Fortellinger om Båtsfjord kommune* (Vadsø: Helfjords Boktrykkeri AS).

Chapter 11

Globalized Reinvention of Indigenuity. The Riddu Riđđu Festival as a Tool for Ethnic Negotiation of Place

Paul Pedersen and Arvid Viken

Riddu Riđđu is a yearly indigenous music and art festival in Gáivuotna (Kåfjord) in the county of Troms in Northern Norway. The 2,241 (2007) inhabitants of the municipality live scattered around a fjord, but mountainous areas behind cover the most of its area. In the early 1980s people were mostly occupied in agriculture and fisheries, often both, or combined with other occupancies. At that time Gáivuotna appeared as a mono-ethnic Norwegian municipality, and an introverted and moderately developed community. In 2008 the same municipality is marketed as a multi-ethnic, outward-oriented and modern place, and the municipality has become a model for how a minority culture can be revitalized and modernized. The local authorities take part in national and international development projects. Thus, the image of Gáivuotna has strongly changed over a period of 15 years. There are many of reasons for the change, but from the middle of the 1990s the ethnic music festival Riddu Riđđu stands out as the most important development agent concerning the regained position of ethnic minorities, as well as modernization and internationalization. From its beginnings as a small barbeque party in 1991 the festival has developed into an international indigenous festival with three to four thousand in the audience per year and an important annual gathering for indigenous people in the circumpolar areas.

Few festivals become societal institutions to the extent Riddu Riđđu has achieved. The festival has emerged within a particular historical setting, engaged in a variety of functions, and was created by a set of young aspiring entrepreneurs. The festival was created in a period of economic crisis which, in retrospect, has shown to have given rise to revitalization and modernization of coastal Sami culture. Behind the entrepreneurial beginnings of the festival was a group of well educated and politically conscious young people. The name of the festival means 'storm from the coast', which is a good description of the character of the festival in the 1990s. The message of the festival, its form and the social behaviour of those attending the festival provoked the local community, particularly the Leastadians, members of a religious sect that has a strong position all over the municipality.[1]

In this chapter the major emphasis will be on the mental and historical significance of Riddu Riddu. The major issue is to what extent and how the festival has contributed to radical reconstructions of Gáivuotna, related to the situation around 1990. This question leads to another: How can festivals influence their surroundings? This normally takes place as a slow process and depends on strong support. If not, the festival will disappear. Over time Riddu Riddu has managed to gather strong support. The question is: what explains its ability to sustain and adapt to changing conditions and contexts? Thus, to understand the special character of the festival, the historical context of the event and its creators have to be considered.

The evidence for this analysis was gathered from in-depth interviews with a series of key persons from the initial phase of the festival from 1991 and onwards. These interviews were carried out during fieldwork in Gáivuotna in 2003 and 2004, and during the festivals in 2003, 2005, 2007 and 2008. In addition interviews have been undertaken with the political and administrative leadership in the municipality and with employees in schools, kindergartens, health institutions, local NGOs and tourism companies. In addition written material such as newspaper articles, white papers and a series of master theses about the festival have been used.

First, a brief overview of festivals as a community phenomenon is given, followed by a theoretical framework for an entrepreneurial analysis of the innovative character of the festival. The coastal Sami situation is then outlined from a historical perspective, before the development of the festival is described, which is organized in sections related to time periods. This is following by looking at the struggle for modernization and ethnic rights and then, in the next section, four functions that the festival has had are discussed: political, identity, innovation and reconciliation. In a concluding section the festival is seen in the light of festival entrepreneurial theory.

Theoretical Frameworks

Understanding festivals

Festivals represent a social institution dating back to ancient times (Falassi 1987; Gold and Gold 2005; Hegnes 2006). Concerning the rationale for contemporary festivals there are several discourses going on. Some festivals are created for the sake of economic benefit, but many festivals have other and normally less secular motives: there is something to celebrate or a reason to have a feast. Many

---

1   The local parish is a pietist version of the Lutheran church called Læstadianism after its founder Lars Levi Læstadius. The sect originated from Northern Finland around 1850 and particularly found became rooted in many Sami communities in Northern Norway.

festivals emphasize historical roots and traditions, others are created to emphasize alternative histories or stakes (Duvignaud 1976). However, as before, festivals are still arenas for pleasure and play, and for celebrations of traditions, customs, myths and beliefs, and of freedom. 'At festival times, people … abstain from something they normally do; they carry to the extreme behaviours that are usually regulated by measure; they invert patterns of daily social life' (Falassi 1987, 3). This tendency may also be strengthened by the fact that most festivals are arenas for art and new ways of presenting traditional culture and customs; arenas for creativity and experiments (Costa 2001). In fact, according to Duvignaud (1976), festivals can be seen as a means for social and cultural innovation, and according to Crepsi-Vallbona and Richards (2007, 120) there are festivals which have changed from focusing on the negative aspects of modernization for local communities, to considering the opportunities that this process presents. As will be shown, Riddu Riđđu falls into this tradition.

Although many festivals are spaces for entertainment, individual consumption and economic benefit, there also seems to exist another environment, for example local festivals based on community initiatives and volunteers or festivals created to strengthen collective identities and local cultures. Such festivals have often an integrative role (Hegnes 2006), at least for the originating group. Many festivals can be traced back to non-governmental organizations and political interest groups. Festivals seem to be a way to get attention. Lesbian and gay parades and New Age events are examples. Such festivals can be more or less political. For instance there are two festivals in Northern Norway set up to create good relationship with neighbouring Russia (Pomorfestivalen in Vardø, and Barents Spektakel in Kirkenes). By modifying Quinn (2005), one can say that festivals constitute arenas where history, cultural inheritance and social structures that distinguish groups from one another are revised, rejected or recreated.

Many festivals act upon the tradition–modernity dimension (Hegnes 2006). Some festivals are put together to keep up traditions, some to revitalize traditions or revive history, and some to create new art, practices or politics. Historically-oriented festivals often present the past through theatre or music plays. However, it is primarily the theme that is historical or heritage related, festivals as such are always modern. Riddu Riđđu is one of these festivals; a hypermodern play with traditions. To reinvent tradition is a way of interpreting the past and creating roots. This is one of the ways cultures develop. Festivals are often also seen in tourism contexts. This is also relevant here with the festival in question, Riddu Riđđu; it is real indigenous tourism as both the performers and the audience primarily are Sami or from other ethnic minorities.

Social entrepreneurship and capital

Creating a festival like Riddu Riđđu can be understood and analysed as a form of collective entrepreneurship. Whereas traditional entrepreneurship is associated with participants that are willing to run risks to maximize profits, collective entrepreneurs are often characterized by caution when it comes to financial risks (Spilling 1998, 2000 Teigen 2004). Although profit is also a motive social entrepreneurs are more interested in serving the local communities in which they live or work. Historical studies show that there are often two main components or motivating factors behind such enterprises (Furre 1971; Teigen 2004). One is financial gain, but in a collective perspective. Enterprises of this kind are often formed in connection with efforts to prevent the local population from being robbed of a resource, activity, or profit. The other component, which often coincides with the first, is the building up or strengthening of a community. Social entrepreneurs deal with areas of activity which in retrospect are considered important, but which had no attention before. A festival has this character. No one thought of making a coastal Sami festival before it developed out of some yearly feasts.

The term entrepreneur is often seen as synonymous with a person with certain characteristics. However, it will help to clarify our understanding if we think of an entrepreneur as a role which a person or a group of persons take on in connection with the implementation of an entrepreneurial event (Barth 1972). Entrepreneurs are often a part of a number of networks, and great significance is attached to these networks (Johannisson 1995). The entrepreneurs' personal network, local network, institutional network, and business network comprise what some have called a stepping stone, a 'gearbox', or bank of resources. The networks function as arenas of discussion, arenas of mobilization, and arenas of support. For analytical purposes it is important to distinguish between two types of networks, the *horizontal* and the *vertical* networks. The context in which the entrepreneurial process takes place has been greatly emphasized in a number of studies in the last decades. This includes social, cultural, and industrial contexts (Malmberg 2004). To be part of a network provides its participants with what has been called *social capital*. Røiseland and Aarsæther (2000) define social capital as the ability, caused by aspects of social life that create confidence, to collectively solve problems. Social capital is, in other words, a collective good which tends to *increase* when it is used. Social capital is initially created as a by-product of other activities, such as through working communities like organizations or festivals (Putnam 1995).

The Coastal Sami Situation

A culture about to vanish?

In order to understand how a coastal Sami festival could grow and develop into an international festival for indigenous people, we must consider the historical roots of the population, the immediate history of the area, and specific events nationally and locally.

The population in Gáivuotna has been ethnically mixed for a long time, and has consisted of Sami, Kvens,[2] and Norwegians. As late as the 1930s they constituted 52 per cent of the population in the municipality (NOU 1985:N 14, 184). In 1970 only 4.6 per cent of the population considered themselves to be Sami (Aubert 1978). There are several explanations for this significant decrease. The Norwegian politics of assimilation became more actively emphasized after World War I, both because of the growing role of the school and the public sector, and because of the modernization of the regional economy. In addition, both public and private agents of modernization spoke of Sami cultural elements as inferior, and without the right to exist in a modern society (Bjørklund 1985; Braastad Jensen 2005). One Norwegianizationing factor was the deep economic crises during the interwar period within fisheries and agriculture – the core of the local economy in the coastal Sami districts (Bull 1979; Eytòrsson 2008). World War II became a turning point in the history of the coastal Sami culture. The entire substance of the coastal Sami culture was destroyed by the German army's use of scorched earth tactics. During the war and afterwards the population also learned that 'the future was Norwegian' (Bjørklund 1985). Children in Sami families were, in contrast to the period before the war, not taught the Sami language (Steinlien 2006). Increasingly, Sami avoided being associated with the Sami culture. It was hidden, actively forgotten, associated with shame, and to a large extent denied. Many of those who grew up during this period had a difficult relationship with their ethnic roots. They became what Høgmo (1986) has called 'a neither/nor generation'. When we stress these circumstances it is to emphasize that although the Sami culture had practically disappeared from the public sphere by 1970, it had not *gone*. There was still a strong historical foundation present for coastal Sami revitalization.

Economic depletion and indigenous rights

Overfishing and the use of damaging fishing equipment in waters close to the coast led to a steep decrease in the amount of fish caught in coastal fishing during the 1980s. The decrease was sharpest in the coastal Sami districts and hit them especially hard because there were few alternatives (Pedersen and Høgmo 2006).[3] Coastal Sami areas were also, for various reasons, especially negatively affected by a fishing quota system introduced by the authorities in 1990. The catch of cod in coastal Sami areas was drastically decreased. In 1991 the amount was only 28 per cent of what it had been in 1980, compared to 77 per cent in areas outside of the coastal Sami districts (ibid.). This led to an atmosphere of deep disturbance in the population that lived off fjord fishing. The frustration and

---

2   Kvens is a label for immigrants from Finland to North Norway from the end of the 1700s.

3   The catch of cod for fishing boats of less than 15 metres was reduced by around 62 per cent in coastal Sami areas, compared to 53 per cent in the rest of the country between 1980 and 1988 (Pedersen and Høgmo 2006).

anger of the fjord-fishers towards the regulations was expressed in a series of articles in newspapers from individuals, more or less official protests from Sami organizations, local groups of fishermen, and eventually political bodies such as municipality councils. Many fishermen ended up in difficult economic situations and from time to time had to seek social security benefits. They experienced that their rights to fish were mercilessly revoked with the explanation that their activity had been insignificant, which was seen as degrading and an injustice committed by an arrogant bureaucracy. The fishing policies of the government lost its legitimacy in this area (Nyseth and Pedersen 2005).

Public recognition and organizing of coastal Sami interests

While these processes were taking place, decisive political breakthroughs occurred at a national level regarding the political demands put forth by Sami political organizations. The minority politics attracted new attention in the wake of the controversial construction of the power plant in the Alta river in the inland Sami (1979–81). The renewed political focus on the Sami situation, led to a series of laws and institutions towards the end of the 1980s (Minde 2005): the Sami were recognized as an indigenous group; the Sami gained some autonomy through the creation of a Sami Parliament (*Sámediggi*); several Sami institutions were formed; and the Sami language was granted equal status with Norwegian. In 1990, as the first country in the world, Norway also ratified the ILO Convention 169, which recognizes the rights of indigenous people to land and water. These arrangements also had great impact on the Gáivuotna municipality.

The argument for the necessity for these legal and institutional developments was to preserve the Sami culture which was on the verge of extinction (Pedersen and Høgmo 2004). The fight for these rights and the fight for protection from overfishing by foreign fishing boats in fjords and waters close to the coast, had already led to the creation of Sami organizations in the 1980s. A local branch of Norwegian Sami Association (Norske Samers Riksforbund) was constituted in Gáivuotna in 1977, and a few years later a local group, Sami National Association (Samenes Landsforbund), which was a competing organization, in particular gained large support among the coastal Sami. The activity of local arts and crafts groups and the restoration of coastal Sami cultural remains, undertaken by Northern Troms Museum, contributed to making the existence of the coastal Sami visible.

Another organization that was formed in this period (1990) was Gáivuotna Sami Youth Group (GNS), which later created and developed the Riddu Riđđu festival. The group was established in a community marked both by a deep economic crisis and an ethnic crisis. These people posed questions about the ethnic status of the community and went public with their own ethnic background. From being a private and hidden matter, people's ethnic roots became a public matter and an issue which demanded a view to be expressed. When various aspects of the language law, and later the Sami curriculum, were to be implemented, this created local ethnic antagonisms which lasted for ten years, and which is inextricably connected to the development of the Riddu Riđđu festival.[4] The areas of conflict were manifold: whether to join the Sami electoral roll, the impacts of the language law giving Sami language a strong position, the use of the Sami flag, the Sami people's rights to land and water, and whether or not the coastal Sami had special rights to fishing in fjords and waters close to the coast. The antagonisms were not only about the content of the regulations, but also about the way in which they were implemented, and to some degree about who had the right to decide over people's everyday lives.[5]

In this situation the Sami youth organization was a visible political participant. The group had a clear political programme, consisting of six main points. In addition to working to promote the Sami language and the coastal Sami culture, the group had a clear environmentalist profile. In this context traditional Sami livelihoods through the exploitation of local resources on a small scale appeared both environmentally friendly and a good way of saving resources. The group quickly gained support, and started a number of activities. It became involved in several areas and was a local driving force for Sami political issues. As a youth branch of the Norwegian Sami Association (NSR), they sent representatives to national meetings, and participated in national and international conferences, and had members that were members of the Sami Parliament (Hovland 1996). It was in this social milieu that the greatest cultural innovation took place. The tool which eventually created a far-reaching and creative social environment in Gáivuotna, started modestly in 1991 through so-called cultural days, which grew into a youth festival (Hovland 1996; Hansen 2008).

The Riddu Riđđu Festival: Setting and Development

The festival setting

The festival area today is situated a couple of kilometres off the main road, but in the middle of village, close to the public school (see Figure 11.1). There is no dense housing close to the festival, but it is surrounded by some farms and

---

4   The organized Sami community was divided on the question of which methods to choose. Samenes Landsforbund, which organized many coastal Sami, was against the creation of a separate Sami Parliament. Samenes Riksforbund, the majority of whose supporters were students and from the Sami who lived off reindeer husbandry, was the driving force behind the new law.

5   The newspapers were full of letters in which the 'Sami activists' were accused of coup-like manoeuvres, and where anger at being subject to Sami public bodies was expressed. The conflict also involved different historical elements, partly connected to the question of rights, but also connected to the psychological history. In some areas it was brought into local elections, and has in reality divided all political parties in Finnmark and Northern Troms.

a magnificent mountainous backdrop. As it is, those living nearest, obviously hear the music played. However, as it is situated, it is somewhat isolated from the village. Internally, the festival area is organized in different sections. Two for accommodation – there are no hotels in the area, people have to stay in tents – one for youth and partying people, and one for families. The accommodation and the stage sections are separated by hedges of hay (see Figure 11.2), the traditional way of preserving the crop for the winter. There is a significant security staff. As it is a family event, people who are obviously drunk or under the influence of drugs are removed. The festival area also includes workshops and stalls for sale of handicrafts and traditional food, and an outdoor internet café. It should also be mentioned that the stages and infrastructure in general are very modern, using the latest in information and communication technology.

Figure 11.1 The festival camp
Source: © Arvid Viken (chapter author).

Figure 11.2 One of the stages – Nenets performers
Source: © Arvid Viken (chapter author).

Defining the content of coastal Sami culture 1991–95

Riddu Riddu started as a celebration of the coastal Sami culture in connection with the annual national meeting of the Norwegian Sami Association (NSR) in 1991.[6] In this year the event was labelled 'Year and Days' (*Jagi vai Beaivvi*) and the Sami profile was more pronounced (Hansen 2007). Those in charge of the event were members of the newly started Sami organization for young people, *Gáivuona Samenuorat*. During the early years of the festival, some strategic choices were taken – informants insisted that they were discussed and decided upon. One decision was of particular importance – the festival should highlight art. There was a tradition of art in the community. Several of the founders reflect on this fact. Hansen (2007, 56), a former festival leader, in her personal account, indicates that this probably was a way of expressing alternative values and thoughts to the strongly religious and narrow values that were predominant in the community. She quotes Weber (1970), who claims that art symbolizes freedom and a secular alternative to religious values. Most years the festival has had an overall theme: northern dance, northern theatre,

---

6 However, as several informants emphasized there had already been some informal annual feasts that constituted a platform before the organizing process started in 1991.

northern trends, storytelling, celebrations and traditional food (cf. Leonenko 2008). One of those who himself had taken part in a former ethnic protest in the 1970s, admitted that the art emphasis was a clever strategy; it was a softer and more inclusive strategy compared to the hard political line they had chosen. As part of the art and culture approach, local artists were involved in the development of the festival and indigenous art and music were given priority in the festival programmes. Another strategic choice was to ask questions and discuss vital local cultural issues. A third strategic choice mentioned in the interviews, was the involvement of ordinary people and the elders. After some scepticism and resistance in the early years, they attended as volunteers, tutors and course holders.

The festival was a balance between tradition and modernity. The focus on traditions gathered local support for the festival, whereas the modernity envisaged through programmes where rock and international indigenous music dominated, gave the festival a youth appeal. In the early years, inland Sami performances and artists had a strong position, reflecting their ethno-political dominance within the Sami society at that time (cf. Leonenko 2008). Later, international indigenous music has been the major profile. Throughout its existence the festival's general profile has given to the coastal Sami content and meaning.

Promoting coastal Sami culture 1996–2000

Over the years the ambitions for the festival grew, and in 1995 the name Riddu Riđđu was chosen. The programme from this year on presented local art and musicians, combined with national artists and internationally recognized indigenous artists. It was also a mixture of music, dance, theatre, art and handicrafts; also of performances, expositions, workshops and seminars. The period is characterized by a promotion of different aspects of the coastal Sami culture, and a beginning internationalization, primarily by including the Northern circumpolar areas. However, the festival was controversial, adding to broader ethnic antagonisms in Gáivuotna that divided families and the local society. The criticisms of the festival concerned accusations of idolatry, drunkenness and disturbance. The festival was blamed for escalating the cultural antagonisms, and even for destroying Sami culture. The organizers were labelled 'plastic Sami', and accused of bringing foreign values to Gáivuotna and for wasting public money. Despite this opposition, the festival gained increasing support. In 2000 the festival area was filled with over 2,000 people from all over the world, and it received a lot of positive press coverage.

Developing into an international indigenous festival 2000–2008

The programme itself was not significantly altered over the years. However, the courses and seminars were broadened significantly, and a film programme was also introduced. The change towards an international indigenous festival is clear. It now opened up to participation from the Southern hemisphere, such as Australia,

New Zealand, Africa, and Central America. In 2002 the festival had a breakthrough media wise, both nationally and internationally. Seventy-five journalists were accredited, among them journalists from *The Guardian, Frankfurter Allgemeine Zeitung*, the BBC, and Botswanian TV. As the drinking trait had been removed due to reorganizing and a professional security system introduced, there was less negative press. In 2004 the festival had 3,500 visitors. The regional newspaper *Nordlys* wrote in the editorial that 'The festival ... is a national event, and now has the opportunity to become the most important cultural festival in Norway in relation to the rest of the world.' The festival had now become an institution which was welcomed and received all round public support. At the beginning of the 21st century it is one of the most important arenas for Sami artists. It is also a main event for indigenous music, particularly within the circumpolar area. The festival is also important for the Sami population – a meeting place. It is almost like a religious gathering – people meet both spiritually and socially, and experience ethnic bonding and communality (Hansen 2008). The international content has contributed to expanding the boundaries of understanding, and has had innovative effects. For the younger inhabitants of Gáivuotna, Riddu Riđđu has become an important event, and a place to be seen at and a place to learn.

Struggles for Modernization and Ethnic Rights

In the discussion above a picture of the most important aspects of the development of the Riddu Riđđu festival has been presented. It was created during a turbulent time and in a society practically without music traditions (Steinlien 2006). In the following, two questions that are closely connected will be discussed: first, why did the festival gain as much support as it did?; and second, why did the festival have such an impact on the understanding or mental image that Gáivuotna is associated with today? However, before doing this, an explanation of why a new generation of young Sami people engaged in a coastal Sami identity is called for, and also why they went back to their home place and fought for indigenous conditions and rights. There are basically three major explanations: one related to education and welfare politics, the other to the situation in fisheries, and the third related to the international focus.

The expansion of institutions of higher education in Northern Norway, and the increasing participation in higher education of young people from coastal Sami is a key factor in the coastal Sami process of revitalization after 1980, and especially after 1990. This process had already begun in the 1970s, but it was intensified from the end of the 1980s. A result of the increased participation at universities and university colleges was that a number of the students became strongly involved in Sami politics at these institutions, especially in Tromsø. But they did more – they also studied their own roots, and learned about tradition and modernity, ethnicity and reflexivity. This contributed to an increased level of knowledge and to a young elite taking back a part of their history of which they had not been properly informed. This gave them roots, a new self-awareness, and a new will to fight. A new generation of highly educated people from the coastal Sami areas entered into positions of local administration, in the service sector, and in special interest organizations during the 1990s. Many of them obtained key roles in local and regional struggles to regain their status as an indigenous people.

Due to low competence and high turnover in the labour market, and an educational level far beneath the national average, the Norwegian Parliament decided that the county of Finnmark and the northern parts of Troms should constitute a special educational political region (established in 1988). This gave the coastal Sami areas a lift. One of the measures implemented was that, in reality, the state paid all costs for education if the person accepted employment in the region after having finished their studies. And other stimulating arrangements were added: among these was there not only a significant increase in the capacity of the colleges and the university in North Norway, but also a quota for students from Sami areas. Those who wanted to take higher education, could now afford the fees and could be enrolled. Together these efforts not only had a motivating effect for entering higher education, but also made coastal Sami areas attractive as areas to settle, since they provided a great financial incentive (Pedersen 2005). This is how the Riddu Riđđu generation was shaped.

The injustice that the fishing population felt when the fishing quota system excluded them from fisheries, made them look for new policies and new allies. The newly established Sami Parliament became such an ally. Already in 1990 the Sami Parliament protested against the new fishing regulations, arguing that it was not in accordance with the government's obligations to protect the material basis for coastal Sami societies and culture. When the Sami Parliament and a number of other local governments joined forces in the demand for a separate Sami fishing zone in 1992, the authorities could not dismiss it with the argument that it was only a minor special interest matter. This action joined the fishermen and the Riddu Riđđu generation together in a fellowship of common interests and arguments. The concept of indigenous people gave legitimacy and a new argumentative force, not only to various demands for preservation, but also to demands for increased efforts in connection with the Sami language and culture. The indigenous perspective was an important part of the way that the Riddu Riđđu generation saw themselves. When the Riddu Riđđu festival assumed an international orientation, this was only a continuation of something that was already present.

The Riddu Riđđu Functions

The gradual increasing support for the festival among several groups in the municipality can be traced to the many functions that the work with the festival fulfilled, and the needs it met which otherwise may remain lacking in municipalities on the outskirts. We will here emphasize four functions: the political, the identity forming, the innovative, and the reconciling.

The political function

The festival first and foremost has a *political function*, although the nature of it changed over time. Riddu Riđđu and its antecedents can be seen as Sami political tools to further the Sami language and coastal Sami culture. The festival shocked and provoked, and was definitely a part of the local fight for recognition of the coastal Sami culture. The festival was something that everyone was compelled to form an opinion about, and it gathered both support and opposition. It contributed to a public debate which revealed prejudices and thereby helped clear the air. The festival as an arena for battle gradually changed as the Sami language and culture found its place and became a part of everyday life in kindergartens and schools, public administration and health care. Since year 2000 the political significance has gradually changed as the festival became politically accepted locally, regionally, and nationally. The festival became an interesting partner for an institution working on relations with Russia in the north – the Norwegian Barents Secretariat – and it was also engaged in international aid programmes. The highlight came in 2008 as the festival was given the status as one of seven national 'core festivals' during a personal visit from the Minister of Culture, Trond Giske. The festival is today the cultural flagship and great pride of Gáivuotna.

The identity forming function

Riddu Riđđu and its predecessor had, furthermore, a clear vision of identity seeking and identity clarification. The work with the festival grew out of insecurity about and a search for what it meant to be coastal Sami and what a coastal Sami identity really was (cf. Viken 2008). The young people involved had their roots in a coastal landscape in which coastal Sami culture was barely visible to an untrained eye. The Sami society had, and still has, a clear hierarchy. The inland Sami culture was depicted as the real Sami culture. Important symbols in the inland Sami culture were a living Sami language, a unique way of living through reindeer herding, unique clothing, and a unique music tradition, the 'yoik'. The inland Sami culture had a hegemonic position, often making the coastal Sami feel inferior. These cultural elements or symbols connected to nature and livelihood did not correspond to the life on the coast. Most people found it difficult to recognize, for example, the reindeer and the tundra as 'universal' Sami symbols, at the expense of symbols from their own lives, with the sea, fishing, farming, and local trade as important categories (Hovland 1996; Pedersen and Høgmo 2006). In the early 1990s, the young Sami in Gáivuotna travelled to the inland Kautokeino to study genuine Saminess, but most of what they learned was rejected locally – it simply was not their Saminess (Hansen 2007). Thus, there was a strong need to clarify what the coastal Sami culture really consisted of. One of the veterans who had participated for more than ten years in the work with the festival said the following:

My main motivation has been the pieces falling into place, that you know who you
are. Eventually I began to understand who I was, and then I discovered all the cultural
treasures that are here. It's a treasure hunt in a way. Another motivation is to get rid
of the Sami pain, as one might call it. Because it is very painful when you have to
go through such a process (change identity). When you discover that you aren't who
you think you are, and that someone (your parents) have lied to you in a way.

The entrepreneurs' choice to 'let all flowers bloom' was important both for
mobilization, and for the search for a content to coastal Sami culture and identity.
They managed to gather and include a wide range of activities in the festival work,
from food, creating life in historic buildings, making local arts and crafts visible,
stories, music, theatre, dance and so on, and they gave it a coastal Sami profile.
This had a mobilizing effect because it coincided with the interests of a large part
of the population, and interests which were already partly organized. When the
work began, people quickly realized that coastal Sami culture was nothing else
than the life that the people in the fjords had lived, and that coastal Sami history
was the history of the local community, which everyone could share.

The innovative function

The development of the festival is in itself a core example of an innovative process. We
have already mentioned the first innovative characteristic – the ability of the founders
to build the festival on a broad foundation. Through involving a large number of
participants the festival contributed to both rejuvination of and innovation of local
cultural elements, and to creating social environments. Since its start the festival has
been an important place to exhibit local traditions, arts and crafts, which eventually
came to represent physical expressions of what coastal Sami culture was and could be.
Another example of the importance and success of the festival was the difficult work on
reconstructing the old coastal Sami festive dress, the Lyngen costume (*Lyngenkofta*).
After the completion of the project in 1995, a regional coastal Sami symbol had been
created which did not require any knowledge of the Sami language. Wearing such a
costume demonstrates one's ethnicity. The Lyngen costume became the festival outfit,
and a main coastal Sami symbol and its recognition as a festive dress, not only in
Gáivuotna, but in the entire region of Northern Troms.

Another main characteristic is the internationalization of the festival. As we
have already shown, an international perspective was a part of the way in which
the Riddu Riđđu generation understood themselves. It is also noteworthy that
Riddu Riđđu became an indigenous festival and not only a Sami festival. Apart
from the genuine interest of some of the founders for the art of other circumpolar
indigenous peoples, there are three other factors which can explain the emergence
of the festival's international profile. First, festivals are like businesses – if they do
not adapt and develop, they die. The founders of the festival were very aware of
this, and they were always looking for ways to give the festival a new direction.
Second, the need for emancipation from the cultural hegemony of the inland Sami,

made the organizers look outwards. In a circumpolar indigenous perspective the inland Sami cultural concept lost its precedence, for example, among other things, its 'language monopoly'. The language of communication was now English. Third, the skill of the founders – they were young academics, used to international perspectives and to using modern strategic tools. Through thorough research, hard work, and a skilled eye for what would work, they managed to create a unique festival. Due to this unique nature and quality, the festival quickly attracted attention from outside of Norway, which has contributed to its continued status as one of the most important yearly meeting places for indigenous people from the entire circumpolar area. The international outlook did not take place by accident but, according to two of the founders, was a strategic choice. However, the innovative character of the festival is not without challenges. I vital question in a looking back session at the festival in 2008 was: 'How can the creativity, innovative power and political contestation of Riddu Riđđu be sustained as the festival is growing bigger, becoming better organized and even integrated in the national web of such festivals.' The answer from one of the organizers was: 'Don't worry, Riddu Riđđu will always be institutionalized anarchy; youth power and rock'n roll.'

The reconciling function

The intense ethnic conflicts surrounding the use of the Sami language and Sami symbols which characterized the municipality throughout the 1990s lessened around the turn of the century and are barely present today. There are several reasons for this, but the Riddu Riđđu festival and the work throughout the year in preparing it has without a doubt made an important contribution. In order to produce the festival, often more than ten work groups have been busy all year through, and during the week of the festival normally several hundred volunteers from the municipality are involved. There have never been any ethnic conditions attached to participating in the work groups or the festival work, although it has been clear to everyone that this is a coastal Sami arena. The members of the work groups had regular meetings throughout the year, and many of the workers came back year after year. The work inspired and united crafts people, artists, farmers, unemployed, Sami politicians and academics. These work groups and the ability of the festival to attract other organized groups, is a prime example of accumulation of social capital. These informal meeting places and networks also functioned as an arena where people from different backgrounds could work through their feelings or traumas concerning the coastal Sami situation. The festival work can be understood as a community or practice (Wegner 1998) where the members, through working on common tasks, acquire standard routines, symbols, notions, and share a common history. Both the preparations for the festival and the arrangement itself have therefore contributed greatly to bringing people together and to reconciling their differences. The festival also represented a sanctuary where hierarchies were, at least temporarily, dissolved, and it became a forum where friendships developed. The festival has also always been an arena for the expression of different kinds of youthful rebellion, often directed at the dominating Laestadian culture, which the younger generations consider to be suffocating and narrow-minded. Things have also changed among the older generation. People are proud of what their children and grandchildren have achieved, and even practising Laestadians now contribute to the practical work surrounding the festival.

Riddu Riđđu: Emancipation and Empowerment

There is long tradition for festivals being created and run in the interest of minorities and opposition groups (Duvignaud 1976). As before, festivals are still arenas for pleasure and play, and for celebrations of traditions, customs, myths and beliefs, and of freedom. All this can be found in the story of Riddu Riđđu. The freedom aspect was particularly prominent in the beginning and there was a tendency to what Falassi (1987, 3) calls 'extreme behaviour'. Riddu Riđđu was an arena for 'sex and drugs and rock'n roll', it is admitted. Drinking, dancing and partying still take place at the festival, but it has grown up and become responsible. Therefore the festival has acquired a recognized status as a meeting place and a forum for the Sami and other indigenous groups.

The free zone side of the festival has been important in many respects. As for most festivals it has provided space for identity negotiations. Festivals tend to create and strengthen collective identities and often have integrative roles, according to Hegnes (2006). Riddu Riđđu has made visible a coastal Sami identity as something separate and different from the inland Sami identity. Two things are important here. The festival revitalized the coastal Sami traditions within many life spheres: traditions which many thought were Norwegian. The other move was the innovative and modernizing effect of the opening up for different forms of art (music, dance, theatre), and for other indigenous people's cultural expressions. But at the same time Riddu Riđđu has also brought ethnic antagonisms to the surface. In the 1980s Gáivuotna was about to become a fully accepted Norwegian community, according to people in the village (Viken 2008). However, this placid state was based on suppression and historical rejection. So, at least the festival cleared the air. Today, there are vital ethnic differences, but people have learned to live with them, and the neither/nor identities have changed to double identities, people are both Sami and Norwegian, or Kvens and Norwegian. The festival has been integrative by unveiling people's ethnicities. Today, they are open about their ethnic roots and priorities. The generation which is growing up in Gáivuotna today is not ashamed of being of Sami descent, but regards such an association with pride. They are a part of Gáivuotna, but they are also a part of the indigenous people of the world. The municipality's multi-ethnic status is accepted. In fact, in everyday life ethnicity is not a problem but a foundation for a vital community.

Somehow many festivals have adopted the character of the carnival. Traditionally, the carnival was a festival that for a short period levelled social differences. From behind their masks people could tell others – including their superiors and supressors – what they felt and meant without revealing who they were (cf. Debord 1998;

Bahktin 1996). Similarly, modern festivals seem to be arenas for self-examining, self-realization, for expressing negative and positive feeling, for announcing new policies, launching new art forms and challenging traditions and truths (cf. Hegnes 2006). Thus festivals are accepted as arenas for social and cultural innovation (Crepsi-Vallbona and Richards 2007, 120). Riddu Riđđu has been an arena for experimenting with ethnic emblems and expressions, seemingly without offending anybody. There has been crticism, not of the festival as such, but of partying, noise and bad behaviour, rather than the ethnic negotiations going on. There, however, is one discrediting note sounded– the organizers have been and still are labelled 'phony Sami' and 'plastic Sami' referring to the fact that many of them only recently have (re-)converted to Saminess. One of the functions of Riddu Riđđu may have been the provision of a particular space for ethnic exposition, negotiation and identification. It can seem that much of the ethnicity in Gáivuotna is exposed during the festival week, but not so much the rest of the year. The festival has changed from a menacing to a regulating function over the years.

The innovative aspects of the Riddu Riđđu festival are overwhelming. First it is obvious that the festival organizers have been social entrepreneurs, and that social capital has been developed; the festival has been a social event, the gain has been social and cultural and not economical. The important role of the founders must also be emphasized. They have shown impressive *social entrepreneurship*. They approached a new area and created an organization (Riddu Riđđu) which turned out to be a successful institution. The satisfaction of creating something, and to get recognition in close networks were the major rewards. The social capital that has been built up is significant; people in Gáivuotna not only have colleagues, friends and networks all over region but also outside the circumpolar world. They make use of these networks when compiling their programmes and provide each other with musicians and other artists. But probably, the Riddu Riđđu story also shows the significance of vertical networking; a growing number of authorities want to take part and support it – obviously also to get a share of the glory of this indigenous festival.

Riddu Riđđu is also an example of political innovation. However, it might be argued that it is more an example of a political band-wagon effect. The 1990s was the decade when the indigenous perspective was seriously put on the international agenda (Minde 2005) and the internal Sami self-governance was expanded. It also became more and more accepted that Northern Norway was a multicultural society and that this was something positive. In other words, the concept that the founders of Riddu Riđđu represented, struck a chord with central trends of their time. After the turn of the century the festival was declared a work of genius in the Norwegian and international press. In political rhetoric Riddu Riđđu became a prime example of how the resources in a multi-ethnic environment can be mobilized, and a model for how ethnicity can be used and converted to cultural, industrial, societal and political development. Gáivuotna today understands and promotes itself as a *multi-ethnic, extroverted,* and *modern* place. This vision, once developed by the

Riddu Riđđu organizers, has now become a strategy for *municipal* development in Gáivuotna which really has been a process of place reinvention.

References

Arbo, P. (2004), 'Kan innovasjon planlegges?', in: Arbo, P. and Gammelsæter, H. (eds).
Arbo. P. and Gammelsæter, H. (eds) (2004), *Innovasjonspolitikkens scenografi* (Trondheim: Tapir akademiske forlag).
Aubert, W. (1978), *Den samiske befolkning i Nord-Norge* (Oslo: Statistisk sentralbyrå).
Bahktin, M.M. (1996), *Rabelais and His World* (Bloomington: Indiana University Press).
Barth, F. (1969), 'Introduction', in: Barth, F. (ed.), *Ethnic Groups and Boundaries* (Oslo: Universitetsforlaget).
Barth, F. (1972), *The Role of the Entrepreneur in Social Change in Northern Norway* (Oslo: Universitetsforlaget).
Bjørklund, I. (1985), *Fjordfolket i Kvænangen* (Oslo: Universitetsforlaget).
Bourdieu, P. (1984), *Distinction. A Social Critique of the Judgement of Taste* (Cambridge: Harvard University Press).
Bull, E. (1979), 'Klassekamp og felleskap 1920–1945', in: Mykland (ed.).
Cant, G., Goodall, A., and Inns, J. (eds) (2005), *Discourses and Silences. Indigenous People, Risk and Resistance* (Christchurch: University of Canterbury).
Costa, X. (2001), 'Festivity: Traditional and modern forms of sociability', *Social Compass* 48(4), 541–8.
Crepsi-Vallbona, M. and Richards, G. (2007), 'The meaning of cultural festivals', *International Journal of Cultural Policy* 13(1), 103–22.
Debord, G. (1998), *The Society of the Spectacle* (New York: Zone Books).
Duvignaud, J. (1976), 'Festivals: A sociological approach', *Cultures*, 1, 13–25.
Eytòrsson, E. (2008), *Sjøsamene og kampen om fjordressursene* (Karasjok: Forfatternes Forlag).
Ekman, A.K. (1999), 'The revival of cultural celebrations in regional Sweden: Aspects of tradition and transition', *Sociologica Ruralis* 39(3), 280–93.
Falassi, A. (1987), 'Festival: Definition and morphology', in: Falassi, A. (ed.), *Time Out of Time – Essays on the Festival* (Albuquerque: University of New Mexico Press).
Furre, B. (1971), *Mjølk, bønder og tingmenn* (Oslo: Det norske samlaget).
Gold, J.R. and Gold, M.M. (2005), *Cities of Culture: Staging International Festivals and the Urban Agenda, 1851–2000* (Aldershot: Ashgate).
Hansen, L. (2007), *Liten storm på kysten. Samisk identitet mellom en lokal og internasjonal arena.* Masters' thesis (Tromsø: University of Tromsø).
Hansen, L. (2008), *Storm på kysten* (Tromsø: Margmedia).
Hegnes, A.W. (2006), 'Feativalenes tvetydighet', *Sociologisk Årbok,* 107–140.

Hovland, A. (1996), *Moderne Urfolk. Samisk ungdom i bevegelse* (Oslo: Cappelen Akademisk Forlag).

Hovland, A. (1999), *Moderne Urfolk – lokal og etnisk tilhørighet blant samisk ungdom. Nova rapport 11* (Oslo: Norsk institutt for forskning om oppvekst, velferd og aldring).

Høgmo, A. (1986), Det tredje alternativ. Barns læring av identitetsforvaltning i samisk-norsk samfunn preget av identitetsskift. Tidsskrift for samfunnsforskning, Vol 27, pp 395-416. (Oslo)

Jensen, E.B. (2004), *Kulturmøter i Nord-Troms. Jubileumsbok for Nord-Troms Museum* (Sørkjosen: North Troms Museum).

Johannisson, B. (1995), 'Personliga nættverk som kraftkjælla vid føretagandet', in: Johannisson, B. and Lindmark, L. (eds), *Føretag, Føretagare Føretagsamhet* (Lund: Studentlitteratur).

Leonenko, A.V. (2008), *Riddu Riđđu, joik or rock-n-roll? A Study of Riddu Riđđu Festivála and its Role as a Cultural Tool for Ethnic Revitalisation.* Masters thesis (Tromsø: University of Tromsø).

Malmberg, A. (2004), 'Teorier og kluster – var står vi i dag?', in: Arbo, P. and Gammelsæter, H. (eds), *Innovasjonspolitikkens scenografi* (Trondheim: Tapir akademiske forlag).

Minde, H. (2005), 'The Alta case: from local to the global and back again', in: Cant et al. (eds).

Mykland (ed.), *Norges historie*, Vol 13 (Oslo: J.W. Cappelens Forlag A/S).

Nilsson J.E. and Rydningen, A. (eds) (2005), *Nord-Norge møter framtiden* (Oslo: Orkana).

NOU (1985), *Samisk kultur og utdanning* (Oslo: Kultur- og vitenskapsdepartementet. NOU 1985:14).

Nyseth, T. and Pedersen, P. (2005), 'Globalisation from below: the revitalisation of a coastal Sàmi community in the northern Norway as a part of the global discourse', in: Cant et al. (eds).

Olsen, K. (2008), *Identities, Ethnicities and Border Zones: Exemplars from Finnmark, Northern Norway.* PhD dissertation (Bergen: University of Bergen).

Pedersen, P. (2005), 'Periferiens siste utvei – betaling for å bo', in: Nilsson, J.E. and Rydningen, A. (eds).

Pedersen, P. and Høgmo, A. (2004), *Krise, kamp og forsoning. Evaluering av samepolitiske tiltak i Kåfjord* (Tromsø: NORUT Samfunnsforskning AS).

Pedersen, P. and Høgmo, A. (2006), *Modernisering og revitalisering i sjøsamiske distrikter i siste generasjo* (Tromsø. NORUT Samfunnsforskning AS).

Putnam, R.D. (1995), *Bowling Alone* (Princeton: Princeton University Press).

Quinn, B. (2005), 'Arts festivals and the city', *Urban Studies*, 42(5–6), 927–43.

Røiseland, A. and Aarsæther, N. (1999), 'Lokalsamfunn og demokrati – Teoretisk og metodisk aspekt ved begrepet sosial kapital', *Norsk Statsvitenskapelig Tidsskrift Nr 2, pp 184-201* , (Oslo).

Steinlien, Ø. (2006), 'Kontinuitet og endring i håndteringen av identitet i et sjøsamisk område', in: Stordalen, V. (ed.).

Stordalen, V. (ed.) (2006), *Samisk identitet og kontinuitet og endring*. Diedut no. 3 (Kautokeino: Nordisk Samisk Institutt).

Spilling, O.R. (1998), *Entreprenørskap på norsk* (Bergen: Fagbokforlaget).

Spilling, O.R. (ed.) (2000), *SMB 2000 – fakta om små og mellomstore bedrifter i Norge* (Bergen: Fagbokforlaget).

Teigen, H. (2004), 'Kollektivt entreprenørskap; eit alternativ også for framtida?', in: Arbo, P. and Gammelsæter, H. (eds).

Thuen, T. (2003), 'Lokale diskurser om det Samiske', in: Bjerkli, B. and Selle, P. (eds), *Samer, Makt og Demokrati*, pp. 265–90 (Oslo: Gyldendal Akademisk).

Viken, A. (2008), *Reinvention of Ethnic Identity – A Local Festival as a National Institution on a Global Scene*. Paper (Polar tourism research network, Kangersuquujak, 21–25 August).

Weber, M. (1970), *The Interpretation of Social Reality* (London). Publisher unknown.

Wegner, E. (1998), *Communities of Practice: Learning, Meaning and Identity* (Cambridge: Cambridge University Press).

Chapter 12
Reinventing Rurality in the North

Mai Camilla Munkejord

Hegemonic discourses in Norway define different areas of the country as more or less rural based on criteria such as location, population density and population size (Berg and Lysgård 2004). Finnmark, being the northernmost county situated 2000 km away from the capital Oslo, with the lowest population size (73,000 inhabitants),[1] and the lowest population density (less than two persons per km^2), is by such discourses defined as the *most rural* region in Norway. The possible interrelations between rurality and urbanity in the North on the other hand, are hardly considered within these hegemonic discourses. This chapter attempts to do so by discussing whether 'rurality', as defined within hegemonic discourses might be useful to make sense of experiences and representations of everyday life of women and men living in an area defined as rural by such hegemonic discourses. Inspired by theoretical contributions from feminist geography in particular, and based on a qualitative study among in-migrants in the small town of Vadsø in Finnmark, this chapter examines the content and characteristics of everyday discourses on rurality and reflects on how these constitute not only a contrast to hegemonic discourses on the rural, but also on how such everyday discourses can be understood as a re-invention of rurality in the North.

The chapter is organized as follows: The first part starts by shortly describing hegemonic discourses on the rural. It then presents relevant discourse, analytical theory on rurality, the empirical context, and the methodology used. The second part explores in-migrants' everyday discourses of rurality revealing that they are conceptually multiple and varied, but at the same time constructed in a particular way. Rurality, here meaning representations of what it is like to live in a small place in Finnmark, is thereby constructed (a) explicitly in the context of other places where the in-migrants have lived, visited or heard of, and (b) implicitly and explicitly in the context of hegemonic discourses on rurality. Hence, I argue that such hegemonic discourses are experienced as 'far-fetched' when it comes to making sense of female and male in-migrants' diverse everyday experiences. The chapter shows that hegemonic discourses on rurality, in other words, are not capable of meaningfully making sense of everyday life and place perceptions in a small town in Finnmark – even if the region in accordance with different hegemonic discourses is geographically 'remote' (from the capital region Oslo),

---

1 Statistics of Norway, 2008, (http://www.fifo.no/finnstat/befolkning/Befolkningsstruktur. htm).

small and sparsely populated. The inhabitants, then, do not at all identify with hegemonic discourses on the rural North emphasizing marginality, periphery and outdatedness. Thus, the chapter shows that a place reinvention is taking place in Vadsø among inhabitants striving to produce other stories of what it is like to live in the northernmost part of the country. The empirical examples show that rurality is reinvented in such a way that what is popularly referred to as rural and urban meanings and dimensions are perceived as interrelated rather than opposed.

Hegemonic Representations of the North

Hegemonic representations of Finnmark have a long history. Already in the travel literature written by European explorers from the 16th century onwards, Finnmark is described as *Ultima Thule* meaning 'the extreme point of the world' (Birkeland 2005, 35). The religion historian Siv Ellen Kraft puts it this way:

> Northern Norway has traditionally been constructed according to a North–South axis, with 'south' as the centre of power and decision-making, and 'north' as a suppressed and exploited backyard (Kraft, 2008, 222).

Kraft adds that the national media until recently have described Northern Norway within a hegemonic discourse emphasizing smallness, periphery, nature and tradition and the people in the area are described as out-of-date and simple (ibid.). The social scientists Stien, Kramvig and Berglund (2005, 84) argue that this type of pejorative discourses on Finnmark/Northern Norway function as a contrast to, and thereby accentuating a Southern Norwegian self-understanding. They further argue that whereas these discourses have been met with laughter and other forms of local resistance, they have also in certain ways grown into and become part of the repertoire of available perceptions of self for people living in the northernmost region of the country – even today. The social scientist Gry Paulgaard (2008, 59) argues the same when she writes that living in the North 'also involves "growing into" fundamental constructions, contrasts and distinctions that are related to both symbolic and natural conditions'.

The geographer Rob Shields suggests the concept 'place images' to shed some light on how hegemonic discourses may mark or brand places and regions. Place images, according to him, contribute to the construction of cultural place-related meanings through dichotomies such as 'north–south' and 'marginal–central' (Shields 1991). Some places can, he argues, be defined as 'social peripheries'. These are:

> marginal places that have been placed on the periphery of cultural systems of space in which places are ranked relative to each other. They all carry the image, and stigma of their marginality which becomes indistinguishable from any basic empirical identity they might once have had (ibid., 5).

Thus, when Finnmark by different discourses is defined as the *most rural* region in Norway, this implies not only 'neutral' connotations related to location, population size and density, but also entails perceptions of a remote, simple, exploited and marginal region that, we may assume, is not able to offer its inhabitants good conditions for a meaningful everyday life.

A useful theoretical starting point to challenge simplistic hegemonic definitions of rural places can be found within feminist geography. Linda McDowell for instance, argues that place, which in our case can be translated to rurality, can be understood as 'a fluid network of social relations that may be but are not necessarily tied to territory' (McDowell 1999, 100). Thus, this perspective challenges attempts to bind sociocultural meanings to a specific territory – that is to define a place as *only* rural or *only* urban. The meaning of a place, and also rurality, should instead be viewed as 'always unfixed, contested and multiple' (Massey 1994, 5).

Analysing Rurality

I take as a point of departure that women and men live and act within hegemonic discourses that delimit what it is possible to think and say (Jørgensen and Phillips 1999; Hammer 2001; Søndergaard 1999; Simonsen 1996). Discourses, as defined by the influential social psychologists Potter and Wetherell (1987, 7), are 'all forms of spoken interaction, formal and informal, and written texts of all kinds'. Discourses 'speak about' the material and social everyday life, but they also constitute models for behaviour.[2] Hence, discourses produce social and cultural effects (Foucault 1989; Søndergaard 2002). Discourses can further be characterized as 'inherently elusive', in the sense that they may contain contradictory aspects (Halfacree 1995, 2). This entails that meaning is floating; that all concepts may make sense in an endless number of combinations of discourses. Instead of establishing fixed definitions of the rural, then, this interpretative project attempts to deconstruct discourses on rurality in order to uncover different kinds of power relations, hoping to expose reinventions of rurality in the sense of new and alternative representations of what it is like to live in a particular northern place defined as rural by different national hegemonic discourses.

Recent qualitative studies focus on how rurality is constructed by women and men by examining the production, practising and contestation of multiple meanings of the rural, both in Britain (Little 2002; Valentine 1997; Pratt 1996; Little and Austin 1996; Halfacree 1995; Massey 1994) and, to a certain extent, in Norway (Berg 2002; Berg and Forsberg 2003; Berg and Lysgård 2004). A gap

---

2 A well-known example from British rural studies is the representation of the rural idyll that in numerous studies is assumed to produce counter-urbanization. A close but somewhat opposite example from Norway, is the consequent media (and academic) representations of the 'rural exodus' that is assumed to contribute to prevent potential in-migrants from actually settling down in the districts.

in Norwegian rurality studies however is that both the north–south dimension as well as the coast–inland dimension are omitted (Munkejord 2006). This chapter attempts to fill this gap by focusing on the everyday discourses of rurality in a northern coastal town.

A well-known discourse analytical model within rural studies for studying rurality as multiple productions of meanings, is developed by the geographer Owain Jones (1995). He argues for the relevance of distinguishing between discourses not on the basis of their content, but on the basis on *who* produces the discourse. This model comprises (a) *lay discourses* defined as '*communication about the rural that people construct and encounter in their everyday lives*', (b) *popular discourses* which are produced in and disseminated through cultural phenomena such as art, literature and the media, (c) *professional discourses* produced by political or bureaucratic decision-makers and planners and, (d) *academic discourses* produced by researchers studying rurality (1997, 38). In this chapter, however, it is first and foremost relevant to distinguish between, on the one hand, lay discourses produced by the interviewed in-migrants in Vadsø and, on the other hand, hegemonic discourses produced from, and by actors in, the South, defining Finnmark as the most rural region in Norway implying connotations as we have seen, such as marginal, peripheral, out of date, and so on. A region or a place defined as 'rural' within hegemonic discourses may in other words not be recognized as such by the inhabitants of the place, and vice versa. In the following, however, instead of the concept lay discourses, I choose to talk about everyday discourses since the actors producing them are themselves highly educated in-migrants being in daily discussion with other types of discourses such as professional, academic and popular. However, the mismatch between everyday and hegemonic discourses leads us to ask: who has the power to define a certain place as rural or urban, and who has the power to define what rurality may be all about? These are important questions that we will come back to in the conclusion.

Rurality – An *Analytical* Concept

When arguing that I study everyday discourses on rurality in Finnmark, 'rurality' should be viewed as an analytical concept not used by the informants themselves. Actually, the concept 'rural' is hardly used in the Norwegian language, and 'rurality', even less. At the same time, in Finnmark hardly anybody (if anyone) would say that they live in the 'countryside', in Norwegian 'bo på landet', and if you live in a small settlement on the Finnmark coast, you would not say that you live in a village, 'bygd', but rather in a 'fiskevær' (a small, but densely populated fishing settlement). The word 'village' ('bygd'), according to my informants, refers to a small *farm*-based settlement in the southern part of Norway or abroad. In Finnmark then, when people use names to speak of places, they specify whether they live on the coast, 'kysten', or in the mountain plateau, 'vidda'. The bigger settlements in Finnmark, such as Vadsø, are conceived as a 'town' by some of its inhabitants, whereas others consider they do not live in a town, 'but in some kind of a township where people combine all kinds of activities'. So, when I wanted to get insight into the everyday discourses of rurality in Finnmark, I was unable to use terms such as rural, rurality, village or countryside, but instead had to ask questions such as: 'Why did you move to Vadsø/to Finnmark?', 'How is everyday life *here*?', 'What is your ideal home place like?' and 'How do you perceive the future?'

The Study

Why in-migrants?

The reason for choosing to study *in-migrants* in Finnmark and their representations of rurality, instead of focusing on 'the return-migrants', 'the locals', or other possible categories, is first and foremost that in-migrants constitute a neglected group among rural inhabitants in Norway in general and in Finnmark in particular. Statistics show that people move to Finnmark, and they show that a little more than 50 per cent of the in-migrants are women (Sørlie 2000; Holm 2004). In spite of a relatively high turn-over, more than one-third of the population in Finnmark today is born outside Finnmark. Interestingly though, hegemonic discourses in research as well as in the media have focused nearly exclusively on the high *out*-migration from Finnmark, particularly emphasizing the high numbers of young women that leave the region.[3] Hence, different academic studies as well as representations in the media have nurtured the popular discourse of Finnmark as 'the region of (female) exodus'. In-migrants in Finnmark and their representations and reinventions of ruralities, are therefore widely neglected topics.

Presentation of the Empirical Context: Vadsø

Vadsø is the name of a small town as well as a municipality situated in the east of Finnmark, a one-hour drive from the border to Finland, and 2.5 hours from Russia. The municipality of Vadsø is vast: 1,259 km², and has 6,122 inhabitants (4.9 persons/km²). Around 5,000 of them live in the town of Vadsø that constitutes the empirical context of this chapter. Vadsø is situated on the mainland and partially on an island linked to the mainland by a bridge. The Vadsø landscape is open with a wide, quite flat and bare mountain plateau facing a large fjord. The settlement

---

3 Different studies that focus on out-migration from rural areas in one form or another are for instance Grimsrud, 2000. Relevant newpaper articles focsing on the exodus from Finnmark, published in *Dagbladet*, the second biggest newspaper in Norway are for example, 'Framtida drar fra Finnmark' (*The future leaves Finnmark*) 24 May 2003 and 'Exit Finnmark', 15 July 2003.

is quite concentrated, so that you can reach the whole settlement within an hour's walk. In the centre, you can find art galleries, some cafes, an Indian restaurant, a cinema and a culture centre offering concerts and plays by local theatre groups as well as by the national ambulant theatre. There is also an indoor football hall, a couple of fitness centres, a swimming pool, a library, food stores, hair dressers, a bakery and a variety of shops selling everything from shoes to electrical articles. From time to time there is what is locally called the 'Russian market' with crystals and other artefacts from over the border.

Vadsø's history as a settlement goes far back. It was registered as a fishing village with a church as early as in 1567.[4] There was a considerable Finnish in-migration to Vadsø during the 19th century, and by the 1875 census, nearly half of the population were reported to be of this origin (Kven[5]) (Stien et al. 2005, 99–100). Today, a large number of the inhabitants is of ethnically mixed heritage. The town centre was seriously damaged during the German capitulation process in 1944, only a few houses survived the bombings. Earlier the most important sectors were agriculture, fishing and commerce. Today, however, as most of the positions related to the Finnmark county administration are placed in Vadsø, the labour market is characterized by what can be called high competence administrative bureaucracy positions.[6] The coastal steamer daily calls at Vadsø, and there is a local airport[7] with flights several times per day connecting Vadsø to other places.

Methods

This chapter is based on empirical material produced during three months of fieldwork in Vadsø during spring 2005. During the fieldwork I did several in-depth interviews with in-migrants from 17 households.[8] The informants were interviewed for three to four hours on average, and all interviews were tape recorded and fully transcribed. The informants are 50:50 men and women, aged between 25 and 60. They are highly educated; two-thirds have studied for four years or more at university. All of them except three have full-time jobs, often within the public

---

4 www.vadso.kommune.no

5 Ethnic minority group from Northern Finland.

6 Fifty-eight per cent of the labour force in Vadsø work within the public sector (against 35 per cent on average in Norway), nearly half of this (25 per cent) work within public administration – whereas the average in Norway is only 6.6 per cent (http://www.fifo.no/finnstat/index.htm).

7 Regional aerodrome with a short runway.

8 Within these 17 households, there are altogether 31 adults of whom I have interviewed 26 and met with another three. Among the 31, 29 were born outside Vadsø and have moved to the municipality as adults. In the cases where the household consisted of two adults I did the first interview with the couple together when this was possible. I selected 19 as my 'main informants', and did a second individual in-depth interview with them in order to obtain deeper and more detailed information for my different fields of interest.

sector, but some are self-employed. They have grown up in all parts of Norway, in smaller and larger places, as well as in countries such as Finland, Russia and Thailand. They have lived in Finnmark between two and forty years. Most of them have social, professional and family networks that necessitate them making trips out of Vadsø on a regular basis.

Structural studies on *migration* in general primarily focus on economic and external conditions that are assumed to push and pull people from one area to another. Within more qualitatively oriented studies on the other hand, migration is conceptualized in a more complex way, often analysed as an inherent component of the individual migrant's total biography (Berg and Forsberg 2003; Halfacree and Boyle 1998; Villa 2000; Wiborg 2003). Applying a biographical perspective, my interviews have focused on the background of the in-migrants in order to find out why they chose to come to Finnmark, why they choose to stay, how they describe their lives in northern Norway, and how they perceive the future. In this chapter I'll present and discuss extracts from the life stories of five in-migrants.

Before turning to part two, where I explore everyday representations of rurality in Vadsø, Finnmark, I'll briefly introduce my informants, particularly highlighting a few gender aspects.

A Gendered Presentation of Informants

British feminists in rural studies indicate that gender culture in rural areas is highly conventional and traditional (cf. Little 2002). Studies from Northern Norway, however, show that this does not apply here (cf. Gerrard 2003; Hauan 1999; Gerrard 2000; Holtedahl 1986; Kramvig 1999; Førde 2004). In fact, a basic premise in Scandinavian society, one may argue, concerns the sex/gender equality (Søndergaard 2002, 195), an ideal that seems to be practised to a certain extent in my material in the light of the large representation of the two-career family pattern. In fact, 28 of the 31 adults in my 17 households do have a full time job – either a steady one or some kind of temporary engagement.[9] In six of the 14 households consisting of a couple with or without children, the partners have around the same income, in another six cases, the male partner earns more, and in two cases, the woman is the main breadwinner. When asked explicitly about gender, nearly all informants start to speak about who does what in the house and with the children. Actually, nine of 11 households with children living at home embraced the ideal

---

9   Among the three who do not have a full time job, there is one man and two women. The man is searching for a job, but with no higher education and health problems, that is not an easy task. Also, this man is married to a woman with a higher university education and a fairly good job. A younger woman is at home with a one-year-old child and she is expecting a second child. The second woman has decided to work part time to have more time for leisure and political activities.

of a 50/50 share of domestic and child care duties. This ideal seems to carry an important symbolic significance.

Feminist rural studies show how gender is relevant when it comes to explaining migration (Little 2002). The reasons my informants moved to Finnmark range from issues related to work, economy, family, to the desire for an adventure or for an exotic framework of everyday life, living too close, or too far away from family and combinations of these. Whereas in Little's study from Great Britain, the woman's job was in no case given as a reason for family relocation (2002, 116), ten of my main informants explain that either her or his job was the decisive reason for moving, the woman's job accounting for as much as one-third of the cases![10] This finding both supports and challenges Little's argument: challenges, because some families say they moved to Finnmark because of her career project; supports, because there is still a strong male bias.

In the following presentation I will attempt to highlight variations in the representations of rurality constructed by the in-migrants in Vadsø.

Presentation of Cases

Distances

An elderly couple, Svein and Eva, were both born in a small coastal community in Finnmark. They moved to Vadsø, which they consider a 'nice town', 12 years ago. When I asked what it is like to live in Vadsø, Svein, the husband, explains that it is better to live in Vadsø 'than in the southern part of the country' because in Vadsø, distances are so short:

> When you finish work, you're home in 5 minutes … You can go to your friends by foot, take a glass of wine and walk home again, whereas in the south your social life is easily amputated by the long distances. That's my experience. I have lived down there for 2–3 years, and we've lots of friends who still do, so we know how it is.

Like many other informants, Svein contrasts the good life in Vadsø to everyday life in 'the South' – a term that in Finnmark mainly refers to the capital region of Norway. Interestingly, this North–South construction is similar to the Welsh constructions of difference between Wales and England, the latter being associated

---

10   In one case, for example, the woman got a relevant job in Vadsø, moved, and was joined by her partner after a few months when he too had got a job there. In two other cases the husband moved together with the wife without having a job as yet. Both men, though, obtained a job within a rather short time, but jobs with a lower status than their wife's job, and with a lower income.

with colonialism, arrogance, and so on (Cloke et al. 1998). According to Svein, distances in the South:

> force people to spend a lot of time travelling to work and bringing children to school, kindergarten and leisure activities. Vadsø on the other hand is constructed as a 'town' so 'small and so compact' that you can walk to your friends and, if you take the car, you can go anywhere within less than 5 minutes.

The good life in Vadsø, according to our informant Svein, is about short distances, no transport time and friends close by. This is interesting, because within the southern hegemonic popular discourse on Finnmark, distances are long *not* in the South, but in the North, and they assume that people in Finnmark have to spend a great deal of time and money to go to places. But while Finnmark is indeed a vast region with long distances between the different clusters of settlement, Svein chooses to focus on the short distances *within* his home place. Svein is not the only one to challenge the popular discourse about distances in Finnmark. A majority of my informants construct rurality in the North as having extra time to 'live and breathe', used as a metaphor for *quality* of life.

A town in the middle of nature

Ann and Tom are in their late 20s and have lived in Vadsø for a few years. They both grew up in the southern part of Norway, Tom in a sparsely populated village and Ann in a rather big town. After studying a number of years in one of Norway's university towns, Tom was the only one to find work, so they both moved to the village where he was employed. Ann was employed by the local primary school there, but didn't like her work very much. After a few months she started to apply for relevant jobs related to her university degree, and soon optained the 'perfect' job in Vadsø. She moved there without hesitation, and after some months Tom too found employment there and joined her. They describe it as wonderful to come to a 'town' with a 'café' where you could buy 'cafe latte', with a 'bakery', a 'cinema' and 'several shops'. They also stress that they appreciate and attend the cultural activities that are offered. Actually, they 'attend more concerts and see more plays with ambulant theatres in Vadsø than [they] used to when [they] lived in [their university town]'. However, in addition to these rather urban activities, the couple says that they very much appreciate the closeness to nature. Ann puts it in this way: 'I love that we are living in a town in the middle of nature: We live in the centre of Vadsø and it takes us only 10 minutes to walk down to the sea shore, and 10 minutes to walk up to the mountain plateau ("vidda").'

This couple are among those who really enjoy outdoor activities such as cross country skiing, kayaking, and taking long walks for hours in the mountain plains or along the shore. They both like to hunt – Ann shot her first grouse last winter – but they emphasize that this is not a passion for any of them. As we can see, Ann and Tom stress the importance of the possibility of *combining* cultural activities, shopping, cafes, *and* outdoor nature-based activities such as hiking, canoeing , hunting and skiing. This *combination* constitutes for them and for a number of other informants the essence of good life in Vadsø.

Before continuing, I would like to add that hunting and fishing are still highly gendered activities in Norway, and Finnmark in particular (Pedersen 2003) . Half of my *male informants* say that they 'like' to hunt, however emphasizing that they only do it a few days per year. Moreover, nearly all men stress that they 'enjoy fishing', while stressing that they normally fish only a few times every year, often together with their children. My *female informants* on the other hand say that they are not very interested in fishing or hunting. Ann is the only 'hunter', but a few tell me that they go fishing from time to time. Some of the women explain that they like to go skiing or hiking 'for well-being', but as many as half of them emphasize that they do not engage in any outdoor activity at all, adding that 'Nature is over-valued'. On the other hand, the female informants, even more strongly than the male, emphasize the scenic and beautiful landscape in Vadsø, adding that such surroundings have positive effects on their mental state. 'The tall sky and the wide open landscape make me breathe', as one of them expressed it. Hence, the male informants seem to represent the landscape surrounding Vadsø as an arena for physical outdoors activities, whereas the women tend to represent it as aesthetic scenery providing a calm and nice atmosphere in their everyday life.

Research on outdoor recreation and adventure shows that this is an area of practice for men more than women, and that their activities largely depend on their female partner staying at home, taking care of the house and children while they are away in the outdoors (Pedersen 2003). However, what I find interesting to include in this leisure context, is that half of the mothers with small children tell me that they frequently do things on their own leaving husband and children behind, engaging in activities such as visiting friends living far away or spending the weekend in a bigger town to go shopping. According to them, the male partner on such occasions takes the full responsibility for housekeeping and children. Thus, staying at home to take care of house and children while the partner is having fun is constructed as a task for both women and men in the everyday discourse. Both the male and the female partner are represented as each other's assistant in the household, and both women and men are represented as actors creating space of their own.

The ambivalence of visibility

Lisa and Peter, aged 35–40, have grown up in smaller places in the Oslo region, and they both have a higher university degree. They decided to move to Vadsø after their studies because they both had good job opportunities there. The fact that Lisa's mother grew up in Vadsø, but left more than 40 years ago, means that Lisa went to Vadsø several times during her childhood. She still has aunts, uncles and cousins living in Vadsø, and her family still has some contact with these relatives.

Lisa explains that Vadsø is the smallest possible place where she would even consider living. She grew up in a village, and says that she does *not* appreciate the feeling that everyone 'watches over you, controlling what you're doing'. The first days as inhabitants in Vadsø were rather shocking. Lisa and Peter came directly from the student hostel in their university town, they hardly owned anything, and went directly to the furniture store in Vadsø. Lisa had rather clear ideas of what kind of furniture she wanted, but when she asked for certain things, the salesmen just 'rolled their eyes and said they didn't sell that kind of stuff'. The next evening Lisa's mother, Mari, calls to say that she has heard about the furniture problems: 'People had talked, you know', Lisa explains, and adds that some of the locals probably had heard that Mari's daughter would move to town, and then someone had told someone else about the failed furniture shopping, and in the end 'another someone' had called Lisa's mother. Lisa tells me that she was quite upset by this phone call:

> I thought that I would never manage to cope with living in Vadsø if everyone, even my mother, would know about every one of my footsteps and all my preferences ...

Eventually, however, things must have gone rather well, because Lisa, Peter and their two children still enjoy life in Vadsø after a few years. Both Lisa and Peter have interesting jobs, and Lisa is, in addition, involved in local activities such as the jazz club. Lisa stresses that it is easy for her as a woman to become visible in Finnmark. She says that

> if you have ambitions and want a position, you will be seen and will get a position more easily here than in a bigger place.

However, Lisa says that she does not live in Vadsø 'with all her heart and all her soul'. What makes her stay, she argues, are the relatively well paid and interesting jobs for herself and her husband, which gives the family economic freedom and a high degree of mobility (two annual travels abroad for the whole family). In addition, Lisa stresses that Vadsø is a good and safe place for her children to grow up in: she reckons that there are less drugs, alcohol and less 'fashion pressure' in Vadsø than in a larger town. Lisa also emphasizes that distances are so short in Vadsø that everyday life runs very smoothly; her children can even go to school alone, and she never loses time in traffic jams.

This case shows the *ambivalence of visibility* that an inhabitant, and particularly a woman, may experience in a small place like Vadsø. *Professionally and politically* Lisa does enjoy being visible since this opens up doors and contributes to giving women space and positions if they have such ambitions. Analytically, I can say that it seems that traditional 'bastions of male hegemony' have now opened up to women that are willing to enter. *Socially* speaking, on the other hand, visibility is experienced as a burden. Lisa sometimes feels that 'everyone' knows everything about her, her tastes, her preferences, and so on. In fact, Lisa's social network is large and includes not only professional colleagues and friends, but also neighbours and relatives on her mother's side such as aunts, uncles and cousins. Lisa is the one who gets the feedback and the reactions from neighbours and relatives if she and her husband break local tacit cultural rules by, for example, not putting up curtains in the kitchen. Lisa describes this social visibility as a *social control*. In Norway, this kind of social control is called 'bygdedyret' ('the rural animal'), and is often constructed as an important aspect of popular, and sometimes even everyday, discourses on rurality (Grimsrud 2000). However, Lisa is the only one in my material speaking about social visibility as having a suffocating effect. Her position as a woman in-migrant with family relationships in Vadsø may be relevant in understanding why this is so.

Easy and pleasant small town life

An elderly lady, Siv, moved to Vadsø from southern Norway 30 years ago together with her husband, also a southerner, and their two children. She is now divorced, and her adult children have settled down in the capital region. Siv has no relatives in Finnmark, but has opted to stay. According to her, this is because she likes the everyday rhythm in Vadsø so much: 'I like the pleasant pulse, it is so easy to live here!' she says. She also emphasizes, like most of the in-migrants, that she really appreciates the 'wonderful and somewhat wild climate', with the midnight sun during two months in the summer, and the blue Arctic winter with lots of northern lights. When describing Vadsø people she says that: 'People are very curious. They want to know everything about who's together with whom and who's divorced from whom, and why and how, but at the same time people are very accepting. Whatever happens is just fine. I really appreciate that!' We should note, however, that the 'curiosity' described by Siv, is rather similar to what Lisa experiences as 'social control'. Why Lisa and Siv experience this 'curiosity' so differently may be because of their different personalities, social positions, age, family situation, and so on.

Moreover, my material shows that divorce, children outside marriage and partnerships (instead of marriage) are constructed as common and accepted practices by my informants. My study of the neighbouring municipality Tana shows the same tendency. In-migrants from southern Norway in Tana stress that they're impressed by the very 'tolerant culture', emphasizing that they feel that locals are less concerned with appearance and less afraid of losing face than what they were used to from where they grew up further south (Munkejord 2005).

A Safe Corner – Linked to the World

One of my informants is Lao, a young woman from Thailand. She is married to a highly educated return migrant. She also speaks very warmly about the beauty of the landscape, and about how much she appreciates the safety there. Her child can run around outside the house without her having to watch over him all the time because there's hardly any traffic in the neighbourhood, and she does not need to lock the door to the house nor to the car. The empirical material, then, suggest that even migrants from non-Western countries have adopted the local discourse about Vadsø as a beautiful and safe place.

When I ask Lao what it is like to live so far away from her family, she says that she is not far away. She explains that she grew up in a small village in a remote part of Thailand, where her family still lives. As a teenager she went to Bangkok to work in a factory, and could only afford to go home to visit her family once a year. After moving to Norway, however, she has visited her parents and relatives twice a year, and is able to phone them every week! This shows the relevance of considering people as belonging to several places at the same time.

Several of my informants in this study speak about mobile lives. They travel during vacations, some of them do a lot of job related travelling as well; they may have relatives in several houses, and their friends and relatives may be dispersed over several places in the country that they try to visit from time to time. The example about Lao shows in addition that even if Vadsø is situated a long distance from the capital region in Norway and from the heart of Europe, it can still be experienced as a central place by its inhabitants. For Lao distance is no longer about kilometres, but about money and possibilities to be mobile.

Reinventing Rurality

This chapter is inspired by interpretative methodology as well as by Owain Jones's analytical model of how to study discourses on rurality (1995). The first part briefly presented central hegemonic discourses on rurality in the North with connotations such as marginality, periphery, exploitation and out-of-datedness. The second part explored different aspects of in-migrants' everyday discourses on the good life in a small town in Finnmark, defined as 'rural' by such discourses.

In the five empirical cases discussed, the in-migrants construct Vadsø in diverse ways: some as a 'town', others as a 'small place', some construct the surrounding landscape as 'beautiful scenery', others as an 'arena for outdoor activities'. Hence, on an individual level, the in-migrant discourses can be characterized as spatially specific, but conceptually incoherent (Jones 1995), in the sense that the same place is constructed in different ways by different inhabitants. However, everyday discourses are also shared and in analysing the interview material, I noted that in-migrants as a group construct rurality in Vadsø by highlighting elements such as 'beautiful landscape', 'direct access to all kinds of outdoor activities', 'safety', 'easy life' and 'laid back lifestyle'. Notably, this representation is quite similar to everyday discourses of the rural idyll presented in studies from the UK (Halfacree 1995; Little and Austin 1996; Pratt 1996; Valentine 1997). However, the in-migrants in Vadsø, very interestingly, insist on also adding more 'urban' elements to their construction of Vadsø. They emphasize aspects such as 'clustered settlement', 'cinema', 'culture stage with concerts', 'cafe latte', 'gender equality' and 'high mobility'. Thus, the good life in Vadsø is constructed by in-migrants as a *combination* of so-called rural and urban lifestyles and activities. Everyday discourses on rurality, in other words, do not refer to elements such as 'distance from the capital region', 'low population size' and 'low population density' to make sense of varied and multiple representations of life in Vadsø. Pejorative connotations related to such hegemonic discourses on rurality, like out-of-datedness, marginality and periphery are, by inhabitants in Vadsø, regarded as even more far-fetched. Everyday discourses produced by inhabitants in Vadsø then, reinvent rurality in the North by combining elements and aspects traditionally referred to as urban *and* rural and *in clear contrast* to national hegemonic discourses produced by actors in and from the South.

The fact that the content in hegemonic discourses on rurality does not at all correspond with everyday discourses on rurality produced by people living in a so-called rural area, compels us to question power relations both within and between different types of discourses: who has the power to define a certain place as rural or urban, and who has the power to define the content and connotations of such concepts? And why is it so important for in-migrants in a municipality with only 6,000 inhabitants on the top of Norway to reinvent the content in the 'rural' label designated to the whole Finnmark region by hegemonic discourses?

These are central but difficult questions. One contribution to an answer consists of highlighting the very different nature of everyday discourses in comparison with the hegemonic discourses referred to in this chapter. Everyday discourses in general refer to communication that people construct and encounter in their everyday lives (Jones 1995, 38), and everyday discourses *on rurality* express the personal experiences and representations that inhabitants articulate in a so-called rural place. Hegemonic discourses, on the other hand, are not based on personal everyday experiences, but draw inspiration from all kinds of discourses (everyday, popular, academic) that are used to develop conceptually precise, but spatially and culturally general definitions of rurality. Moreover, the main difference between everyday and hegemonic discourses, as far as I see it, may be that the latter, are constructed to abstract, think and explain, whereas everyday discourses are constructed as acceptable life narratives. Likewise, the producers of everyday and other discourses are likely to be in different power positions: the producers of everyday discourses are often less powerful and influential than those who produce the other types of discourses. Therefore hegemonic discourses (for example academic and popular discourses in the media), tend to absorb and marginalize everyday discourses which deviate.

While this would explain why some discourses become hegemonic in different ways, it does not make clear why hegemonic discourses on rurality in Norway continuously emphasize pejorative aspects such as remoteness, backwardness, periphery and marginality. Creed and Ching (1997) call attention to a relevant point insisting on the tendency of thought to be structured in binary oppositions.

They claim that rurality as a cultural category is mentally and unconsciously associated to rusticity, in the senses of 'backward' and 'outdated', whereas urbanity is associated with sophistication, in terms of the 'modern' and 'distinguished'. In other words: the 'urbanity–rurality' dualism constitutes a hierarchical deep-structure (situated in the back of our Western minds) where urbanity occupies the hegemonic and more valuable position.

But, if so, how can we explain that the hegemonic discourses on 'rurality' is constructed by the inhabitants in Vadsø not only as something to reject, but also at the same time is being reinvented through positive stories, experiences, dimensions and characteristics? The most fruitful perspective is perhaps to be found in Murdoch and Pratt's critique (1993) which argues that it is 'the *distinction* between rurality and urbanity that gives power to both' (1993, 415, quoted in Jones 1995, 45). Along this line this chapter argues for the need to understand rurality and urbanity as interrelated rather than opposed in order to make room for reinvention of place perceptions as rural and urban at the same time. Thus, a rural–urban debate as well as a critical questioning of possible consequences of an uncontested hegemonic power of definition of rurality and rural places, is not unique for Finnmark. Publications from different places around the world problematize negative aspects of a clear urban–rural distinction, and points to how urbanity and rurality are interconnected in different ways, both socially, culturally and spatially (Tacoli 1998; Thompson 2004). As the social scientist Tacoli (ibid., 147) puts it: 'The distinction between rural and urban is probably inescapable for descriptive purposes … In reality however, things tend to be far more complex.' This complexity is continuously translated by inhabitants of so-called rural places into new experience-based everyday discourses. Related to this, the social scientist Gry Paulgaard shows in her research that the Northern Norwegian identity project of today is not first and foremost about constructing differences or contrasts but, on the contrary, about emphasizing *similarities* between places and cultures in the South and the North (Paulgaard 2008). This chapter supports this argument by showing that everyday discourses on rurality by in-migrants in Vadsø is reinvented in contrast to hegemonic pejorative discourses, but at the same time by a combination of rural and urban aspects when representing what it is like to live in a small place in the northernmost part of Norway.

References

Berg, N.G. and Forsberg, G. (2003), 'Rural geography and feminist geography: Discourses on rurality and gender in Britain and Scandinavia', in: Öhman, J. and Simonsen, K. (eds), *Voices from the North. New trends in Nordic Human Geography*, pp. 173–89 (Aldershot: Ashgate).

Berg, N.G. and Lysgård, H.K. (2004), 'Ruralitet og urbanitet – bygd og by', in: Berg, N.G., Dale, B., Lysgård, H.K. and Løfgren, A. (eds), *Mennesker, steder og regionale endringer*, pp. 61–76 (Trondheim: Tapir Akademisk Forlag).

Birkeland, I. (2005), *Making Place, Making Self. Travel, Subjectivity and Sexual Difference* (Aldershot: Ashgate).

Cloke, P., Goodwin, M. and Milbourne, P. (1998), 'Inside looking out; Outside looking in. Different experiences of cultural competence in rural lifestyle', in: Boyle and Paul, H.K., (eds), *Migration into Rural Areas. Theories and Issues*, pp. 134–50 (Chichester: John Wiley & Son).

Creed, G.W. and Ching, B. (1997), 'Recognizing rusticity. Identity and the power of place', in: Creed, G.W. and Ching, B. (eds), *Knowing Your Place. Rural Identity and Cultural Hierarchy*, pp. 1–38 (London: Routledge).

Førde, A. (2004), *Svaler som gjer nye somrar kreative kvinnepraksisar i provencalsk og nordnorsk landbruk*, Monography for the Degree Doctor Rerum Politicarum (Department of Planning and Community Studies, University of Tromsø).

Foucault, M. (1989), *The Archaeology of Knowledge* (London and New York: Routledge).

Fredriksen, S. (2001), *Distriktskvinnescenarier 2010. Å tyde distriktsveier på kvinnefremtid*. (Oslo: Norsk institutt for by- og regionforskning).

Gerrard, S. (2000), 'The gender dimension of local festivals: The fishery crisis and women's and men's political actions in north Norwegian communities', *Women's Studies International Forum*, 23, 299–309.

Gerrard, S. (2003), 'Må det bo kvinnfolk i husan? Nye levekår, levemåter og nye utfordringer', in: Haugen, M.S. and Stræte, E.P. (eds), *Ut i verden og inn i bygda. Festskrift til Reidar Almås.*, pp. 143–58 (Trondheim: Tapir Akademisk Forlag).

Grimsrud, G.M. (2000), Kvinner på flyttefot. Lillehammer: Østlandsforskning, ØF-rapport 13.

Halfacree, K. and Boyle, P. (1998), 'Migration, rurality and the post-productivist countryside', in: Boyle, P. and Halfacree, K. (eds), *Migration into Rural Areas. Theories and Issues*, pp. 1–20 (Chichester, New York, Weinheim: John Wiley & Sons).

Halfacree, K.H. (1995), 'Talking about rurality: Social representations of the rural as expressed by residents of six English parishes', *Journal of Rural Studies*, 11(1), 1–20.

Hammer, S. (2001), 'Diskursbegrepet i sosiologisk relieff', *Sosiologi i dag* 31, 7–24.

Hauan, M. (1999), 'Velkommen, du kjører no inn i Harryland! Kystens menn i urbanitetens diskurs', in: Gerrard and Balsvik (eds), *Globale kyster. Liv i endring, kjønn i spenning*, pp. 157–67 (Kvinnforsk: Universitetet i Tromsø).

Holm, S. (2004), Bosatte i Finnmark etter bosted pr. 01.01.04. Statistics from Statistics of Norway, produced on request on 7 September 2004.

Holtedahl, L. (1986), *Hva mutter gjør er alltid viktig: om å være kvinne og mann i en nordnorsk bygd i 1970-årene* (Oslo: Universitetsforlaget).

Jones, O. (1995), 'Lay discourses of the rural: Development and implications for rural studies'. *Journal of Rural Studies* 11 (1): 35-49.

Jørgensen, M.W. and Phillips, L. (1999), *Diskursanalyse som teori og metode* (Fredriksberg: Roskilde Universitetsforlag).

Karlsen, U.D. (2001), *Ung i spenningens land analyser av preferanser knyttet til valg av utdanning, yrke og bosted blant nordnorsk ungdom*, Monography for the Degree Doctor Rerum Politicarum (Department of Pedagogy, University of Tromsø).

Kraft, S.E. (2008), 'Place-making through mega-events', in: Bærenholdt, J.O. and Granås, B (eds), *Mobility and Place. Enacting Northern European Peripheries*, pp. 219-232 (Aldershot: Ashgate).

Kramvig, B. (1999), 'Ære og verdighet: kvinnelighet og mannlighet i et fiskerisamfunn', in: Gerrard, S.B.R.R. (ed.), *Globale kyster. Liv i endring, kjønn i spenning*, pp. 63–77 (Kvinnforsks skriftserie 1: Universitetet i Tromsø).

Little, J. (2002), *Gender and Rural Geography. Identity, Sexuality and Power in the Countryside* (Harlow: Prentice Hall).

Little, J. and Austin, P. (1996), 'Women and the rural idyll', *Journal of Rural Studies* 12, 101–11.

Massey, D. (1994), *Space, Place and Gender* (Cambridge: Polity Press).

McDowell, L. (1999), *Gender, Identity and Place. Understanding Feminist Geographies* (Cambridge: Polity Press).

Munkejord, M.C. (2005), Det gode liv i Deatnu/Tana. En undersøkelse om Tanaværingers tanker om Tana som bosted og om Tanas omdømme. HiF-rapport 6. (Alta: Høgskolen i Finnmark).

Munkejord, M.C. (2006), 'Challenging discourses on rurality: Constructions of the good life in a rural town in northern Norway', *Sociologia Ruralis*, 46, 241–57.

Paulgaard, G. (2008), 'Re-centring periphery: Negotiating identities in time and tpace', in: Bærenholdt, J.O. and Granås, B (eds), *Mobility and Place. Enacting Northern European Peripheries.*, pp. 49–59 (Aldershot: Ashgate).

Pedersen, K. (2003), 'Discourses on nature and gender identities', in: Pedersen, K. and Viken, A. (eds), *Nature and Identity. Essays on the Culture of Nature*, pp. 121–50 (Bergen, Kristiansand: Høyskoleforlaget).

Potter, J. and Wetherell, M. (1987, *Discourse and Social Psychology: Beyond Attitudes and Behaviour* (London: Sage).

Pratt, A.C. (1996), 'Disourses of rurality: Loose talk or social struggle?', *Journal of Rural Studies*, 12, 69–78.

Shields, R. (1991), *Places on the Margin. Alternative Geography of Modernity*, ed. (London/New York: Routledge).

Simonsen, D.G. (1996), 'Som et stykket sæbe mellem fedtede fingre. Køn og poststrukturalistiske strategier', *Kvinder, Køn og* Forskning, 5, 29–51.

Skålnes, S. (2001), *Distriktskvinnescenarier 2010. På leit etter ei framtid*, (Oslo: Norsk institutt for by- og regionforskning).

Søndergaard, D.M. (1999), 'Destabiliserende diskursanalyse: veje ind i poststrukturalistisk inspirert empirisk forskning', in: Haavind, H. (ed.), *Kjønn og fortolkende metode. Metodiske muligheter i kvalitativ forskning*, pp. 60–104 (Oslo: Gyldendal Akademisk).

Søndergaard, D.M. (2002), 'Poststructuralist approaches to empirical analysis', *Qualitative Studies in Education*, 15, 187–204.

Sørlie, K. (2000), *Klassiske analyser. Flytting og utdanning belyst i livsløps- og kohortperspektiv* (Oslo: Norsk institutt for by- og regionsforskning).

Stien, K., Kramvig, B. and Berglund, A.-K. (2005), 'Finnmark – arbeid, velferd og kjønnete lokale strategier', in: Berglund, A.K.et al. (eds), *Med periferien i sentrum. En studie av lokal velferd, arbeidsmarked og kjønnsrelasjoner i den nordiske periferien*, pp. 78–112 (Finnmark: Norut NIBR).

Tacoli, C. (1998), 'Rural–urban interactions: A guide to the literature', *Environment and Urbanization*, 10, 147–66.

Thompson, E.C. (2004), 'Rural villages as socially urban spaces in Malaysia', *Urban Studies*, 41, 2357–76.

Valentine, G. (1997), 'A safe place to grow up? Parenting, perceptions of children's safety and the rural idyll', *Journal of Rural Studies*, 13, 137–48.

Villa, M. (2000), 'Livsfasebygda', in: Husmo, M. and Johnson, J.P. (eds), *Fra bygd og fjord til kafébord?*, pp. 175–85 (Trondheim: Tapir Akademisk Forlag).

Wiborg, A. (2003), *En ambivalent reise i et flertydig landskap. Unge fra distriktene i høyere utdannelse*, Monography for the Degree Doctor Rerum Politicarum (Department of Social Anthropology, University of Tromsø).

Chapter 13

The Narrative Constitution of Materiality

Arvid Viken and Torill Nyseth

Introduction

This book deals with reinvention of small towns and settlements in the rural North. The chapters point at a series of processes and events that are taken as evidence for change. It can however be argued that this is quite evident, that the character of the phenomena in focus is change; place, culture, industries are all dynamic elements. Thus, there might be a tendency to over-interpret signs of change; there may be stability beneath. Changes are often a necessity; industries and businesses adapt to changing circumstances to survive and authorities urge change to keep up employment and settlements patterns. So there is always a question of what is change, reinvention, revitalization, restructuring and so on. This is an argument put forward by Hoggart and Paniagua (2001) from a study of rural restructuring in England. According to them:

> Some of the processes now referred to as restructuring have been with us a long time, albeit having been re-invented and re-presenting themselves in new packaging every decade of so ... [R]e-packaging that lacks fundamental distinction from the past is not 'restructuring' (Hoggart and Paniagua 2001, 55).

They also claim that the term 'consumption countryside' is to 'suggest a too high level of transformation' (ibid. 35). This is partly the stance also in this book; changes can be observed, but absence of change is just as evident. Or rather, there is dialectic between change and not-change, and some communities exist due to changes in the ways they are presented and interpreted. In fact, this has been the focus in this book, how materiality as landscapes and industrial base and their representations are tied together, and how social constructed narratives create activities and reinvent places.

The book has aimed at understanding the significance of place rhetoric as conveyed through place promotion, images and identities. If it is socially accepted that a place is flourishing, it is presumed a good place to live. In the introduction (Chapter 1) the materiality and symbolic perspectives on place was presented. However, it is also emphasized that all this is, could or should be governed by politics. Although the focus has been on processes where social constructions of places appear, these processes are often intervened by political discourses and priorities.

For the analyses of place we have introduced the concept 'place reinvention'. Place reinvention is related to the overall changes going on, also beyond the economic sphere, involving place perceptions, how people identify with place and how place conceptions are manipulated through place narratives. In the preceding chapters the place reinvention concept has been developed further, through the analytical dimensions, material, symbolic and political production, with places on the northern rim as evidence. A basic question has been to what degree has the place reinvention concept produced new knowledge of place development? This chapter is devoted to this question.

In this book place has been understood both as geographical and physical location, as landscapes and townscapes, as sense of place – the subjective experience people have of a place, and as a social context and arena for everyday life. All these features are seen through the lenses of informants and authors. Their place construction processes are not neutral and natural, but take place within the frames of grand and small narratives, academic and professional discourses and public parlance. Thus, the book primarily contains interpretations and narratives of events, policies, development trajectories, promotional efforts and identity negotiations that add to the constitution of the places in question. The narratives can be organized under the following headings: (re)industrialization or cultural and experience economy turn, place promotion, identity, urban rurality and centre–periphery. Towards the end the narrative reinvention of places will be discussed.

Material Productions of Place

Modes of (re)industrialization

Several of the chapters in this book show that places seem to have one aim overarching all others: job creation. And as most of the places in the book are small towns originally founded by industrialization, a vital concern for most of them is how to create or sustain the industrial base. There are four ways in which the processes of (re)industrialization take place. The first way is *traditional industrialization*. One particular example of this is Fjarðabyggð in Iceland, where small-scale industry is substituted with a large modern aluminium plant, bringing the town into the industrial modus that most towns have left. Benediktsson, somewhat ironically, calls this process a second-hand modernity. The second type of process can simply be called *reindustrialization*; towns like Kirkenes in Norway and Kiruna in Sweden where they keep on their same industrial path, in both cases mining. The third form of process that has been observed in this book can be called *transforming industrialization*, referring to processes through which one industry is substituted with another such as changes from fishery to tourism, and from farming, fisheries and mining to cultural economies. The studies show that these processes often are troublesome, as they have been in Egilsstaðir in Iceland and in Pajala in Sweden, at least in towns with traditions of heavy industries. The fourth type is *diversifying industrialization.* The three mining towns referred to in the book have all taken the step from being exclusively mining and harbour towns to places of multiple production. Traditional industries are, however, still important but the industrial base is diversified and service industries and governmental employment are just as essential as the industries themselves, so there is a mixture of new and old industries that constitute the local economies. The small industrial towns in the North have not been restructured into spaces of consumption (Lash and Urry 1994), rather they show that production and consumption in the postmodern society more or less go hand in hand (cf. Thrift 2008).

The rhetoric on reindustrialization is also diverse. This rhetoric is situated in different types of discourses: public, political and academic. One is rooted in old social democratic values, valorizing industrial labour and manufacturing industry. This is *the industrial mantra,* a kind of masterframe that discredits alternatives. This has been observed both in Fjarðabyggð and Kirkenes. A second type of rhetoric is about *prosperous industrial futures*; it is about all opportunities related to local or regional resources, or to the town's position in trade systems. This has been observed in Fjarðabyggð, Kiruna and Kirkenes, Narvik and Båtsfjord. A third rhetoric is related to industrial crises, and is about *restructuring* or *development.* There are several cases of this type: Egilsstaðir, Pajala and Sørøya for example. The fourth rhetoric observed is about *obstructing industries*, which Throgmorton (2003) calls ghost narratives; it is about how old industrial structures and cultures are obstacles for modernization and development. This rhetoric was particularly used in Kirkenes, among those who wanted change and new industries to be prioritized, but is also observed in Egilsstaðir and Pajala.

Emerging experience and cultural economies?

Concerning cultural economy there are a whole series of interpretations of the term, stretching from the cultural implications of production and marketing, creating the stage on which modern human beings are playing, to the fact that to produce, sell and consume art and other 'cultured products' is all included in a growing part of the economy (cf. Amin and Thrift 2007). It is in this more narrow way, as an area for art and popular culture, that the term has been used in this book. However, there are not many examples of art-related production substituting traditional industries. The chapter discussing Egilsstaðir and Pajala points to the appearance of such a cultural economy, but at the same time the chapter shows that it is a difficult path, since as previously mentioned industrial inheritance tends to be a barrier. Another explanation for the restriction on development of a cultural economy can be the lack of a market for products – the Egilsstaðir case is an indication of this.

In several chapters the value of cultural production related to a place – as novels, films and marketing materials – is discussed. Such exposure creates attention and obviously has marketing effects. Berlevåg and Pajala both are places that have received significant media exposure because they are related to successful movie films. And of course the value of culture is mentioned as a factor creating a thriving environment and well-being. For instance in Vadsø, a small rural town, a variety of cultural offers makes an urban life possible.

There is an alternative label describing contemporary economies, namely 'experience economy'. Among the cases in this book there are particularly two that are an example of adaptation to the experience economy: Egilsstaðir and Sørøya. In Egilsstaðir a couple of special interest tourism activities can be identified, one related to a film and art festival, another devoted to sports hunting. On Sørøya fishery seems to be on the way to being replaced or supplemented by fish tourism. This is an interesting change; in fact it means that the value added by the local resources is multiplied. However, this is not a change without challenges: for fish tourism to succeed, it must rely in part on traditional fisheries that provide the sport fishing sector with boats, know how and a fishing environment.

There is also another example in the book of adaptation to the experience economy: Arboga. In its town planning priority is given to the town's medieval origin, and the well-preserved wooden houses from the 18th and 19th century. This falls into a well-known pattern: old harbours, streets, mines, plants and farms are transformed into shopping areas, theme parks, cultural institutions, tourist attractions or other forms of experience facilities. Such processes have also taken place in the North, but note there is only one flagship project among the cases, and that is to come in the future. In the discussion about moving the centre of Kiruna, the grid pattern, the town hall and the church must be saved because, it is argued locally, they are monumental signs of the old town. Such considerations and projects relate to a process that has been called 're-enchantment' (Ritzer 1994), and it also represents a landscape becoming tourist centred. It is claimed that tourism has substituted agriculture as a major rural industry in Great Britain (Sharpley 2003), and in Norway many fishing villages have been transformed into tourist resorts. However, for the northern rim, re-enchantment and becoming tourist centred are modest trends, probably due to the fact that the number of inhabitants in most places are too low to be economically beneficial.

The symbolic side of the cultural and experience economy paradigms are strong; it often feels as though it represents an ideology. And often the empirical evidence for such shifts is rooted in local stories, and it is argued that the changes are rhetorical or a question of redefinition. Activities, such as teaching, data processing and hair-dressing are re-categorized as culture or experience production. And often, the acquisitions are small. The case studies in this book support this; the new types of production in Egistadir and Pajala have had troublesome times, and Berlevåg, which had much media exposure due to the film made about the male choir in the town, has not seen an increase in investment or in-migration afterwards. Overall, the conclusion concerning industrial change on the northern rim does not quite fit the description Lash and Urry (1994) made in the early 1990s of a change from an 'economy of consumption' to an 'economy of signs and space', that also involved the 'production' of place. To make towns and villages more agreeable, welcoming and so on (see below) is also a well-known discourse in the North, but it is more about re-enchantment than about renewing townscapes. Thus, the most important signs of such transformation in this book are the appearances of small niches of production: art, handicraft and culture, tourism, border-related activities and the mere production of representations and fictions that add to the diversity of activities.

Symbolic Production of Place

Place marketing and urban entrepreneurialism

Modern places compete; therefore they have to make themselves attractive to a range of actors, from their own inhabitants to tourists. Two ways of responding to these needs have been shown in this book. The first is related to activities such as urban design, urban regeneration and other ways of reshaping places. There is only one case in this book where this has been on the agenda – Kiruna – and that is because of a need to relocate the centre of the town to provide space for the expanding mining industry. Regeneration is very much a large city approach, although place development has been a topic in rural Scandinavia. However, an alternative trend is the phenomenon called 'heritagization' based on a societal urge for nostalgia (cf. Urry 1996) or what above has been called re-enchantment (Ritzer 1994; Viken 2001).

What has been more visible in this collection, is that all places are inscribed into the modern discourses and masterframes: about a global world, a network society, the experience, cultural or border economy. In some cases these ascriptions have taken place as local industrial transformation, as in Fjarðabyggð, Sørøya, Kirkenes and Pajala. In other places the changes are primarily of a rhetorical character; for instance in the search for uniqueness. Often uniqueness is based on local culture, heritage or nature. Arboga promotes its heritage. In Narvik it's nature, the town's steep mountains are reflected in the new image of the town. In Pajala place profiling is linked to the Finnish language and culture that makes the town special in a Swedish context, but also to the slogan the 'Cultural Municipality'. Also as an old industrial town Pajala can be regarded as unique. But new industry can bring uniqueness too, as with the aluminium smelter at Fjarðabyggð.

So, the examples of this book fit into the well-known postmodern patterns of place competition: urban entrepreneurialism and place branding. This has also to do with a demand for an aesthetic environment, more accentuated since the 1990s than in previous periods – it is said a re-aesthetization of everyday life has taken place (Featherstone 1992; Lash and Urry 1994).

The second response is related to the imageries and representations of the towns. Therefore, place marketing, place promotion and place branding have emerged both as a political and as an academic field. Place promotion is the use of publicity and marketing to relate selective images of specific localities targeted at specific populations (Gold and Ward 1994). Place marketing is primarily an outward-oriented activity, but it is also a matter of generating local pride, identity, self-confidence and counteracting negative perceptions (Bramwell and Rawding 1996). Place promotion can be an intentional activity, but there will always be activities that are made for other purposes that have similar effects.

Among the intentional examples of place promotion in this book is Narvik. Granås shows what a complicated process place marketing can be; there is a desire to stand out as unique, far away and extreme but at the same time as being ordinary, close and accessible. Thus place marketing takes place within discourses such as those of urban–rural, centre–periphery, north–south and so on. And often the marketing somehow takes a stance in these discourses, for instance, as in Narvik, cementing the periphery image of the town. In another chapter Førde shows how a fishery community has changed both its means of production and its image, from a backwards island to a world centre for sport fishing, and how a group of women have created this image of 'The Land of the Big Fish' and successfully promoted it. Locally, self-perception has changed. Becoming well known and attractive within a particular sphere – as that of sport fishing – generates pride and self-confidence.

Most of the cases presented in this book concerning place marketing are unintentional accounts. There are several examples of novels or films that add to the images of the places from where they originate. The novel and a film from Pajala in Sweden has given this town tremendous publicity, but as shown by Júlíusdóttir and Gunnarsdotter, this positive image has a negative counterpart; it tends to be both sexist and biased. Another chapter shows how film added to the image of Berlevåg. However, this is a movie film distributed in cinemas in many countries. The film obviously plays on the hillbilly perception held about this area, but it also shows that these people have problems and challenges in their lives that are of a universal character.

Identities as narrative reinventions

Place or local identity has been a topic in several of the chapters in this book. The book refers to life experiences that people have gathered, and show how they permeate their perception of themselves. Twigger-Ross and Uzzell (1996, 207–209) identify four different ways in which place can be relevant in relation to individual identity, all represented among the cases in the book. Firstly, a human being achieves distinctness by being associated with a place, because the place is special or because of the special lifestyles associated with that place. Places can be distinct because of aesthetic conditions (nature and cultural landscape), history and traditions, but also because of representations that are associated with the place, such as books, films or stories. There are a whole series of examples in this book: in Båtsfjord and Kirkenes strong identities related to the history of the place, whereas in Berlevåg a renewed local identity can be observed, related to the cinema movie mentioned above. One aspect of distinctness is that people from other places are designated as belonging to other groups, although the inner coherence of one place-group and the differences with others are often exaggerated. There is an excellent example of this in the book; in the construction of their own identity people in Båtsfjord present a contrast to people in neighbouring Vadsø. Secondly, a place represents continuity, and being attached to a place is thereby a stabilizing factor. People retain their ties to a place because their life history is connected to it, or to a certain type of place. There are examples of this also in Båtsfjord where people, according to Moldenæs, highlight their roots in the place, although these roots for many only go a generation back. Thirdly, being connected to a place can be of importance to one's self-esteem. People are proud of living near a beautiful site, at a place with a famous history or cultural monument, or in a place with a particular atmosphere or unique environmental qualities – conditions that have been described as being the 'sense of place' (Shields 1991). People of Sørøya are proud of their origin of the culture of the place; Førde describes how they rejected a proposal of a performance change to please German tourists. Fourthly, being connected to a place can be important when it comes to opportunities for *self-realization*. Many people choose to live in places suited for particular activities such as an urban life, outdoor activities or artistic work. In the book it is shown how these aspects are important to new settlers in Vadsø in Norway, and that Egilsstaðir in Iceland attracts people due to a film production milieu that has emerged.

The concept of 'identity' is a product of the modern age and according to Kellner (1992), in the era of postmodernity, identity to a much lesser degree is a given quantity and much more diverse, flexible and situation-dependent than in earlier phases of modernity. In this book Fjarðabyggð, Berlevåg and Sørøya provide evidence from this stance. According to Holstein and Gubrium (2000, 105), 'the question of identity is moving away from traditional queries into who am I, to progressively become a question of when, where and how I am'. And one could add, 'Who I want to be'. A local identity is a bond between a human being and his or her surroundings based on acquired experiences, understanding, feelings and the place's symbolic meaning (cf. Stedman 2002). In this book, this has particularly become evident in the chapter about Båtsfjord and Kåfjord. In Båtsfjord people are very aware of successes of the fishing industries, and the town's position in the fishery sector, both nationally and internationally. In Kåfjord the identity is tied to ethnic background, and for many the experiences of being excluded from the Sami culture and to the new symbols that have been developed. But in their chapter Pedersen and Viken also show the significance of modern higher education, politics and internationalization in the creation of a postmodern ethnicity. Thus, Kåfjord is also an example of identity negotiations being related to prevailing ideologies, politics, discourses and trends.

Place is one of those remaining mechanisms that stabilize the postmodern society, according to Florida (2002). A meta-interpretation of the cases presented in this book supports this position; people are obviously attached to the places where they live. This, for instance, contrasts with a widely held perception that place has lost power as an identity platform and marker. Pile and Thrift (1995,

11) claim that the 'roots' metaphors have been replaced by a 'route' metaphor (cf. Clifford 1997). The only case giving indications in this direction is the discussion about in-migrants in Vadsø. Although Munkejord's informants more or less moved to the town recently, they seem to identify with the place – thus adopting a Vadsø identity. But, their stories can also be interpreted as if the place identity is not so vital, if their cultural or recreational needs are satisfied. This can mean that identities related to lifestyle are more important than those attached to place. It may be that this is a sign of local identities being situational; change of place means reinventing the identity related to place.

Urban Rurality

The cases presented in this book are situated in rural areas, some places are locally perceived as towns, others as villages. Rurality does not necessarily refer to agricultural districts or places; in several of the places in this book most people have traditionally lived off fisheries, some other places are mining towns. All cases are in processes of transition or reinvention. This falls into a global pattern: 'Throughout the developed world, rural areas are in economic, social, and visible *transition*. The traditional economic base provided by resource industries is typical decline' (Milward et al. 2003, 9). What the cases here show only partly confirms this; it is also obvious that the traditional industries strive for and succeed in sustaining their place, particularly the mining sites; and in Fjarðabyggð in Iceland the new aluminium plant is based on a natural resource: water and hydropower. But this collection also demonstrates new industries emerging: for instance tourism, cultural production and border-related business. In part, the evidence presented in this book fits the description given by Halfacree (2006, 311, quoting Marsden 1999):

> The countryside is no longer seen primarily as a food factory, but as a place for leisure and residence; it services the 'external' (Marsden 1999) demands of urban residents. Consequently countries in the global North are seeing the emergence of a multifunctional rural regime, an increasingly regionalized rural.

The importance of the rural districts for leisure activities is shown in several of the chapters in this book: Egilsstaðir, Pajala, Narvik, Sørøya and Kirkenes in Norway have had some success in the tourism market, 'serving' urban residents that go to the countryside for vacation and recreation. However, concerning Vadsø, Munkejord shows that the in-migrant inhabitants have similar leisure interests: the town's surrounding nature and recreation opportunities constitute a reason for living in the town. This is also a general trend, locals and tourists having similar interests, undertaking the same type of leisure activities (Urry 1995). In various places there has been mention of the fact that the towns in question, for instance both Kiruna and Narvik, have become important in supporting the surrounding districts with goods and services. Although this is not discussed explicitly in the chapters, there is an 'increasingly regionalized rural' (cf. Viken 2001). What is shown in most of the chapters in this book is that places have become more multifunctional than they used to be: Kiruna and Pajala in Sweden, Egilsstaðir in Iceland, and Narvik and Kirkenes in Norway all fit this description of the contemporary rural.

In her chapter Munkejord shows how many living on the northern rim, in a rural district, live a rather urban life, and that the urban–rural dichotomy probably is not particularly suited for the picturing or the ordinary life in this town. Munkejord refers to an ongoing discourse on the topic, about how rurality is socially constructed in public and academic discourses. She also refers to Little (1999) who discusses the othering of the rural. Othering descriptions are often linked to scales of values, preferences and interests, and thus have persuasive power. Whereas rural and urban are nominal differences, the dichotomy is often interpreted as providing an unequal status; the urban as the normal, the rural a deviance, the urban as modern, the rural as traditional. Thus, the othering processes often produce prejudices and stereotypes. There is a risk related to a book like this, in that it adds to such stereotypes. The chapter by Paulgaard shows how such stereotypes have been reproduced in films. However, the analyses Paulgaard makes of the film about the men's choir in Berlevåg shows how such stereotypes can be turned into a universal human description, and thus giving the place of origin for the film a positive image. Munkejord shows the incapability of the rural–urban dichotomy to capture vital aspects of daily life in Vadsø. It is also been shown in several chapters how rural locations do not hinder being important in global affairs, as the fish industry in Båtsfjord, the space industry in Kiruna, and the dreams of Kirkenes of becoming a hub in a global transport network. And in the view of inhabitants of several of the places described in this book, their home towns are central in many respects. This may be true for a specific area, but also reflects a counter-rhetoric, and thus, can also be seen as a coping strategy to resist centrally-created hegemonic narratives of the rural as backward and being in the past. Another way of understanding this is of course that narratives of rural urbanity are desparate efforts to be something else than rural dregs. The urban–rural dichotomy is a multilayered hegemonic structure that is difficult to reinvent.

Centre–Periphery

It is common to see the northern rim of Europe as a periphery. For most people – and they live in central areas – the North is far away. Periphery is defined in relation to centre or core, not the opposite. There is a whole set of characteristics attributed to geographically peripheral areas. Therefore it is widely regarded that there is a whole symbolism or semiotics related to the term, among these are questions of distance, population density, resource situation, degree of modernity, and power. For example, is periphery closely related to marginality (Hall 2007,

21)? And often the periphery is perceived as a burden and a problem. First and foremost, in the view of the public, the periphery is different. To be treated as something different, deviant or other is a process called 'othering'. To be tied to the periphery is to be treated as the 'Other'. Thus, the centre–periphery is a 'thick' dimension filled with prejudices and stereotypes.

The stereotyping of the term periphery can be illustrated by an article written by Hall, concerning tourism in the periphery (2007). There he states that the peripheral areas are located far from market, lack political control, have migration outflows, lack of innovation, are subject to state interventions and are less informed. Such statements may contain some truths, but also represent doubtful generalizations. Concerning these variables there are obvious variations: the distance to the market is not necessarily a problem; and if what is sold is raw material, then there is a market as long as the society demand the resource; and in tourism remoteness is in fact a selling point. With reference to political control, Kirkenes represents an example in this book of a periphery becoming a political centre. Migration outflow is of course a problem, but several of the places described in this book, for instance Kirkenes and Narvik, have retained their population size, despite many problems in the 1990s, mostly due to the fact that new industrial activities have been created. The periphery's lack of innovative power can also be contested (Aarsæther 2004). There are examples in this book of new industries, tourism in several places and within the cultural sector in Egilsstaðir and Pajala. State interventions take place everywhere, including, in remote areas, but there is always freedom to invent, to create jobs and new industries through merging resources from the public, private and civil sector. And if the periphery is generally regarded as less informed, this is certainly not true for them all. Therefore the term 'periphery' is highly contested, as illustrated in a book called *Mobility and Place* (Bærenholdt and Granås 2008). As it is published within the Anglo-American sphere, it bears the subtitle *Enacting Northern European Peripheries*. In one of the chapters Paulgaard (2008) discusses one of the impacts of this ordering of society; the othering of the periphery: 'The North becomes a zone of otherness, fundamentally different to other territories and places in the south representing the centre, essentially different, whether it is figured as idyllic or troubled, mythological or more backward and weakly developed' (Paulgaard 2008).

The Narrative Reinvention of Place Materialities

Circulating narratives

Throughout this book there are lots of examples of realities and materialities that come out of place perceptions, future ideas and hopes. Somehow, this is how reinvention takes place; someone gets an idea, makes a plan and implements it. As indicated in the introduction to this book (Chapter 1), this may be both intentional and unintentional acts. Often, what is being observed is a result of more or less rational people and ideas crossing each other's trajectories. What this book also shows is that narratives of different types seem to embody and empower; there is a narrative reinvention of place going on – in the book also presented as small narratives from places on the northern rim.

There are different ways the narratives perform. First, there are the intentional narratives, for instance those created in and by the people living there, and narratives that are created about them by a particular narrator. The creation of the project 'The Land of the Big Fish' on Sørøya is an example of this first type; through local negotiations the idea of fish tourism and its profile took shape. And it was implemented, with a particular eye to sustaining the traditional heart of the island. Another example is the branding of Narvik, a project run by actors owned by the municipality; this ended up in new logos and the slogan 'extreme experiences'. However, the result is contested, creating an awareness of the limited opportunities for the town as a ski destination; the mountains are too steep and scare as much as they attract. Thus the reality that comes out of this process may be a more realistic vision concerning the tourism outlook. A third example is Pajala, promoted as a 'Cultural Municipality', that only to a minor degree has become a reality, showing that a slogan is not enough, there must also be a will and priority. Culture seems to be a female matter in the eyes of many, and not something creating 'real' jobs.

A second intentional type of narratives is those created about a place or a community. Also these seem to have material impacts. The examples are the novels and films made about Pajala and Berlevåg. Although the direct impacts of these narratives are contested, they enhance self-perceptions and image. Particularly the film about the male choir in Berlevåg has produced local confidence and pride. The place has become well known, the choir national celebrities, and a curiosity that has increased tourism. The media exposition of Pajala due to the novel made by Mikael Niemi, and the film based on the book, is more problematic, as the narrative is playing on and even giving rise to new prejudices of the North. This, is an unpredictable side of narratives, they tend to live a life of their own and can be rather authoritarian (cf. Ricoeur 1992), also producing negative realities.

The second major types of narratives are the unintentional ones, and some of them are not even seen as narratives locally. The narratives are put together and presented by the researchers. One of the examples is Båtsfjord where there is a collective perception about the town as a successful and international fishing site of which the inhabitants obviously are proud. This self-esteem is important as a platform for industrial developments: this is a place where people experience success and where private initiatives are appreciated. Another example is Kirkenes, where Viken and Nyseth have observed a series of narratives, partly competing, partly supporting each other, in giving the town an image as industrial, international and future-oriented. In the chapter it is shown how such ideas materialize in a series of activities, of an industrial, cultural and social character, and not least, these activities keep the narratives alive and make them circulate.

The book also contains other examples of narratives that may be important for the material world, for instance ontological or public narrative from a place

(Somers 1994), narratives about family genealogy or local history and culture. Such knowledge can constitute grounds for place awareness, creativity and reinventional processes. A major example is Kåfjord (Norway) where the silence of the ethnic background, made young people curious. Behind the silence they found a strongly-rooted Sami culture, having been suppressed for some decades, due to authorized narratives about prosperous futures as Norwegians. They created their own story, of Gáivuotna as Sami, multicultural and international. It has become a success story, and the new public narratives have given the municipality a strong push forwards; it has become a model for the governance of ethnic diversity.

Contextualizing narratives

Narrative analysis has been acknowledged as having a position in social sciences that is long overdue in arriving. In place analyses narratives are vital. Narratives are of course of different types; they are more or less a good story, they are more or less weaved into meaning universes and webs of power and politics. This is also the case with the narratives observed in this book. Some of these narrative aspects need a comment. First it should be said that the term 'narrative' is used in this book in a broad sense and not just referring to stories with clear plots (Czarniawska-Joerges 1995; Bowman 2006). Many of them are diffusely circulating among people, and have been made into narratives by the authors. But there are also chapters that refer to stories, like the film of Båtsfjord, and the novel and film referred to in the presentation of the Pajala case. And, there are chapters in this book also having the plot form, with a beginning, a core and an ending – the stories about fish tourism in Sørøya, the self-confidence in Båtsfjord and the emergence of Gáivuotna as a Sami municipality all have this form. Most other narratives presented do not so thoroughly follow the story script.

Secondly, there is a wide diversity in the book, concerning the status of the narratives referred to. Some are based on public talk, some on plans and other official documents, and some on history and other academic disciplines. For instance, there are examples of what Bridger calls heritage narratives which 'give temporal persistence of a community by providing an account of its origins, the character of its people (both past and present), and its trials and triumphs over time' (1997, 69). This is a good characteristic of many of the cases in this book. The interpretation by the author of the heritage narrative in some way or another is central in Arboga, Kiruna, Pajala, Kirkenes, Båtsfjord, Sørøya and Gáivuotna. For instance in the Gáivuotna case there are strong accounts of origin, crises and triumphs.

There are several examples also of contemporary official narratives, narratives from planning and about planning. The Kiruna case is about a future replacement of the town centre, and actually how relaxed people are concerning this issue; there is a strong prevailing narrative in Kiruna about a caring mining company that share the interests of the people. There is also the Arboga case, where people are asked about preferences concerning their town, as part of a planning process.

It is in fact recommended to use academically based survey methods as a means of inhabitant participation; Berglund and Olson claim that representative samples give a voice to everybody. It can of course be asked how innovative such narratives can be. There are also other examples of narratives derived from planning processes: fish tourism in Sørøya, the industrial development in Kirkenes and the branding of Narvik. The case of Kirkenes is also an example of planning being a form of persuasive storytelling (Throgmorton 1992), at least it has an aim of ordering the society (cf. Doolin 2003, 751–70).

Narratives are dynamic and contextual. One of the contexts is discourses. Many of the narratives referred to or presented in this book refer to particular discourses. Hardy et al. (2000, 1234) gives a description of how discourses provide people with a particular analytical approach, concepts, categories and theories. In this way local narratives are structured and inscribed in discourses (cf. Somers 1994). An excellent example is Gáivuotna, where young people confronted the silence about the ethnic background of the community with discourses of ethnicity, heritage politics, and reflexivity. This case also shows how these discourses more or less produce a new reality: a Sami and multi-ethnic community. This case also shows how the discourses provide people with positions: in the festival, in the Sami world, in international indigenous networks and so on. Some of the discourses that are important in this case can also be called meta-, master or grand narratives (Somers 1994). They relate to big questions such as religion, democracy, human rights and so on. In the Gáivuotna case discourses about indigenous peoples, ethnicity, nationality, suppression and democracy are all being more or less explicitly referred to.

Narratives are related to power and hegemonic positions. In Kiruna the hegemony is in the hands of the mining company, and it is not contested. In Kirkenes there is a struggle of hegemony going on between the industrial narratives and border-related narratives, and between political narratives and identities and more neutral bordered positions (Viken et al. 2008). However, it seems as though the struggles are creating a positive dynamic in the town, and that it adds to a cultural and industrial diversity that is widely acclaimed. The Gáivuotna is another example, the ethno-political controversies obviously have come out on the positive side, although the battles were fierce during a period in the 1990s.

Lastly there also is a performative side of narratives: they are enacted and to be found in the material sides of places. The performative side of narratives is partly a product of their circulation; as narratives are told and retold, they change and new dimensions are added. Probably the story of Båtsfjord is an example of how narratives circulate and metamorphose in which Moldenæs gives an autobiographic description of how such narratives are created. But narratives are also materially reproduced in texts, technologies and organizational arrangements – this is often what makes narratives a factor in stabilizing arrangements. In Kirkenes there is a strong material element; there is a heritage from the mining period that is visible, and so are the new institutions coping with border issues. In this town the narratives of a political and international place also materializes in strong iconography, and in several of the towns described there are landscapes and townscapes telling stories about industries, crises, modernization and globalization.

Conclusion

Place reinvention in this study has been used to capture how places change meaning as a consequence of continuous and strategic processes of place making and identity building. Place reinvention directs attention towards the relationship between symbolic and imaginative changes, and the planned regeneration or place making initiatives. Place reinvention is a concept that perhaps only can be addressed at a very abstract and aggregated level. At the same time it involves processes that are very concrete, physical and material in the sense that places actually are being changed through these processes. Places are reinvented through continued practices. Place relates both to materiality and to identity (Hillier 2001). Signs, meaning and materiality come together. The total congregation of people and materiality creates a patchwork of meaning that people assign to this material reality. These meanings are symbolic representations as well as the product of direct experiences. The change of 'place image' or 'place identity' is, however, linked to such place making in various forms.

In this study we have been concerned not so much about this broader picture of global enforced change in itself, but about how places in the North are reinventing themselves within the context of a globalized and changing economy. In the postmodern society the place as such has become more important; it is more important than ever to appear as attractive towards newcomers, investors and tourists, but also in the eyes of its own inhabitants. Hence, the sense of place, place identity and place image have become vital issues. In this book place has been understood both as geographical and physical location, as sense of place – the subjective experience one has of a place, and as a social context, that is as an arena for everyday life. The dichotomy between materiality and social constructions of life on the one hand, and its many representations on the other, has been analysed from narrative perspectives pointing at industrial structures, place promotion, identity, rurality and periphery.

The message of this book is that there exists a materiality that is strongly influenced by the rhetoric within which it is wrapped. The materiality is a social construction, not only as a matter of communal perception, but through the narratives that circulate among people and gives expression to their thinking, networking and action. There is whole series of cases showing how people, plans and circulating narratives have agency. This certainly goes into the discussion of structure and agency (Giddens 1984), and the contributions here are a demonstration of how the narrative level constitutes a layer in-between. The important side of this is that the narratives tend to be constitutive, at the same time as they are very sensitive to contextual changes. There is also, with reference to cases from the northern rim, a political message in this – for instance how the Sami reinvented their identity in Gáivuotna or how a group of women changed the spirit to one of optimism and positive change on Sørøya – and that is not to take the public narratives for granted, they can be changed and often they should be changed. Narratives can transform reality and give a prosperous future.

References

Aarsæter, N. (ed.) (2004), *Innovations in the Nordic Periphery* (Stockholm: NORDREGIO).

Amin, A. and N. Thrift (2007), *Cities. Reimagining The Urban* (Cambridge: Polity Press).

Baerenholdt, J.O. and Granås, B. (eds) (2008), *Mobility and Place* (London: Ashgate).

Bowman, W.D. (2006), 'Why narrative? Why now?', *Research Studies in Music Educations*, 27, 5–20.

Bramwell, B. and Rawding, L. (1996), 'Tourism marketing images of industrial cities', *Annals of Tourism Research*, 23(1), 201–21.

Bridger, J.C. (1997), 'Community stories and their relevance to planning', *Applied Behavioral Science Review*, 5, 67–80.

Clifford, J. (1997), *Routes: Travel and Translation in the Late Twentieth Century* (Cambridge, Mass.: Harvard University Press).

Czarniawska-Joerges, B. (1995), *Narratives in Social Research* (London: Sage).

Doolin, B. (2003), 'Narratives of change: Discourse, technology and organisation', *Organization*, 10(4), 751–70.

Featherstone, Mike (1992), 'Postmodernism and the aestheticization of everyday life', in: Lash, S. and Friedman, J. (eds), *Modernity and Identity* (Oxford: Blackwell).

Florida, R. (2002), *The Rise of the Creative Class: And How It's Transforming Work, Leisure, Community and Everyday Life* (New York: Basic Books).

Giddens, A. (1984), *The Constitution of Society* (Cambridge: Polity Press).

Gold, J.R. and Ward, S.V. (1994), *Place Promotion: The Use of Publicity and Marketing to Sell Towns and Regions* (Chichester: Wiley).

Halfacree, K. (2006) 'From dropping out to leading on? British counter-cultural back-to-the-land in a changing rurality', *Progress in Human Geography*, 30(3), 309–36.

Hall, C.M. (2007), 'North–south perspectives on tourism, regional development and peripheral areas', in: Müller, D. and Jansson, B. (eds), *Tourism in Peripheries. Perspectives from the Far North and South* (Wallingford: Cabi).

Hardy, C., Palmer, I. and Phillips, N. (2000), 'Discourse as strategic resource', *Human Relations*, 53(9), 1227–48.

Healey, P. (1997), *Collaborative Planning. Shaping Places in Fragmented Societies* (Hong Kong: Macmillan).

Hillier, J. (2001), 'Imagined value: the poetics and politics of place', in: Madanipour, A., Hull, A. and Healey, P. (eds), *The Governance of Place. Space and Planning Processes* (London: Ashgate).

Hoggart, K. and Paniagua, A. (2001), 'What rural restructuring?', *Journal of Rural Studies,* 17, 41–62.

Holstein, J. and Gubrium, J.F. (2000), *The Self We Live By. Narrative Identity in a Postmodern World* (Oxford: Oxford University Press).

Kellner, D. (1992), 'Popular culture and the construction of postmodern identities', in: Lash, S. and Friedman, J. (eds), *Modernity and Identity* (Oxford: Blackwell).

Lash, S. and Urry, J. (1994), *The Economies of Signs and Space* (London: Sage).

Little, J. (1999), 'Otherness, representation and the cultural construction of rurality', *Progress in Human Geography*, 23, 437–42.

Marsden, T. (1999), 'Rural futures: the consumption countryside and its regulation', *Sociologia Ruralis*, 39, 501–20.

Milward, H., Harrington, L., Ilbery, B. and Beesley, K. (2003), 'Milieux, viewpoints and processes of change in the new countryside', in: Beesley, K., Milward, H., Ilbery, B. and Harrington, L. (eds), *The New Countryside* (Canada: Brandon University/St. Mary's University), pp. 9–23.

Paulgaard, G. (2008), 'Re-centring periphery: Negotiating identities in time and space', in: Bærenholdt, O.J. and Granås, B. (eds).

Pile, N. and Thrift, N. (1995), *Mapping the Subject: Geographies of Cultural Transformation* (London: Routledge).

Ricoeur, P. (1992), *Från text till handling: en antologi om hermeneutik* (Stockholm: Brutus Österlings bokförlag Symposion).

Ritzer, G. (1994), *Enchanting a Disenchanted World: Revolutionizing the Means of Consumption* (Thousand Oaks: Pine Forge Press).

Sharpley, R. (2003), 'Rural tourism and sustainability – a critique', in: Hall, D., Roberts, L. and Mitchell, M. (eds), *New Directions in Rural Tourism* (Aldershot: Ashgate).

Shields, R. (1991), *Places on the Margin: Alternative Geographies of Modernity* (London: Routledge).

Somers, M. (1994), 'The narrative constitution of identity: A relational and network approach', *Theory and Society*, 23, 605–49.

Stedman, Richard C. (2002), 'Toward a social psychology of place – predicting behavior from place-based cognitions, attitude, and identity', *Environment and Behavior*, 34(5), 561–81.

Thrift, N. (2008), *Non-representational Theory. Space, Politics, Affect* (Oxon: Routledge).

Throgmorton, J.A. (1992), 'Planning as persuasive storytelling about the future: Negotiation and electric power rate settlement in Illinois', *Journal of Planning Education and Research*, 12, 17–31.

Throgmorton, J.A. (2003), 'Planning as persuasive storytelling in a global-scale web of relationships', *Planning Theory*, 2, 125–51.

Twigger-Ross, C. and Uzzell, D.L. (1996), 'Place and identity processes', *Journal of Environmental Psychology*, 205–20.

Urry, J. (1995), *Consuming Places* (London: Routledge).

Urry, J. (1996), 'How societies remember the past', in: Macdonald, S. and Fyfe, G. (eds), *Theorizing Museums* (Oxford: Blackwell).

Viken, A. (ed.) (2001), *Turisme. Tradisjoner og Trender* (Oslo: Gyldendal Akademisk).

Viken, A., Nyseth, T. and Granås, B. (2008), 'Kirkenes: An industrial site reinvented as a border town', *Acta Borealia*, 25(1), 22–44.

Index

Illustrations are indicated by **bold** page numbers.